# THE CRISIS IN
# AMERICAN
# DIPLOMACY

# THE CRISIS IN AMERICAN DIPLOMACY

## SHOTS ACROSS THE BOW OF THE STATE DEPARTMENT

By

### SMITH SIMPSON

THE CHRISTOPHER PUBLISHING HOUSE
NORTH QUINCY, MASSACHUSETTS
02171

PRINTED IN

THE UNITED STATES OF AMERICA

*To Henriette*

*Who has been a part of the Great Adventure*

# PREFACE

I can remember standing on a slope of the Arlington National Cemetery as a teen-ager, one Christmas Day, down apiece from the broken mast of the battleship *Maine* and, as I laid a wreath on the grave of an ancestor, vowing I would do whatever I could the rest of my life for good will and peace among men. From that day this has been my consuming interest. The broken mast of the *Maine* has been a kind of compass needle by which my private and diplomatic life has been guided.

What one person can contribute is little, but if each contributes that little, the confluence of little streams can produce a mighty river which can sweep all obstacles before it. It is not a vague, impossible dream, this one of peace on earth, good will toward men, if each human being adds his little bit persistently, mindful, of course, that breachers of the peace are always among us and must sometimes be restrained by force. Common sense need not desert us in this elevated quest and, indeed, if we ignore its counsel we but invite defeat and subjugation by those ambitious to reduce others to their political and economic bondage.

Along with many other developments since the end of World War II, our China move reiterates the warning which has pounded insistently upon our door to take a hard, analytical look at the nature and quality of diplomacy which the United States must achieve in the interest of national survival and the needs of the world community.

We must perceive diplomacy as an international political process, often subtle, overheard rather than directly and distinctly stated, and demanding superior political instincts and talent. These include an ability to combine strategic thinking and planning with tactical moves, fuse learning and techniques with personal skills and blend the organizational dimensions of modern diplomacy with individual initiative. This perception of diplomacy is not widely held in this country, not even in our diplomatic establishment—the Presidency, the State Department and the Foreign Service—which is only dimly and superficially aware of it. As a result, the diplomacy we practice is woefully inadequate to the needs of our national security and those of the world community.

When I became an author of one of the real, enduring reforms of American diplomacy—the establishment of a labor attaché program in the Foreign Service—and wound up being commissioned in that Service, I saw this as opening up an opportunity of making good on that teen-age commitment to contribute to international understanding and peace. That was in 1944 and thus began, in the midst of war, not simply a career liaison but what I considered a direct service to country and at the same time to the great cause of understanding, cooperation, and peace among nations to which our own was pledged.

Anyone entering our diplomatic service at that time with such a commitment could not but quickly spot alarming deficiencies in our diplomatic performance. From the earliest days, mystified by what I saw, I began to inquire, examine and analyze and then to seek ways of correcting the shortcomings, more and more convinced as the years passed that the United States not only *could* but *must* do far better in conducting its worldwide affairs. I cannot say I got very far in reform efforts, but at least I could and hopefully did set an example. When eventually I found myself in charge of consular posts, I could see to it that the performance of entire posts was jacked up.

With each succeeding year I became more and more frustrated by the State Department's inclination to mosey along with its traditional ways of conceptualizing and doing things, little interested in any analytical approach to its responsibilities and resources for discharging them. Apart from Edward R. Stettinius and George C. Marshall, Secretaries of State in 1944-45 and 1947-49 respectively, no Secretary of State under whom I served took much interest in spotting, analyzing and correcting the deficiencies of our diplomatic establishment. Stettinius had too little national and international experience and too little intellectual capacity to get far with the reforms he launched during his nearly fourteen months as Under Secretary, and he lasted but a short time thereafter as the Department's head. General Marshall served only two years and while he innovated some improvements, he, too, served too short a time to deal with many appalling inadequacies crying for correction.

It was not until 1958-61 that I acquired a fulcrum on which to rest a lever of reform of any breadth, when serving as a participant in the National Security Council machinery. I then made some contribution to modernizing our African policy and diplomacy. Facing the prospect of losing that fulcrum as the normal process of rotation closed in upon me and completely fed up with the antiquated notions and ways of our diplomatic establishment, I took an early retirement in 1962, determined to fire, and keep firing, warning shots across its bow. Articles in the following three years attracted some attention, including that of the Deputy Under Secretary of State for Administration who was also convinced that the establishment could not continue its old, haphazard ways. He called me back to the Department as a full-time consultant for a year to work on some of the reforms I was urging. I reluctantly agreed, reluctantly because I was not persuaded that the very top leadership of the State Department was seriously interested in reforms. I thought, therefore, that I could be of more value in my lonely task of conceptualizing and arguing them.

My doubts proved all too well founded. Neither the Secretary, Dean Rusk, nor his deputy, George W. Ball, the

Under Secretary, appeared interested and we lacked their support.  Both of these men would have made top-notch State Department officials prior to World War I, but both had failed to catch up with World War II and the kind of systematic diplomatic organization and officer quality and performance demanded of a world power.  As far as I was concerned, that year of hard work was a waste of my time and the taxpayers' money and as I came to perceive this, I began omitting whole days in my weekly reports of time spent so as to reduce the drain upon the Treasury.

The following year, 1967, my book *Anatomy of the State Department* appeared and attracted some attention.  When, as a result, I appeared on the "Today" television program, Dean Rusk, an inveterate watcher, heard what I said but was still shaking his head bewilderedly on his arrival at his office, where he confessed to associates: "I don't understand what Smith Simpson is saying."  A lot of Americans did, however, and I was encouraged to persist in what I was calling a "campaign for quality," of which the following essays are illustrative.

Our move to normalize diplomatic relations with the People's Republic of China and the triangular relationship which this sets up between the United States, the Soviet Union and the P.R.C. demands a quality of diplomacy which we have rarely achieved and therefore a hard, hard look at what diplomacy is and how well our diplomatic establishment is equipped to practice it.  If these essays, written with the insight of a former participant, assist in that hard look, I shall be happy to have made such a contribution.  Our national security and the peace of the world are at stake.  We should make no mistake: we are in a tough bind in the world and we need the best diplomacy we can devise to pull us through.

*Annandale, Va.*                              *Smith Simpson*
*August, 1979*

# CONTENTS

# THE CRISIS IN
# AMERICAN
# DIPLOMACY

# Part  I
# DIPLOMACY

I wish to express my gratitude to Professor Waldo H. Heinrichs, Jr. who was kind enough to read the following essay and give me the benefit of his helpful comments.

# 1.

# THE NATURE AND DIMENSIONS
# OF DIPLOMACY

Diplomacy is not much written or thought about in this country; but, nevertheless, it constitutes our principal alternative to war and an essential ingredient of our national security.

We Americans over the years have failed to understand the nature and value of diplomacy, either expecting too much of it and, when it fails, dismissing it as "a slow, plodding way of doing things" as Andrew Young described it when resigning as the United States Ambassador to the United Nations, August 15, 1979, or conceptualizing it, as have many of our practitioners and scholars, in such incomplete terms as to drain it of its dynamic nature.

In recent years, academians have become aware of this neglect and have turned to the study of diplomacy but, approaching it piecemeal, by analyzing some of its components such as negotiation and conflict resolution, have neglected others of equal importance, such as the frustration of negotiation and conflict promotion. They have therefore been less than realistic and overlooked important factors in the breakdown of the American diplomatic effort.

Needed at this critical juncture is a realistic definition which will characterize diplomacy as it is—a many-dimensioned form of political action—and thus assist in a more accurate appraisal of its potential and its limitations, the resources it demands, and those we are lacking.

Diplomacy is the political process by which governments seek their strategic—or what we call "policy"—objectives. It is the process by which foreign policies are converted from rhetoric to realities, from mere pronouncements of principles to the everyday promotion of the national interest. It is the means by which nations seek influence and security. From an international point of view, it is the means by which adjustments are effected peacefully, so that accommodation takes the place of war.

What, specifically, is this means? It consists of daily and methodical gathering and reporting of information, explanation or concealment of policies and clarification or misrepresentation of intentions, efforts to gauge and anticipate events, problems and crises and moves to meet these according to national interest, all directed to strategic ends and involving tactical maneuver. Since strategic objectives may be to promote understanding or misunderstanding, international unity or division, order or revolution, the interest of the international community or a government's own narrowly-conceived interests, it follows that diplomacy is not necessarily what many Americans imagine it to be—an instrument of international understanding and peace. Whether it is, depends upon the strategic objectives and tactics of governments.

In its best form, it is a quiet process, a subtle process. It is a kind of political chess game in which one tries not only to think out his own moves but to guess the moves of a competitor, and to weigh in advance the consequences of each. It is therefore a process of calculation and method, of system, rather than inspired improvisation, although this is by no means absent. It requires patience and a thorough familiarity with the modalities of the game. At its best, it is muted and ingeniously suggestive rather than exhortatory or evangelical. *Pas trop de zèle*, as Talleyrand observed, is its admonition. While an active and dynamic process, in which the advantage is with players of initiative, resourcefulness and well-coordinated effort, as in any group undertaking, from athletic teams to corporate enterprise, it works best in the absence of grand-stands and publicity. It abhors a stage as nature abhors a vacuum and emerges upon one only when its work is done. When reasonable players are involved, it evolves most effectively through *tête-à-tête*—on the park bench, at a café table, in the quiet of a room, at a small dinner party. A subject which cannot be handled this way raises three questions: (1) is it a fit subject for diplomacy or (2) is the other party amenable to reason and (3) if not, what other resources of diplomacy than reason would be worth bringing into play?

Diplomacy is a navigational process, demanding eru-dition—a knowledge of the political seas, their mingled winds, currents and tides—political intuition and good judgment, shrewd anticipation of problems and crises, an understanding of the limitations of available resources, as well as quickness and adroitness in the exploitation of any opportunity for advancing the interests of govern-ments. It is the quiet art of the practicable, with all the scientific elements which politics possesses.

Many of the qualities, skills, techniques and tactics needed for diplomacy, therefore, are displayed in everyday relationships. They appear in a parent's quiet, firm but tactful handling of an obstreperous child (it is amazing how often statesmen behave like children), and in a sales-man's skill in overcoming resistance to his wares. They appear in the noiseless maneuvers of one university depart-ment to gain the upper hand over another in a disputed area of learning or sphere of interest (governments also have spheres of interest) and in a labor union's unpublicized maneuvers with other unions and employers. They are to be found in an architect's persuasion of government offi-cials and private property owners to accept redesign of Pennsylvania Avenue in the nation's capital. They are to be found in a lawyer's skillful use of psychology, learning, common sense, intuition and experience in analyzing and persuading a jury. They appear in the log-rolling man-euvers and arm-twisting which occur in every town and county council, State legislature and Congress.

In the relationships of national governments, the use of such resources is called "diplomacy," and the personal factor can be a considerable one. The best diplomats—the Jules Jusserands, Lord Bryces, Dwight Morrows, David K. E. Bruces, Charles E. Bohlens and Anatoly Dobrynins—have, as individuals, added so much to their official status as to acquire an extraordinary influence not only with the foreign governments to which they have been accredited but with their own as policy shapers. Personality, character, learning and intuitive grasp of what to do, when and how, greatly determine a diplomat's role and thus, in no small measure, his government's capacity in world affairs.

The distinction between diplomacy and the manifestation of many of its attributes in homely relationships is four-fold. Diplomats represent national governments which are responsible for the welfare and security of their states. Secondly, it follows that diplomacy is an integral part of national defense. Thirdly, diplomats must live and function cross-culturally. Fourthly, they must also live and function cross-historically, since peoples of the world are at various stages of social, cultural and economic development. These differences present the diplomat with problems and responsibilities not confronting private citizens and organizations.

Even so, the demarcation line between the diplomatic activity of governments and the activity of individuals is not always clear. There is an infinite variety of transnational relationships between individuals, between private organizations, between state corporations, and between all these and national governments where private and official activity overlap. For example, when a private lawyer negotiates with the Soviet government the exchange of a Soviet spy for an American U-2 pilot with the knowledge and cooperation of the United States government but with no conferment upon him of diplomatic status, this is substantially, though not formally, diplomacy. So, too, when the chairman of the Federal Reserve Board attends a meeting of government bankers, exchanges views, and explores how central banks will react to developing problems, he is engaging in an exercise indistinguishable from diplomacy save for the fact that he lacks a diplomatic passport. When the chairman of the House of Representatives' Ways and Means Committee end-runs the President of the United States, who has long been trying to extract from the Japanese government a voluntary control of textile shipments to this country, by himself negotiating with the Japanese ambassador in Washington, he is engaging in diplomacy without the credentials. Organizationally, Article 71 of the United Nations Charter contributes to this gray area by providing for a consultative relationship between its Economic and Social Council and private organizations. The International Labor Organization institutionalizes it by associating representatives of employer and labor organizations with those of governments —none of whom are accorded diplomatic credentials—in the negotiation and adoption of international labor conventions and recommendations.

If all of this suggests that the subtleties of differentiation which set diplomats apart confer upon them no supernatural role, it nevertheless remains that they have a far greater role and influence upon events than most people imagine. If diplomats are doing their job, they are not mere messenger boys at the end of a teletype or transoceanic telephone system.

### The Political Dimension

Being a governmental activity, diplomacy is politically motivated and directed to political ends. It is, in a word, international politics. (I am using "politics" in a broad sense which includes social and humanitarian objectives. Such objectives, when pursued by governments, become political objectives.)

Since, therefore, it consists essentially of action, it possesses strategic and tactical elements. While this should be evident and these elements have generated considerable literature on their military application, they have generated none on their diplomatic. Nevertheless, in its political dimension, diplomacy consists of seven elements: grand strategy, strategy, grand tactics, lesser tactics, techniques, personal skills and logistics.

**Grand Strategy** consists of the larger objectives sought by governments in their diplomacy, such as world domination or world influence, or, as in the case of Woodrow Wilson, world order. The promotion of the forces of freedom or those of repression throughout the world, the promotion of change by violence or by peaceful means, or the preservation of the status quo, would be other examples.

**Strategy** consists of objectives of lesser rank, needed to promote grand strategy. These could be the promotion or discouragement of:

— international law

— of a particular international organization or the general system of international organization

— the arms race

— a nation or bloc of nations

— a peace treaty between two hostile governments.

Strategic objectives could thus include the encirclement of an oil producing region, the subversion of another government, the building of an alliance system or the weakening of a hostile alliance system.

**Grand tactics** consist of means more specific than those of strategy for achieving a government's objectives. Since national and international problems are intertwined, such tactics include moves by a government within its own society as well as in the international community.

The line of demarcation from strategy is not always clear but in general it is the difference between an objective and an action. The decision, in principle, to intervene in Africa belongs to strategy but the choice of means is tactical. Any particular move of intervention is therefore a tactic. So, too, with the decision to gain control over an oil-producing region and a move to do so by subverting one or more governments. The decision to promote a Law of the Seas conference would be part of a government's strategy—either grand or lesser, depending on how the conference was conceptualized—but the actual moves to initiate and obtain support for such a conference would be tactical.

**Minor tactics** consist of steps taken to set or keep grand tactics in motion. While a grand tactic might be to initiate or support the holding of a conference, moves in the conference itself to promote its success would constitute minor tactics. So also would action to induce allies to chip in a larger share of the costs of an alliance system. Minor tactics include naval visits to "show the flag," thereby giving visible expression of the interests of the sending power and promoting good relations through accompanying occasions of mutual hospitality. The deployment of naval force as a deterrent would belong to grand tactics.

Strategies or tactics of whatever grade can be spoiled by those of a hostile government and hence diplomacy consists of not only positive but defensive or checking moves.

**Techniques** are the means by which minor tactics are accomplished or spoiled. For example, as a tactic, the diplomat of one country wanted to spoil the cooperation between the representatives of two other countries at an international conference. In a private meeting of the three, he discussed a plan, presented to him by the other two, in a way to divide them. Whereupon, one of the two proceeded to tip over the cart on which the drinks were resting, thereby bringing the discussion to an abrupt end.[1]

**Logistics** is the branch of the science of diplomacy that deals with all aspects of personnel recruitment, education and training, procurement of supplies and facilities, assignment of personnel and equipment, and the provision of services.

Diplomacy, therefore, is far from an ordinary bureaucratic process.    From this it follows that a diplomatic service is not simply a projection abroad of a domestic civil service, as experts in public administration have tried to insist.    The political functions of diplomats, and the performance of these in a cross-cultural, cross-historical environment, set the two distinctly apart.    It is equally clear that substituting for diplomacy such terms as "overseas administration" and "implementation of foreign policy" is as inapt as trying to describe national politics as "administration" or "implementation of campaign promises."    Such nonsense deters us from coming to grips with diplomacy, which is, I repeat, *politics*.

It is important to recognize that while action is of the essence of diplomacy, there are times when it is best—as in personal relations—to abstain from speech and action. The wisdom articulated in Ecclesiastes is as profound as ancient—"to everything there is a season, and a time to every purpose . . . a time to keep silence and a time to speak."    In the years of the frequently precipitate and peripatetic John Foster Dulles, his subordinates sometimes longed to convey to him the admonition which they exchanged *sotto voce* among themselves: "Don't just *do* something: stand there!"    While the tactic of withholding action or expression can be a sound one, silence or inactivity because of a lack of preparation for events is something else.    This is not diplomacy.    It is an abdication of diplomacy.

Equally    important    is    recognition    that    the    political action    which    is    the    essence    of    diplomacy    involves    not simply Presidents, Secretaries of State, ambassadors and other senior officers but junior officers as well.    It involves not only diplomatic but consular officers.    If there is one aspect of diplomacy not grasped by the American public, or    indeed    by    much    of    our    diplomatic    establishment itself and White House budget trimmers, it is the political contribution of consular posts.

This was one of the factors in our failure to judge more accurately    the    Iranian    situation    under    the    Shah.    Our consular posts in Iran were not adequately staffed or used, because they were not seen by the State Department and Embassy Teheran as important listening and evaluation posts. Entirely too much dependence was placed upon the Embassy's and CIA's limited contacts with officials in the capital, with the result that we completely misjudged the strength of popular and religious opposition to the Shah over the years. For want of a nail the shoe was lost.

   As State Department administrators and budget-cutters in the President's Office of Management and Budget close down consular posts on the ground of economy, arguing that their passport, visa and protection service can be performed in distant embassies, one is struck by how little understanding of diplomacy is reflected in these decisions. The significance of the problems encountered in the protracted negotiations and ratification of a consular convention between the United States and the Soviet Union in the 1960's, although clearly registering the political dimension of consular posts, seems to have passed over the heads of many of our government officials.[2]

## Domestic aspect

The political dimension of diplomacy has acquired crucial domestic thrusts. Whole governments are involved. In getting the executive bureaucracy to respond to world developments adequately and promptly, the diplomat must become a bureaucrat of sorts, but a bureaucrat politically motivated, foreign-environment-conscious, and strategically oriented, with many of his end results sought in overseas societies. In being thus compelled to synthesize domestic and overseas actions, with an eye always to strategy, the diplomat is, again, plainly a different breed of government employee from the ordinary civil servant.

Just with respect to the State Department, the American diplomat can face a sizable task. Much of his success abroad—and in his own capital, when assigned there—depends upon his ability to cope with that Department's peculiar attitudes, including its aversion to organizational efficiency and thus its often rambling and chaotic ways of dealing with information and with the conflicting, sometimes irreconcilable strategic considerations often involved in decisions, necessitating extensive consultation between bureaus. He must solicit the cooperation of his own Departmental colleagues by the very same tactics, techniques and skills which he employs overseas in enlisting the collaboration of foreign officials. Getting the action he needs from his own headquarters within the time required by fast-paced events can be no mean feat. If, when stationed abroad, the diplomat is unable to get it, he must decide whether to act on his own responsibility.

Not the least of the confusions with which he must cope have been introduced in recent years by the President's Special Adviser on National Security Affairs, who presides over a staff of the National Security Council. In some respects this resembles a little State Department, with an obvious potential of duplication and rivalry in the formulation of strategies and tactics. Were the position clearly conceptualized and its incumbents seasoned in diplomacy the potential of confusion would be appreciably reduced, but in recent years the position has been held by academicians with neither diplomatic experience nor good political instincts, but rather a seemingly insatiable thirst for power. They have therefore tried to convert the position from a staff to a line status, inordinately complicating the work of Secretaries of State and their career associates in Washington and abroad by constantly meddling in diplomacy. They have negotiated with foreign ambassadors in Washington, traveled abroad for discussions with other governments and set up NSC committees arrogating the function of coordinating our government's conduct of foreign affairs which properly belongs to the State Department.

These problems are multiplied with respect to the executive branch as a whole. Practically all government departments and agencies have a stake in foreign affairs. Each has its own little State Department. Each must not only be reasoned with but cajoled, pressured, stimulated and carried along with the State Department's initiatives. The moves of each must be coordinated and harmonized with the strategic decisions of the President and Secretary of State. While in our government the State Department shares some of this responsibility with the staff of the National Security Council, it has residual, hour-by-hour coordinating functions to perform, as do diplomatic and consular posts abroad. When, in a given area, the NSC has a staffer who is less than expert, the State Department's burden increases.

Too rarely are diplomatic officers capable of responding imaginatively and effectively to this bureaucratic challenge. None are trained for it systematically. What each learns he generally picks up on the run, and since he is frequently rotated his experience is very limited with respect to any given subject.[3] Other departments and agencies being well aware of this, the diplomats all too often lack the standing, respect and influence needed for leadership in the Washington bureaucratic game. All of these short-comings strikingly coalesced in the Operations Coordinating Board created by President Eisenhower to provide the kind of policy integration and harmonization of activity which successful diplomacy requires. The Board was placed under the chairmanship of the State Department but so great were the latter's lamentations over this burdensome role that President Kennedy abolished the Board.[4]

This bureaucratic factor accounts for some of the weird things that happen in modern diplomacy. It explains such misadventures in our own as "Camelot" and "Skybolt,"[5] the botching of a relatively simple attempt of a Lithuanian seaman to defect from a Soviet ship in U.S. territorial waters in 1970,[6] and the repeated failures of the U.S. government to deal skillfully with the governments of state-controlled societies which are capable of a tightly knit diplomacy.

On the domestic front, the problem of dealing with Congress is as complicated and confusing as any. A spirit of congressional independence bred by our separation-of-powers system is aggravated by a lingering frontier disdain of diplomacy, an astonishing failure of State

Department representatives to conceptualize and present to congressional appropriations committees their financial needs in terms of national defense and the rotation of diplomatic officers, who find themselves chronically unable to answer questions relating to matters dating back more than two or three years. From this amalgam comes a congressional sense of frustration in dealing with our diplomatic establishment, an impulse to find out for itself what is going on in the world and a brash, olympian disregard of what the diplomats are struggling to accomplish.

Lobbies seek to influence Congress in foreign no less than in domestic affairs. The size, varying economic interests and polyethnic composition of our nation, together with a government of separated powers, have produced a vascular system of lobbying which periodically creates something very close to anarchy in our foreign relations. Pumping this system are private organizations of both economic and ethnic character, with the Jewish and Greek foremost among the latter. Others of myriad number become active when something develops of interest to them and new ones are appearing. One has crystalized around African interests. There will undoubtedly be an Hispanic; and there are incipient signs of an Arab.

Our system of checks and balances and tradition of lobbying encourages similar activity by foreign governments. Embassies in Washington entertain congressmen extensively so as to provide occasions for suggesting and pressing matters of interest. By combining with an ethnic organization in the United States, an embassy can develop considerable clout. Success along this line, however, depends upon the degree of discretion and skill with which the relationship is managed. Too obvious a coordination could eventually prove self-defeating.[7]

The discreet activities of embassies in Washington and sometimes not so discreet lobbying attempts by foreign intelligence agencies[8] are supplemented by those of American citizens hired by embassies or their Chiefs of State. Like lobbyists for domestic interests, these citizens are lawyers, "public relations counselors" or people with prestigious names. They can intervene in legislative matters without appearing to be meddlesome foreigners. Any overzealousness or awkward maneuver can be repudiated by clients without embarassment. *Persona non grata* and recall procedures never have to be invoked. They constitute a kind of local diplomat without diplomatic credentials, shadowy, elusive, operating in that mysterious gray area between diplomacy and private activity so difficult to penetrate and yet so highly influential.

Our system of government and political processes thus enable other governments to accomplish by overt contractual arrangements what the CIA must seek to do abroad by covert means.[9]

As formidable as are the obstacles which lobbyists place in the way of the State Department in its efforts to keep our foreign relations pointed in the direction of our national interests, there are others. Congressmen have been known to conduct discussions with ambassadors resident in Washington on matters under active negotiation between their own governments. They invite ambassadors and visiting foreign officials to lunch on Capitol Hill to obtain information and views directly from them to supplement what they obtain from the State Department and sometimes consider themselves better informed and more prescient than the Executive Branch. All in all, a governmental and political system more calculated to reduce diplomacy to a shambles could hardly be devised.[10]

Congressional interaction with diplomacy occurs not simply in Washington but in other parts of the world. Congressmen are members of U.S. delegations to international conferences and, as committee members, travel extensively overseas. So do their staffs. So do their committee staffs. Between them, they penetrate almost all areas of the world and all subjects, probing U.S. foreign policies and diplomatic moves, overseas conditions, the likelihood of crises and what should be done about them. They must be entertained, briefed and introduced to foreign dignitaries by our diplomatic and consular officers.

They freely dispense opinions and advice, are tempted to accept gifts from government officials and when they do so complicate diplomacy, all the while contributing to the overseas image of America and Americans. They thus perform many diplomatic functions and of course, get in the way of those appointed by the President to do so, adding to everyone's confusion. They do not perceive that if parliamentarians of all countries emulated their example, the burden upon diplomatic establishments and government officials around the globe would be magnified to awesome proportions.

All of this, of course, can bewilder foreigners, whose parliamentarians enjoy no such privilege. At a cost of considerable confusion and sometimes loss of respect for the United States and its national legislature—when manners and particularly behavior under the influence of liquor come close to frontier standards—congressmen get to be fairly well informed, although often lacking the background to put their information in perspective. Their familiarity with our overseas diplomatic operations sometimes exceeds that of a Secretary of State who, except in the early years of the nation, has not been drawn from our diplomatic establishment, never gets around to more than a few of our posts and, for lack of time, even then cannot inquire into their operations.[11]

Congressmen and their staffs of shabby ethical standards can do much to complicate and even destroy the careers of officers, lower morale and reduce the quality of our diplomacy. Senator Joseph McCarthy, his staff assistants Roy Cohn and G. David Schine, and Congressman Richard Nixon brought ruin upon some of our "China Hands" and they are only the more egregious examples. There is a wide range of undercutting and denigrating of our diplomatic officers by Congressmen, their staffs and lobbying groups that work with them.[12]

Diplomatic complications occur when congressmen blurt out some piece of confidential information. When done to make headlines, this can be in cynical disregard of the national interest, but it can also be done to place

before the American public something of national importance which a congressman has sought in vain to impress
upon a President or the State Department. In either
case, unfortunately, it soars before the world public as
well and diplomats have to do what they can to clear up
the falling debris.

## Public clarification

Factors inherent in the evolution of democracy have
created for free societies another facet of this dimension:
what one might call public clarification. It overlaps the
organizational dimension, for managers are needed to
ensure that the responsibilities which it generates are
assumed by the diplomatic establishment.

By "public clarification" I refer to diplomacy, which is
my subject, not to foreign policy. With certain exceptions,
like Vietnam, the Panama Canal treaties recently negotiated and Southern Africa, we have generally had an
abundant public clarification of our foreign policies.
We have had little or no clarification of our diplomacy or
anyone else's, or even of diplomacy in general as the process of international politics on which we are depending
as our first line of peacetime defense. What John Stuart
Mill said of eloquence and poetry is applicable to policy
and diplomacy—the one is heard, the other overheard.
It has long been time to let more diplomacy be overheard.

The importance of this cannot be exaggerated. Diplomacy is our principal alternative to war. Upon it and its
quality rest the lives of all of us. Yet, unlike civics, diplomacy is not taught in our high schools, and not much
concerning it is taught even in our institutions of higher
learning. Since the State Department assumes no responsibility to fill in this gap, we induct into our diplomacy
men and women who lack the foggiest idea of it. The
general public, unfamiliar with its nature and resources, is
vulnerable to appeals that our government resort to force
when an effective diplomacy could do the job or to es-

calate the use of force in situations like Vietnam which are susceptible only to a political solution.

Not only the nature but the strategic and tactical substance of contemporary diplomacy needs to be overheard by the public. I am not pleading for "open diplomacy" so much as for greater ingenuity in conveying contemporary developments to the citizenry by other means than congressional shouting from the roof-tops, irresponsible leaks, and piece-meal reporting by the mass media. We are ingenious enough to invent systematic ways of keeping our people better informed concerning a process so vitally affecting them. If, for example, the State Department worked with the political science departments or interdisciplinary faculties of our colleges—and of our high schools—to stimulate the teaching of diplomacy, collaborating with them in the development of teaching materials, we would get on with the task of reconciling the demands of democracy with those of diplomacy and of conferring upon the latter a prestige it does not now enjoy because of prevailing ignorance.

## The Intellectual-Cultural-Psychological Dimension

Because diplomacy is practiced across national, cultural, psychological and historical boundaries and even across different stages of civilization, it possesses an intellectual-cultural-psychological dimension which affects every function a diplomat performs. This is at the root of his problems of gathering and evaluating intelligence, reporting to his government thousands of miles and perhaps a whole historical period and civilization away, explaining his government's policies and the character of his nation, and performing his wide-ranging public relations work. It is a determinant of his ability to command respect from foreign nationals, as well as from his own, manage posts and programs intelligently, resolve conflicts and negotiate. It affects his role as a trade promoter, particularly in sophisticated societies. It affects not only his resourcefulness as a tactician but his ability to rise to the level of strategic thinking which in turn affects his competence to advise his government and the host government on policy issues.

It is this dimension which does much to explain the extraordinary capacities of the Benjamin Franklins, Thomas Jeffersons, Jules Jusserands, Lord Bryces, David Eugene Thompsons, Dwight Morrows, David K. E. Bruces, Ellsworth Bunkers, Chip Bohlens, Anatoly Dobrynins and all the other outstanding contributors to diplomacy. These have been men of unusual intellectual capacity, cultural breadth and depth and psychological insight.

Consider Jules Jusserand. He was the French ambassador in Washington for thirteen years, from 1903 to 1915, after having spent some years in the French diplomatic service in London, Constantinople and Copenhagen. Note, first, the length of service in Washington. Then take note of his publication in 1889 of a study of *English Wayfaring Life in the Middle Ages*, six years later a *Literary History of the English People* and in 1898 *Shakespeare in France*. If one is inclined to raise his eyebrows over the relevance of English wayfaring life in the middle ages or literary studies to 20th century diplomacy, he is betraying an ignorance of the cultural depth and subtleties demanded for diplomatic competence. He may be suggesting the very reason American diplomacy so seldom gets off the ground on the various continents of the world. And if he wonders how, today, a diplomatic officer of ours could possibly engage in such cultural pursuits, he may be raising one of the vital questions concerning the quality of our diplomacy and our problem of world leadership which the American public, the President, the Congress and the State Department itself are failing to address.

Jusserand became a close friend and adviser of an American President, one generally considered so ebulliently self-confident as not to be in the market for much advice, especially from a foreigner. But when Theodore Roosevelt had a particularly difficult question to resolve, whether domestic or international, he came to seek the counsel of the French ambassador. When Secretary of State John

Hay fell ill and the President wanted the best advice he could get on some foreign affairs question, he turned not to the Acting Secretary of State, nor to a member of his Cabinet, but to this learned, perceptive, personable emissary of France. Remarkable was this relationship and it could not have evolved from anything the French Government could have done save dispatch this exceptionally competent diplomat to Washington. Such influence could not have been exerted in Paris either by the President of France, her Premier or her Minister of Foreign Affairs and any attempt to do so would have been brusquely rebuffed in Washington as "intervention" in American affairs. It could only be developed in the overseas capital itself by an erudite and empathic emissary. Here lies the subtle secret of influence and leadership in world affairs.

Since dictatorships are numerous these days, let us consider the mission of David Eugene Thompson. At a critical time in the history of Mexico, this Nebraskan was appointed our ambassador there. He was described by an American diplomatic officer who served with him as "a man of powerful personality, of large intelligence and shrewd judgment, and of sharp and forthright tongue . . . . By the lifelong exercise of a naturally strong intellect on a vast number and wide variety of books, he had, for all his lack of formal schooling, made himself into an unusually well-educated man . . . . His great value to his country lay in the fact that he possessed, as no other man possessed, the absolute confidence of the aging Mexican dictator, Don Porfirio Diaz . . . and the friendship between them illustrates the great and beneficent power a North American diplomat could, if he were trusted and well-liked, exercise unofficially in Spanish American capitals." Now observe what this produced: "Aware of the relationship between the President and the Ambassador, State Governors, generals, police officials, federal judges and even judges of the supreme court would drop into the Embassy to consult him about any case that might happen to involve Americans or American interests."[1][3]

Here is influence—indirect, indeed, but effective all the

same and indeed the greater because not exerted directly. It arose from respect. It therefore carried no taint of intervention. Is this not the secret of diplomacy? Is this not what diplomatic influence is all about? Is not this the kind of representative the United States should be sending abroad in all ranks of its diplomatic service—men and women of personality, large intelligence, culture, and shrewd judgment, people articulate, well-liked and trusted?

James Bryce, who served as the British Ambassador in Washington for six years (1907-13), although he had not held previously any diplomatic post, was well seasoned as a scholar, professor, party leader and government official, and had published a celebrated two-volume study of the United States, *The American Commonwealth*. His knowledge of the strengths and weaknesses of our society being profound, he was one of the most sentient and popular ambassadors ever to serve in this country. He was in great demand as a speaker and he spoke with typical British substance and grace. Wherever he went, he represented the best of British culture and did much, therefore, to nurture that pro-British sentiment which was to prove so useful to his government when the first of the world wars descended upon it. Here again, is not this the kind of favorable view and good will which the United States should be seeking throughout the world by sending its best people to represent it? What does it gain by sending second- and third-rate people and even clowns? (If the example of Bryce suggests that a government should appoint no one as ambassador who has not written a perceptive book on the country to which he is to be sent, one can see considerable merit in the idea. One could only add that exceptions should be made for the Thompsons, Bunkers, Bohlens and their like.)

This has been a hard dimension for Americans to grasp. The frontier attitude, which continues astonishingly resistant to extinction, is that diplomacy is a push over, something that can be done by anyone of common sense, with little or no preparation, no particular cultural depth, no particular ability to articulate his thoughts, and no training whatever in strategy and tactics. Its principal occupation is conceived by the frontier mind to be telling other people what they should do to pull up their socks. It is because of this attitude that we elect Presidents with no experience in foreign affairs and Presidents, in turn, appoint inexperienced and incompetent people as ambassadors and State Department officials, even as Secretaries of State. We have recently had one Secretary of State with such enormous psychological problems he could not trust and extensively draw upon, much less mobilize and improve, our diplomatic establishment but, instead, dealt it demoralizing and crippling blows.

Few Secretaries of State, indeed, are anything but dimly aware of this dimension. Being themselves often unseasoned in diplomacy, they appoint, or set policies which permit subordinates to appoint, inexperienced and sometimes incompetent people to the State Department and Foreign Service. So far has this extraordinary practice been carried that since 1967, under an Equal Opportunity Program pushed by Secretaries of State, unqualified ethnics have been systematically named to the Department and the Foreign Service in total disregard of the political and intellectual requirements of diplomacy. (This point is expanded on pages 281-282).

There was a time early in our history, when we managed our foreign affairs with far better political judgment. Presidents of the United States served previously as Secretaries of State and Secretaries of State acquired their position only after diplomatic experience abroad. They thus brought to the two top positions of our government a good working knowledge of foreign affairs, skills sharpened by apprenticeship and an appreciation of the preparation which effective diplomacy requires. The period lasted from the election of Thomas Jefferson until the frontier mentality achieved ascendance in our political thinking with the election of Andrew Jackson in 1829.

One sees much of the Jackson frontier swagger in the human rights campaign of the Carter Administration. It hit the international trail with a kind of covered-wagon, muleteering drive under the leadership of young, un-traveled, inexperienced zealots who rudely brushed aside all other strategic considerations and sensitivities, not to add a weighing of how private human rights organizations could be utilized and strengthened. In all our history, with all our faults and failures to measure up to our own declared ideals, no government—apart from the Soviet, which is *sui generis* in a number of respects—has publicly upbraided us for our shortcomings, well understanding it would be bristlingly resented and thus prove, in all prob-ability, counter-productive. Even our horrible institution of slavery other governments let us work at in our own way and resolve in our own time. But this kind of sensi-tivity does not appeal to frontier minds, which make a fetish of direct, rude, flambuoyant action and lack the slightest sense of ordonnance.

Much of our frontier approach to diplomacy was evi-dent, also, in our decision to go to the rescue of the South Vietnamese. This was a nobly conceived crusade to give the South Vietnamese a freedom of choice, supported by what were considered strategic interests, but at no time was any inventory made of the diplomatic resources needed for such a complex nation-building strategy, which of these our government possessed and what should be done to supply those we lacked in advance of intervention. Whether such a matching of diplomatic resources to com-mitment would have turned the trick in the short term no one can say, but to embark on such a venture with major emphasis upon military and CIA resources was the height of frontier folly. This astonishingly low-grade strategic and tactical thinking sealed the fate of the inter-vention and its failure opened up a Pandora's box of division at home and irresoluteness in diplomacy which the Soviet Union proceeded to exploit in its African and Afghanistan adventurism.

As to both of these crusades, the results of our nation-building and human-rights-building in Cuba and the Philip-pines after the Spanish American war, under far more favorable conditions than Southeast Asia presented, should have been a warning. Except in rare cases, such as colonization, a nation simply cannot export its own values and institutions. The results of such efforts are short-term at best and are eventually overtaken by the character of a people, which determines the kind of government they will have and what human rights their government will observe. Any blatant, brash, tub-thumping evangelism by a foreign government will accomplish little more than temporary relief at the cost of much resentment and irritation corrosive of other important strategic interests.

This is not to say that governments cannot quietly and shrewdly exert a variety of pressures to correct the more obvious cruelties inflicted by governments upon their citizens and that private organizations cannot be greatly bolstered. Nor does this mean that the ideological battle should not be waged. Not at all. The question is how to wage it adeptly and shrewdly, with wisdom and finesse, how much should be waged by words and how much by example, how much by governments and how much by private organizations stimulated, encouraged and assisted by governments. But to tax diplomacy with an overt, chiding, hostile, tub-tumping interventionism is to impose upon it something for which it is not suited and therefore invite not success and relief of many victims of injustice but ill will, eventual failure and the discredit of the government engaging in it.

I am aware that this word of caution will not satisfy everybody, including the naive, "can do" frontiersmen and many decent people who look with horror upon evil in the world, but we must seek always the courage to do the possible, the willingness to accept the impossible and the wisdom to distinguish the two.

It is evident that the political and intellectual-cultural-psychological dimensions interact and this interaction does much to determine the quality of a nation's diplomacy and thus the extent of its power in international affairs. In view of our present situation it may sound odd that a few years ago foreign writers were propagating the notion that the United States is a modern Rome intent upon building a global empire, but the politically damaging results of this widely publicized view required that the United States' diplomatic representatives—of all ranks—be prepared with maximum intellectual resources to cope with it. No such effort was made and our traditional, pedestrian conception of the diplomatic function of "representation" has been wholly inadequate to cope with this and other equally subtle factors affecting the international climate.[14]   Whatever the factors at work against us in the world community, they demand a quality and an activity of diplomats more dynamic and more ingenious, more active and more profound—beyond the walls and desks of embassy and consular offices—than any which we have envisaged heretofore.

*Types of diplomacy*

From this intellectual-cultural-psychological dimension it follows that there is not one type of diplomacy but many—as many as there are histories, cultures, psychologies and combinations of these. Although Western diplomacy has many values and objectives in common, United States' diplomacy is not the same as Britain's, nor Britain's as France's, and these types are not the same as Japan's, Japan's as the Soviet Union's, the Soviet Union's as Zaire's, South Africa's or Mexico's. Diplomacy, thus, is not a single but a psycho-sociological phenomenon.   What justifies the use of a generic word to cover so many types are the basic elements of strategies, tactics, techniques, personal skills and logistics, which are common to all.

The failure to recognize this variety causes Americans much confusion in international politics, particularly in their dealings with the Soviet Union, which has its own history, psychology and culture, not to add ideology. The two countries conceptualize diplomacy differently and employ different types. Americans think of diplomacy as an instrument for promoting truth, understanding and peace; the Kremlin, as an instrument as useful for deception and promoting misunderstanding, rivalry and confusion as for any other purposes. Our conception leads us to think of détente as a friendly relationship or at least one free from prevarication, cheating, and aggressive fomentation or exploitation of instability in underdeveloped countries—a kind of Eden of decency. The Kremlin thinks of it in no such terms but simply as a tactic to lull another country into a relaxed attitude so that the diplomatic contest can be pursued more advantageously to itself. It is all a matter of history and geography, psychology, ideology and therefore strategic interests and tactical values.

There are governments which apply not only in their military but their diplomatic operations von Clausewitz's dictum: "Be audacious and cunning in your plans, firm and persevering in their execution, determined to find a glorious end."[15] Any government failing to compete with such a government shrewdly and boldly, firmly, perseveringly and with a sense of high mission must inevitably lose. One type of diplomacy must be met by a competitive type —not necessarily the same type—if the vying of values and interests that goes on in the international political process is not to be one-sided.

Diplomacy, then, does not take place in the tidily buoyed channel marked for striped-pants navigators so long imagined by frontier-minded Americans. If there is some validity to that figure of speech, there being limitations upon the activities of diplomats in exchange for their privileges and immunities, the channel is of markedly varying width and depth in different societies. It can also swirl with different and conflicting currents, including religious, tribal and ideological, presenting unexpected turns and bars. Like a sand-strewn African river, diplomacy confronts the practitioner with a constantly shifting course and the necessity of demonstrating quickness of navigational judgment and skill, shrewdness and sometimes boldness. Under these circumstances, the policy he is steering makes its way with difficulty and on occasion, like an African river-boat, has to be ingeniously turned around so as to let the current swing it stern first through the twist of a shifting channel in order to emerge prow first—and right side up—for the next challenge.

The different histories, cultures, and psychologies of people ensure these eccentricities of channel and current. But individual navigators add their own. It is wise to keep in mind *si duo faciunt idem, non est idem* (if two people do the same thing, it is not the same thing). This is not just a matter of style but depth of learning, differences in background and psychology, and degrees of skill, and therefore differences in perspective and grasp of the art and science of political navigation. No one would maintain that the diplomacy of a George Marshall was the same as that of a Jules Jusserand, that of Jusserand as that of Lord Bryce, a David Eugene Thompson or a Dwight Morrow, except in the basic elements of tactics and techniques and such qualities as tact, resourcefulness and decisiveness.

### The Dimension of Overseas Projection

It is a peculiarity of diplomacy that it is politics projected beyond national frontiers, into—to change the figure of speech—a brier patch of conflicting interests, ethical standards and actions by other governments. It must clear a way through that thicket for a government's interests and policies.

To clear that path, a government operates diplomatic missions and consular posts. Because they know the local thicket better than their distant principal, they are the best judge of which policies and tactics will work and which will not, what steps need to be taken to facilitate them and at what time. As obvious as this may appear, it is difficult for some Americans to grasp, including officials from Presidents and Secretaries of State on down. The zealots of human rights posted in the State Department by the Carter Administration have plunged into the brier patch, rejecting all counsel of caution, brushing aside the advice of seasoned diplomats on how to proceed and all but reduced their country's foreign relations to tatters.

Because of the importance of this dimension a wise old diplomat, François de Callières, once counseled would-be diplomats to travel extensively abroad, not as tourists but as students, to learn the social systems and values that govern foreign countries. Unless one did so, he warned, one would never learn that the institutions and concepts of foreign countries are often fundamentally different from one's own and discover how to cope with them.[16]   Perhaps the only thing that need to be said in criticism of zealotry in diplomacy is that it is practiced by untraveled people.

It is only common sense that governments should weigh carefully the reports of its overseas posts and elevate to the highest appropriate levels of decision-making their insights, warnings and advice.   It is also necessary, by suitable techniques, to keep these before decision-makers over the years.   Events are not a series of disconnected happenings but a continuum and they can be understood and crises anticipated and managed only in that context. Crisis management in diplomacy requires a familiarity with the background of the crisis.   A government surprised by developments in Iran in 1978 of which it had been warned by its diplomatic mission in Tehran fourteen years earlier is not effectively exercising power.[17]   A Secretary of State who imperiously brushes ambassadors aside when he visits the capitals in which they are posted, refusing to take them with him in discussions he has with local officials not only displays a flabbergasting ignorance of diplomacy: he is a dangerous official.

That this overseas dimension places a heavy burden on any government department goes without saying and since the department dealing with foreign affairs is racked by a constant rotation of personnel, the burden becomes sizable indeed, demanding unusual measures and resources to cope with it.   The relationship of this problem to research and retrieval is plain and one of the more severe indictments that can be made of our State Department is that its officials have signally failed to recognize and accept its challenge.

A government's relationship with its overseas operators being a crucial factor of its ability to act alertly and intelligently, the State Department's failure to give it more than casual attention has cost this country many reverses. Opportunity after opportunity for timely action has been lost and leadership constantly eroded.

Illustrative of this is the experience of an American ambassador to Libya in the early 1950s. He has recorded it as follows:

> ... The Prime Minister [of Libya] had resigned and flown off to Rome, his nerves frayed by the thankless task of guiding a newborn state. The king was ill, in seclusion; there was a rumor in the bazaars that he might abdicate. The whole government structure seemed about to collapse. I had just reached a vital point in negotiations for an air-base agreement. So when the Libyan cabinet asked me to fly to Italy and persuade the Prime Minister to return I cabled the Department urgently for permission to make the try.

> Time was of the essence, yet the hours ticked by without response. In Washington, the wheels ground methodically. Committee met with committee, weighing the pros and cons of my recommendation. The Pentagon had to be consulted. Policy factors had to be considered; so did tactics, in the light of progress to date on the air-base negotiations. Suggestions at a lower level had to be referred to a higher level for further discussion. I sent a second cable. No reply.

> Finally I decided to act on my own. I boarded the plane of my Air Attaché, flew to Rome, and called on the Prime Minister at his hotel. With all the eloquence I could muster, I urged him to come back and steer the ship of state through the storm, pointing out that the fate of his country—and our delicate negotiations—rested in his hands alone. He heard me in silence, still smarting from the political wounds which had caused him to resign. He would think it

over; he would give me his answer that evening.

At eight o'clock I was again at the Prime Minister's door. His face was wreathed in smiles. He would do as I asked, and to mark the occasion he invited me to dine with him downstairs. With a load like lead off my mind, I was enjoying the repast when I spied an officer of our Rome embassy discreetly waving a piece of paper from behind the potted palms. I made my excuses, rose, and went over to receive the message—a priority cable to Tripoli, repeated to Rome for information. At long last, Washington had moved. There were my orders. *Under no circumstances* was I to follow the Prime Minister to Rome, for that, the Department feared, might be interpreted as interference in the domestic affairs of a sovereign country.[18]

Earl E. T. Smith argues that while he was ambassador to Cuba during the guerilla activity of Castro the important issues that activity raised were not adequately presented to the Department's summit and never (as far as he knows) to the President or the National Security Council.[19] Since he was trying to put together a group which would provide the Cubans with a third alternative to Batista and Castro, it was important that this effort be adequately understood at the highest levels, either approved or rejected there, and if approved be given all possible support. Had Smith succeeded in Cuba, all necessity of a Bay of Pigs and a missile crisis with the Russians might have been avoided. Those on the front line can be stymied by the inadequacies of the ministry of foreign affairs at home.

Not only do these cases draw attention to the difference between diplomatic officers and civil servants and to the need of recruiting only the most gifted and enlightened people to serve in a diplomatic establishment, but they suggest how much of the strength and weakness of a nation in international affairs lie in this dimension—in other words, how much a nation's "power" resides in its diplomatic skill. For in this dimension resides a government's ability to act quietly, intelligently, without fanfare, yet efficaciously. Here, much of the respect and confidence of other governments is won or lost. Grand pronouncements of interests do not provide leadership in world affairs. Sophisticated statesmen know full well that the extent to which and the skill with which pronouncements are followed up by diplomacy determines their value and that this, in turn, rests in no small measure upon the willingness of a government to respect and utilize the judgment and initiative of its diplomatic and consular officers.

Much of the morale of a diplomatic service and hence the quality of its performance is determined in this dimension. A service not kept well informed, denied the freedom of appropriate initiative and treated with scant respect is not only aware that it is carrying little weight but that other governments are aware as well.

Other sources of frustration abound in this dimension. Few missions are totally satisfied with either the policies or the perceptions of their government or indeed the perceptions of their principal officers. Differences in education and specialization, in extensiveness and kinds of local contacts, in precision of knowledge, in experience and in political judgment—even in linguistic competence—account for divergencies of view. An age of revolutionary change such as our own multiplies these differences in perception. With missions located at a distance from headquarters and staff members enjoying different degrees of access to that headquarters' echelons of authority, the tasks of reporting, analyzing and developing advice and courses of action can be difficult indeed. Only the best and most seasoned minds are good at this. And when the reporting, analysis and advice runs counter to the prevailing views at headquarters the risks of misunderstanding and penalization are multiplied.

There is, of course, a minimal coherence and discipline which a mission must seek in its reporting and advice. For headquarters to receive varying intelligence, and contradictory evaluations of what the intelligence means and advice on what actions should be undertaken is not a bad thing up to a point. But if a mission cannot itself agree on what is going on, what is coming up over the horizon and what action is demanded confusion and paralysis can result. There is a nice line to be drawn between the fertilizing effects of dissent and bewilderment. This is why relatively few political appointees, with the scantiest knowledge of the countries to which they are sent, make good chiefs of mission. But this does not mean that career officers are necessarily good at it, either. It takes very special instincts, education, training and experience.

When the task of a diplomatic or consular officer posted abroad is complicated by the intrusion of congressmen and lobbies in questions of policy and diplomacy, by a general climate of public opinion at home and by a stupidity or spinelessness of key officers at headquarters, he can be frustrated, penalized and even ruined. Such is what happened to some of our China specialists a generation ago. As one of them has observed of a colleague:

> When the Sino-Japanese War commenced and the Japanese occupied Shantung in 1937 and 1938, our consul in Tsingtao was Samuel Sokobin. He was a capable, conscientious officer—a China specialist of long experience. As is often the case, he had come to have a genuine liking and respect for the Chinese. Eventually, Chinese guerrillas began to be active in Shantung. Soon the Chinese press was carrying dramatic accounts of heroic exploits in crippling the Japanese-held railways and denying the Japanese the important agricultural and mineral resources of the province. In his post at the main port, and making intelligent use of excellent contacts in shipping and business circles, Sokobin came to realize the gross exaggeration in these claims. The Japanese were maintaining and increasing the flow of these strategic materials to Japan.
>
> Sokobin did not consider that a responsible officer needed to be told when (or what) to report. He

commenced a series of reports thoroughly document-
ing the success of the Japanese in countering the guerrillas and in exploiting the resources of their occupied
territory. He should, of course, have been commended;
but the reaction his reports received was very different. He was upsetting the picture, then the accepted line, of a Chinese resistance not only brave but
also effective. Sokobin's reports were harshly depreciated. He was cruelly and ridiculously accused of
being "pro-Japanese." And, with a perverted idea of
justice, his transfer was arranged to Kobe, Japan.
He was never returned to service in China.

Sokobin's career might never have reached the
heights—one can never know. But in 1947 he finished
33½ years of loyal service as Class 3 and consul in
Birmingham.

This was long before McCarthy had become a
senator. The United States was neutral in the Sino-
Japanese War, and there was no outside high level
pressure. It was entirely an internal State Department
affair: in fact, it was done by the China branch to
one of their own. Perhaps, in valuing the integrity
and honesty of field reporting, few of us are beyond
reproach.[20]

The persecution of the China Hands was outrageous, but
the use of assignments in an establishment of rotating personnel as a penalty for dissent, or a device of personal
vengeance, has not been restricted to them. So greatly
have personnel problems flourished in the American diplomatic service as to make it astonishing that only in recent
years have steps been taken to give officers abroad direct
official access to Washington redressment of grievances.
A "dissent channel" has been established which permits
officers to convey to the Secretary of State views which
dispute superiors' or call in question United States policy.
As for personnel grievances, these can now be submitted
to a Washington board whose members are independent of
Department administrators. Such procedures should pre-

vent such injustices as were heaped upon the China Hands and correct many another. Operating such systems in a world-wide establishment involved in a dynamic political process and therefore demanding a certain amount of discipline is not one of the easier diplomatic tasks, and until the State Department creates a truly professional educational program the system may serve better the grievances of individuals than the needs of the establishment as a whole.

Women's liberation has produced stresses in the American diplomatic service unknown in the past. Traditionally, wives of the diplomatic officers of all nations have actively participated in the diplomatic process, sharing in the professional interests of their husbands, promoting the interests of their countries and making a contribution, if such be the objectives of their governments, to international good will, understanding and peace. This has involved extensive entertainment, community (including charity) work and, in the case of wives of American officers, service on committees dealing with various facilities of the American community, such as schools. Through these activities they have usefully supplemented their husband's sources of information and appraisal of local happenings, thereby assisting their government's gathering of intelligence. When sufficiently sophisticated, they have also been participants in their government's tactical moves. Repeatedly thrown into a strenuous inter-cultural, inter-political situation requiring energy, tact, ingenuity and rapid accomplishment in establishing a family in a new environment, as well as contributing to their nation's representational resources abroad, wives in the past have found their role to be an exhilarating adventure.

Since there never was financial remuneration for any of this, some American wives today regard these as heavy and onerous duties, with champions of women's liberation denouncing them as exploitative. It has not occurred to them that wives of Presidents, Congressmen and other public officials are not remunerated for their active participation in their partners' political careers. But the State

Department has not rejected their quixotic notion in the diplomatic arena. It has refused to take a firm stand in accordance with a clear conception of the diplomatic process, cringing and retreating, even to the point of forbidding all evaluation of wives and their contribution to our diplomatic effort. They can now be the worst possible representatives of their country, doing the opposite of what the wives of Jusserand, Bryce, Thompson, Bruce and Bohlen have done for their countries and for the international community, but no report of this can be made and no action can be taken to relieve their husbands of their commissions. A wife is now free to do her own thing which, needless to say, has depreciated the diplomatic establishment in comparison with the military and struck people abroad as naive, producing one more question whether Americans are really up to the demands of international leadership in as highly competitive a business as international politics. The absurdity of the notion that in a part of our national defense system a wife can behave as though she were an independent individual, on a "me generation" lark, with no responsibilities to her country, is but one more symptom of our diplomatic crisis.

## Rotation

Because diplomatic officers serve abroad, they must be rotated at least between overseas posts and their headquarters, in order to avoid loss of their national roots. But the existence of undesirable, even unhealthy and otherwise dangerous locations requires that a certain amount of rotation also occur between posts. Thus, it is a feature of diplomatic establishments, unlike most civil services, that officers rotate periodically.

As in the case with the military establishments in peacetime, rotation over the centuries has been a way of avoiding in diplomatic establishments a sedentary mentality. It has also discouraged diplomats from succumbing to the seductions of a foreign country and acquiring sentimental attachments destructive of objective judgment or commercial attachments favorable to future employment. Finally, it has been a way of broadening perspectives.

These were once valid reasons, when distance and poor communication made it difficult for governments to keep tabs on their diplomats and for the latter to follow events beyond their limited horizons. This has changed. Communication is now easy and rapid, virtually instantaneous; inspectors periodically make their rounds; and a host of other means, including the mass media, exist to prevent parochialism. But the fetish continues with officers normally transferred to new posts every three or four years, and oftener if special need arises. This succession of assignments undoubtedly broadens the diplomat's perceptions of policy and diplomacy, but this could be accomplished in other ways, such as reading programs, a slightly more generous staffing of posts to provide leisure to study and reflect beyond the immediate environment, and sabbaticals. The disadvantages of frequent rotation are serious, beyond the financial cost. It permits only superficial knowledge of foreign countries, deprives the diplomat of as wide a range of influential contacts as he could otherwise build and as modern diplomacy demands, and often renders language proficiency impossible, further reducing ability to communicate and persuade.

The length of Jusserand's and Bryce's tours of duty in Washington have been mentioned. The Soviet Union has kept Anatoly Dobrynin as its ambassador in Washington for an even longer period, seventeen years as of March 1979.[21] In these notable instances, governments, finding their representative well chosen, acquiring an acute understanding of the host society and expanding his influence through a widening circle of contacts, wisely discarded the ritual of rotation.

### The Dimension of Policy Making

These three dimensions combine to produce a fourth, for they make any diplomat worth his salt an incomparable resource of advice in his government's formulation of foreign policy. He can provide useful interpretation not only of the information which he himself supplies but of that which reaches his government from a myriad of sources. His insights, which only a close observer stationed abroad can acquire, are essential to correcting the limitations of home-bound officials. The "best and the brightest" of such officials can make tragic mistakes of foreign policy, as we learned from Vietnam.

There are times when a Chief of State knows he must act but does not know what action to take. Furthermore, his policy decision must be carried out and one of the tests of a policy's soundness is whether indeed it can be carried out and, if so, with what consequences. In all these stages of policy formulation, diplomatic experience counts. Llewellyn Thompson, a career diplomat, was an integral participant in the various stages of policy formulation by President John F. Kennedy in the Cuban missile crisis. Other diplomatic officers took part, but Thompson, a former ambassador to the Soviet Union, could give "advice on the Russians and predictions as to what they would do" which "were uncannily accurate." His "advice and recommendations were surpassed by none."[22] It was an acute analysis by George Kennan while serving as counselor in our Embassy Moscow which crystalized thinking in Washington about the Soviet Union in 1946, incidentally effecting his transfer to Washington and eventual chairmanship of a newly established Policy Planning Council in the State Department.[23] When serving as the U.S. Ambassador in Paris, David K. E. Bruce received from the State Department a telegram proposing a policy with respect to European defense which he considered seriously flawed. Through a skillfully worded telegram in reply, he steered the Washington decision-makers to a different policy.[24] Wise indeed is the government which recruits superior people for its diplomatic service and consults them fully in the development of policies.

While this is one of the more important admonitions of experience, I would not be so rash as to suggest that the United States government invariably heeds it. As noted

before, we have had a Secretary of State in recent years
who deliberately flaunted it. He kept much of his senior
Department staff at arms length and when he traveled
abroad neither conferred with our ambassadors nor took
them with him in his talks with government officials.
This one-track behavior of course diminished his own resources as well as those of his government, eroding the
esteem of host governments for our ambassadors, thereby
reducing their effectiveness, and decreased respect for the
United States as a diplomatically competent country. As
noted earlier, the human rights zealots have also acted
as though this dimension did not exist.

## The Military Dimension

Diplomacy has always existed in a symbiotic relationship with force. From the earliest dawn of human existence, grunts of discourse have been accompanied by the
brandishing of whatever objects were available for conveying interests and intentions to defend them. With the
rise of nation states, war became an expression of national
policy by other than political and economic means.
Accordingly, when a nation's strategic considerations
include a recognition of war as likely or inevitable, as
occurred in the Japanese preparation for the attack on
Pearl Harbor, diplomacy shades off indistinguishably into
a stage of military tactics. Even in the best of times,
diplomacy, as an integral element of national security,
must be closely associated with military resources for the
assertion of national interests and the enforcement of
international law.

"Gun boat diplomacy" was an expression of this symbi-
osis, with consular as well as diplomatic officers authorized
to call in a vessel of war to protect the lives and property
of their nationals. While this authority no longer exists,
governments still deploy naval vessels as a diplomatic
tactic. When a signal is conveyed by one government to
another of a readiness to use force—as in the maneuver
of naval, army or air units—a gray area arises between

diplomacy and military action, which can shade into war itself, as those involved in the Cuban missile crisis well understood.

With diplomacy intimately tied to national security, diplomats have always been used as intelligence agents. It was only in the late nineteenth century that military attachés were added to embassies to provide specialists in the military field, but a continued overlapping of political and military intelligence was ensured not only by the fact that the employment of military resources in international affairs is a political decision but by those social factors which determine military capability and convey military intentions. The intelligence agencies of military services have grown correspondingly, with considerable supplementation from civilian intelligence agencies, including the diplomatic. *Pari passu*, diplomatic establishments draw upon military intelligence agencies for much information of a socio-political nature.

Side by side with the natural affinity of diplomacy and force has come an extraordinary evolution of the military into a negotiating instrument. In our case, this occurred in our navy in its earliest years,[25] and in our army in its dealings with the Indians, nation-building efforts in Cuba, Puerto Rico and the Philippines after the Spanish American war and participation in the Hague disarmament conferences; and in our air force since World War II. This negotiating function has reached such impressive proportions that it is no longer accurate to view the military establishment as simply a military establishment. It has become a vast, complex, social institution with the broadest possible negotiating relationships with not only its own but foreign societies.

At home and abroad the military negotiates with producers of military equipment and supplies, with local citizens and communities wherever military posts are located, with the academic community over research programs—sociological as well as scientific—and with Congress for appropriations and policy support. It participates with the State Department in negotiations with foreign governments concerning military assistance and bases and, from base rights, negotiations spread like an oil slick over an extensive area. The very employment of foreign nationals at its far-ranging installations obliges the military to negotiate not only with them but their labor organizations, with local communities, and with national ministries of labor, welfare, finance and sometimes foreign affairs. It operates schools for dependent children and radio broadcasting systems which, by attracting a local audience, greatly amplify the American impact. The administration of justice at such installations involves the military in sensitive negotiations with the local authorities. Not only the public relations officers but a broad range of the command hierarchy can be as deeply involved in the substance and art of diplomacy as diplomats.

This is also true in the interesting interaction of military and political objectives which comes to a focus in the use of military assistance to strengthen democratic values and processes in underdeveloped countries. As a part of its training and equipment exercise, our military has designed "civic action" programs to put the military forces of backward countries to work helping peasants build schools, clinics, and roads to markets. In some areas, the indigenous military groups dispense medical treatment to the general population and organize civilian groups advisory to the military, which have served to bring it face to face with the social problems of the civilian population. With democratic interests and attitudes in the military establishments of backward countries thus encouraged, a forward thrust has been given to popular government not available from diplomatic resources. Missing, however, has been a thorough knowledge of these efforts by our diplomatic officers stationed in such countries and a skillful synthesis of diplomatic and military efforts.

The "civic action" program has reinforced within our military establishment an awareness of the deep sociological forces which must be reckoned with in overseas interests and operations and given impetus to the increasing sophistication of that establishment's research and training efforts. A facet of this surfaced in the "Camelot" affair. Perceiving the need of developing ways of measuring and forecasting the causes of revolution and insurgency in underdeveloped countries, the Army sponsored a research project for the purpose at an American university. The research was to be conducted in Latin American countries, under the code name "Camelot." When its existence became public knowledge in Brazil and Chile in midsummer 1965 it was viewed there as a brazen *Norteamericano* intrusion in domestic concerns. An emotional and noisy brouhaha ensued; the State Department stepped in and the project was canceled. Thus, a useful and constructive undertaking was scotched for lack of political sensitivity in our Department of Defense and a timely diplomatic smoothing of the way by the State Department.[26]

Other instances of the military's failure to grasp the diplomatic dimensions of its decisions have occurred, as in its termination of "Skybolt," an air-to-ground missile with a nuclear warhead. As the missile was in course of development, the U.S. agreed to provide it, when completed, to the British government, in order to solve the latter's problem of maintaining a strategic deterrent. The British adjusted their national defense plans accordingly. On a cost-effectiveness basis, our Defense Department decided late in 1962 to abandon the missile, but the British were not notified and given a chance to work out an acceptable alternative. The Pentagon's announcement of its decision came out of the blue sky; a political crisis erupted in London; a conference on the highest level was held in Nassau, the President of the United States and the British Prime Minister attending. There the problem was resolved.

Bewildered over how the political system of the Defense Department could have produced such a diplomatic blunder and desirous of avoiding a repetition, President Kennedy commissioned Professor Richard E. Neustadt to do a study of it. The result was as illuminating as the episode itself. The Neustadt inquiry focused narrowly on the relations of the American Secretary of Defense and his British counterpart, with only side glances to the British ambassador in Washington and the State Department. The question why the military as a negotiating instrument had not been effectively married to the diplomatic establishment was not investigated. It was a classic case of American failure to identify the diplomatic dimension of a military decision.[27] Had that been explored, raising the issues it posed, and its warnings brought to the attention of the proper officials, the whole Southeast Asian blunder, which soon followed, might conceivably have been scotched. For that, too, presented the crucial issue of diplomatic restraint upon military decisions.

The military participates in the negotiation and implementation of security treaties and when this implementation involves an organization like NATO, the military's horizons become very broad indeed. Acquired in the process is a seasoning in and an influence upon political, economic and social concerns of a range not much less extensive than the diplomats'.

Through its role in the negotiation of arms limitations treaties with the Soviet Union and discussions directed to a reduction of forces in Europe, our military acquires a familiarity with Soviet objectives, bargaining psychology, techniques and tactics not very different from the diplomats'. Obversely, these negotiations have likewise generated broader perspectives within the Soviet military-industrial complex, with dialogue becoming an accepted component of Soviet military thinking rather than viewed as a trick foisted on the U.S.S.R. by a devious and hostile West.

It is because a military establishment in a free society has acquired broad social functions and experience that, in the case of the United States, generals and admirals are not infrequently appointed to diplomatic positions. One has served as Secretary of State—General George C. Marshall; another as Under Secretary of State—General Walter Bedell Smith; a third as Assistant Secretary of State—General John Hildring; and still others as ambassadors. While this is a departure from common practice in the international community, such appointments being seen by other governments as conveying a military message they consider undesirable, the departure is symbolic of the broad functions and proficiencies of a modern military establishment. *Pari passu*, the military has recognized the intellectual-cultural demands of its role in its educational and training programs, one of the results of which is that many colonels hold doctoral degrees in international relations. That this would have an effect upon the scale and use of military intelligence could be expected.

On its part, our diplomatic establishment has encountered difficulty, particularly at crucial turning points, in asserting the primacy of political interests and objectives and the need of taking stock of diplomatic resources in mapping strategy. This has become a continuing source of weakness in the conduct of our foreign affairs and thus of our present diplomatic crisis.

### The Dimension of Covert Activities

The Western concept of diplomacy as it evolved in the last century or more, apart from totalitarian regimes, came to abjure clandestine activity, and hence to view that activity, as overt war, as a projection of policy by other means. The "tidily buoyed channel" of Western diplomacy defined as unacceptable not only covert operations such as financial assistance to friendly political parties in other countries and "dirty tricks" against hostile governments, but clandestine intelligence gathering and all that goes with it, including bribery and paid informants. Any diplomatic officer caught violating these norms was promptly declared *persona non grata* and his recall requested.[28]

Hence, confronted by fascist and communist assertion of a contrary code, Western governments turned to special agencies for conducting such activities. The operatives of such agencies work without the limiting symbols of sovereignty, the values of civilization, and the norms of decorous behavior which define the channel of diplomacy. By the same token, their work represents an unhappy retrogression to less civilized times. In fighting fire with fire, the more civilized nations have been forced to point one of their governmental agencies backward in the direction of barbarism.

Totalitarian governments view covert activities as a dimension of diplomacy and therefore do not hesitate to cloak their operatives with diplomatic and consular credentials and to utilize their nationals on the secretariats of international organizations for the purpose. Thus, the activity of foreign intelligence agents in the United States is extensive. The Soviet Union's KGB, Yugoslavia's Administration for Research and Documentation (UID), and the comparable intelligence agencies of Chile, Iran under the Shah, the Philippines, South Korea, Taiwan and others, are directed to the silencing of critics, influencing American opinion by propaganda and undermining the relations of the United States with other countries. The Taiwan Government, for example, worked hard in the United States to delay our diplomatic recognition of the Peoples Republic of China, infiltrating college campuses and student organizations, conducting large-scale propaganda campaigns through front organizations and staging anti-Peking demonstrations.

All of this activity is designed to have a chilling effect upon public discussion and attitudes, prevent officials and citizens from obtaining accurate information from émigrés and foreign students about conditions in their home lands and deter U.S. diplomatic moves. Some intelligence agencies carry this effort as far as assassination of dissident émigrés, as did the Soviet Union in the cases of Leon Trotsky, who had taken refuge in Mexico, and General Krivitsky in the United States. The problems and stresses of diplomacy are thus multiplied, as are those of a free society in ensuring constitutional guarantees of free discussion and assembly.

The discouragement and prevention of defection by their diplomats and other citizens is one of the principal functions of a totalitarian government's clandestine service and this can present many problems to the diplomacy of free societies. The frequently massive presence of KGB agents in Soviet embassies is designed not only to conduct intelligence and counter-intelligence operations against the host government, propagandize, recruit spies and silence defectors but to watch and control the movements and decisions of Soviet diplomats and other citizens of the U.S.S.R. This factor is obscured from general view and there are times when our government officials act as though they are unaware of it as well. Thus, in August 1979, when moving to ensure that Ludmilla Vlasova, the ballerina wife of the defecting Bolshoi dancer, Alexander Godunov, would be interviewed by U.S. government representatives under circumstances guaranteeing her the right to choose freely whether to remain in the United States or return to the Soviet Union, U.S. officials acted as though they were oblivious of the KGB's role in Soviet diplomacy. They relied upon the assurance of the Soviet Embassy in Washington that Vlasova's right would be respected, taking no precautions on the possibility they were dealing with KGB people at the Soviet Embassy or with diplomatic personnel incapable of restraining KGB action. As a consequence, Vlasova was spirited out of her New York City hotel by Soviet guards and whisked aboard a Soviet plane at Kennedy International Airport. Thereafter, U.S. diplomacy never regained its lost ground. After a stand-off of several days, during which the Soviets refused to permit Vlasova off the plane for an interview and the U.S. refused to let the plane depart for Moscow, the compromise was reached to allow a mobile lounge vehicle to be joined to the Soviet plane and in it, with six Soviet representatives (and an equal number of American) present Vlasova was questioned. This overwhelming Soviet presence was inconducive to any real freedom of choice for Vlasova. The efficiency which KGB agents give to Soviet diplomacy was once more attested.

While there are important differences in the objectives of the KGB and the CIA—the primary one being between the suppression and the promotion of freedom—and in philosophical values, there are disturbing similarities in tactics. The CIA, like the KGB, has been admitted to the diplomatic dimension, nestling in our diplomatic missions and consular posts, its operatives provided diplomatic and consular titles for cover. While it cannot openly defy diplomatic and consular superiors or take charge in crises as can the KGB, it *is* a secret agency and as such has been permitted an extraordinary freedom to meddle—often with a kind of adolescent, frontier exuberance—in the internal affairs of countries, decide on its own whom it would support among available parties and individuals, sometimes undercutting those backed by the State Department, gravely misconceive and mismanage major projects, as the Bay of Pigs, and even foment and conduct undeclared wars. Little by little it has edged into an area of decision and action reserved by the Constitution to the President alone, spreading contradictions and confusions in our foreign affairs. Clandestinity is not something we have learned to master but, rather, all too often, it has mastered us.

So it will continue until our diplomatic establishment trains its officers more thoroughly in intelligence gathering and evaluation, uses them (including those in consular posts) more effectively, provides them with the banks of computers and specialists needed to operate more efficiently in the intelligence area, expands its officer corps and support personnel commensurately, and jacks up its general organizational competence. Until then, a vacuum will continue to exist between our foreign affairs needs and our diplomatic resources which a secret agency, amply provided with funds and staff, will move to fill. The challenge of modern diplomacy is to achieve such efficiency as to compress that vacuum to a minimum.

### Parliamentary Dimension

Just as bureaucracy has invaded diplomacy from the angle of the national government, so it has invaded from the international angle. Never have international affairs been so extensively organized. The annual list of international conferences presents a staggering number. The multiplicity of organizations and conferences, their size, financial demands, legal and management problems and agenda have created a new dimension of diplomacy requiring some ministries of foreign affairs, such as our State Department, to create a whole new bureau to deal with their activities.

With this has come a parliamentary diplomacy, indistinguishable from the maneuvering, tactical manipulation of procedural rules and debate, cloak-room and corridor cajolery, arm-twisting and log-rolling which characterize national parliaments, state legislatures and city councils.

This has greatly extended the diplomatic arena once preempted almost entirely by bi-lateral relationships and has brought into existence a new breed of diplomat versed in parliamentary politics. However, while the terrain is different the basic elements of diplomacy underlie the activity—those of strategy, tactics, techniques, learning and personal skills. While a new dimension has come into existence, the fundamentals continue with international secretariats bringing them to sharper focus in recurring forums. Where the State Department has fallen down is in its failure to recognize this dimension in its training programs, our skill and success suffering as a consequence, even to the point of our being routed from one of the organizations.

### *The Dimension of Research, Analysis and Retrieval*

All of these dimensions demand a research and analysis back-up performance of gigantic proportions. As never before, the diplomat must be served by the gathering and analysis of information on broader and deeper scales than he or his associates in any given office or post abroad can command. There are also problems of communication, of leisure to absorb the fruits of headquarters' research and analysis and of imaginative retrieval and circulation of analyses so as to keep before policy makers and operators insights which tend to disappear in filing cabinets. Two wholly neglected facets of this dimension deserve emphasis:

(1) research and analysis of diplomacy itself, its strategies and tactics, techniques and other resources, and the situations in which it can be effective, and those in which it cannot, and (2) maintenance of an inventory of the diplomatic resources which a government possesses, those in short supply, and those lacking altogether. "Know thyself" is a good motto for a diplomatic establishment.

I often think of a remark that President Kennedy made to an associate early in 1962 after some disappointing experiences with the effective execution of our foreign policies. He ruefully observed: "To prepare for this Administration we had a task force on foreign policy—and a good one. But why did no one think of having one on the resources we need to carry out policies?" One thinks again of Vietnam. I am quite sure that had we stopped to inventory our diplomatic resources for rendering assistance to an inchoate nation in Southeast Asia and for preserving diplomatic (that is, political) control of that assistance, including its military segment, we would have backed off fast from the contemplation of massive inter-vention.

As a part of the inventory process, mistakes in foreign policy and diplomacy should be analyzed. Rarely has the State Department paused to look backward, and never searchingly and systematically, with all possible resources at its command, to ascertain why it failed in any situation or why things did not go as hoped. When the Navy loses a ship, it automatically creates a board of inquiry to ascertain why. Subtler, of course, are lapses and losses in the diplomatic field, but the same need to inquire and learn is no less acute. Only in this way can the repetition of mistakes be avoided. The State Department needs a Standing Review Committee for the purpose. It is time for the role of analysis to be applied to diplomacy through such a committee in the Research and Analysis Bureau or as part of the Policy Planning staff.

Many other organizational and procedural problems await a similarly tough analysis. How, for example, are the lessons of failure and success which come from a

Review Committee to be imparted to diplomatic officers, so that all may learn from the errors and successes of some? Even the simplest information needed for the discharge of immediate tasks encounters what I call a "transfer of experience" block. It is accentuated by the proclivity of all diplomatic establishments to rotate their officers from position to position, country to country, even continent to continent. In our case, organizational size is a factor, as is a leanness of staffing which makes rare indeed any overlapping of officers so that an incumbent can adequately brief—that is, transfer the benefits of his experience to—his successor. This problem is not insoluble, but it requires identification and analysis by imaginative people, adequately trained and furnished with sufficient funds to effect the needed communication of experience.

Planning has always been viewed by the State Department as related to the policy process. Common sense suggests that it is equally related to the diplomatic. Neither the Policy Planning Council staff nor the offices concerned with the administration of personnel have given hard, systematic thought to the development of the resources, human and other, needed to carry out policies. They do not think in terms of strategies and tactics and hence "diplomacy" is something not clearly grasped. It survives from hand to mouth. It lives in a "by guess and by God" fashion. To make policy-decisions, to enter commitments (as we did in the Southeast Asian Treaty Organization), and to decide important moves (as we did in Vietnam), without stopping to inventory our resources and to bring our diplomacy into equilibrium with our policy decisions, is the rankest folly.

Perhaps these two dimensions of research-analysis-retrieval planning and management should be viewed as coalescing in a "mobilization of resources" dimension.

There are those who bemoan the large share of U.S. research and development that goes for the military component of national defense. The Federal government finances about half of all American research and development and half of that goes for military purposes. It is a fact, however, that that half for the military is no conscious apportionment by any President, any congressional committee or any director of the Office of Management and Budget. Each federal agency decides what portion of its proposed budget goes to research and development and it does this through a combination of inertia, prejudices of tradition and occasional new thinking. Unhappily, in the case of the State Department, new thinking is rare and its failure to conceptualize diplomacy and therefore its diplomatic challenges and responsibilities means that even its limited research funds have not been focused sharply on those challenges and responsibilities. None of the issues raised in these essays has ever been tackled by the Department's research offices and only sporadically by reformers who unhappily are migratory.

The Defense Department has learned since World War II that sustained and substantial investments in research and development are the only way of keeping abreast of the growing demand for delivery of their services. The civilian agencies of the government—including the State Depatment—have not. What Elliot Richardson, as departing Secretary of Health, Education and Welfare in 1969, criticized as that department's failure to discover "wholly new capital and manpower technologies" to meet its needs could be said also of the diplomatic establishment. Civilian agencies, including the State Department, simply do not possess modern, disciplined programs to explore, promote and apply new ideas and new systems for delivering their services. The research they do or finance in academic institutions and think tanks is disconnected from operating problems and systems. There is no continuing research tied to finding specific solutions to operational problems. The shame which anti-war, anti-military citizens try to load upon the Pentagon for constantly exploring new ways of being effective should be directed to a diplomatic establishment which is *not* evincing that interest.

### The Dimension of Attitudes

How one views his calling or profession is a determinant

of how he practices it. Two persons of equal abilities will perform at different levels of competence according to the way they visualize their role. This factor of conceptualization is of basic importance, yet our diplomatic establishment has paid not the slightest attention to it in its recruitment and training of officers. The result has been a much lower quality of performance than one would expect from an organization possessing a great number of intellectually and politically able officers.

With little attention paid to diplomacy as a political science in our universities, candidates are accepted in our diplomatic establishment with no clear view of it. Most vaguely think of it in primitive, frontier terms, not as an art and science deserving serious, systematic study but rather as something to be picked up on the run, like a craft to be learned through an on-the-job apprenticeship. Thus, they do not visualize it in professional, dynamic, political terms. They go at it in the manner of plumbers and carpenters, their thinking and activity committed to particular jobs in particular places, determined largely by the day's demands. Performance therefore tends to be pedestrian rather than dynamic, routine rather than imaginative. Sufficient unto the day are the events thereof and, since there is never any shortage of events, officers tend to be overwhelmed by them rather than anticipating and moving to change their course. They thus allow other governments to preempt the place and time of moves rather than compelling a contest of skill and wit at times and places of their own choosing.

I am focussing primarily on the American diplomatic establishment as it is our crisis that concerns us, but the general proposition holds with respect to all, that attitudes determine the quality of performance. In other words, they are a significant ingredient of national security. A mistaken strategy can sometimes be salvaged from ruin by a corps attitude of alertness and ingenuity, free from bureaucratic routine. By the same token, a sound strategy can be ruined or dissipated by adverse attitudes.

For this reason much of diplomacy, as much of military activity, is intelligible not in organizational terms alone but

in simple human terms. The outward circumstances of
diplomatic success and failure are often deceptive and
the reasons for success or failure cloaked in obscurity
for want of an adequate analysis of the character, personality, qualities, skills and attitudes of the performers. A
case study on this is presented in a later essay (see pages
272-297), but the importance of attitudes will be found
cropping up throughout our consideration of the crisis
which grips our diplomacy, including an analysis of those
inhibiting reform of our diplomatic establishment. (See
pages 203-211).

A common attitude rendering impossible a perceptive
approach to diplomacy is found in relatively new countries—
our own included—of ignoring the past. Among such
countries a common unwillingness exists to study the
past for gleanings of the essential nature of diplomacy,
unaware that its basic elements are as old as the hills.
This is a serious error. Just as military officers study the
battles of ancient times as well as those of the Napoleonic
period and our own civil war to perfect their skill in sort-
ing out the elements of military strategy and tactics, so
must diplomatic officers study the maneuvers and skills of
the most proficient diplomatic performers of the past with
a view to detecting the elements of diplomatic success
and failure.

The increasing number of memoirs published by American diplomats since World War II, to which we refer in
a later essay (see Chapter 15), makes it possible to analyze
American diplomacy as never before, but one needs to
keep in mind that diplomacy is not simply an American
or a recent phenomenon. Much is to be gained from the
study of diplomatic maneuver by other governments in
other times. Indeed, our situation with respect to the
Soviet Union has so much in common with that of Athens
in its dealings with Philip of Macedonia that we could
acquire useful perspectives from studying them and we
could learn also from the tactics and techniques of the
Byzantine Empire in coping with the tribes occupying
what is now the Soviet Union and its neighbors which
sought the Empire's destruction.

No other calling excites greater intellectual-political activity than diplomacy. It is preeminently the profession of intellectual and cultural action in political form, complex in its combinations, varied in the historical, cultural, political and economic terrain on which it maneuvers and diverse in the cross-historical time-spans in which it is practiced. No profession offers more intricacy, none is more difficult to master; hence the attitudes it demands are those of curiosity, scientific inquiry and self-discipline. Since appropriate periods of study and reflection are not as readily available as in the days of Metternich, Jusserand or Bryce, but are as necessary as ever, ways must be found to provide them.

The curious attitudinal aberration caused in the American diplomatic community by advocates of "women's liberation" has been referred to earlier. Since it demonstrates a lack not only of a sense of duty to country but of any understanding of the nature and importance of diplomacy as an ingredient of national and international security it is clearly a debilitating factor. It is not apparent that the wives of diplomatic officers of any other country share this view, in which case their governments possess an advantage in international politics.

National attitudes influence the climate in which a government's diplomacy is conducted and affect its quality as much as those within the diplomatic establishment. Indeed, the two consort with one another, in a mutually advantageous or debilitating partnership. In our case, a frontier mentality continues to exercise an enormous influence upon our national attitude toward diplomacy. It leads us to elect Presidents with no experience in international (or indeed in national) matters. It leads Presidents to appoint Secretaries of State with little or no experience in diplomacy and little familiarity with its many and complex dimensions. It leads to the appointment as ambassadors of inexperienced people from outside the diplomatic establishment and the promotion of incompetent people within that establishment. It leads to the commissioning as Foreign Service officers of wholly un-

prepared people from minority groups. It generates a tendency to think of diplomacy as simply the activity of high
officials in Washington and to ignore the global vascular
system which keeps the diplomatic process working day
and night in every country of the world. It explains the
prevailing lack of respect for diplomats and the lack of
interest of Secretaries of State in effective organizational
management of the diplomatic establishment, as well as
opposition to the idea of a permanent general manager
of that establishment.

It leads to the excruciating complication of diplomacy
by Congressmen, through voluble criticism of other governments, a constant legislative intrusion into negotiations,
blabbing of secrets and even negotiations with foreign
ambassadors situated in Washington, not to mention
confusing conduct when traveling abroad.

It leads to a blustering attitude toward other governments on the simplistic assumption that "all peoples are
alike," hence other societies and cultures should be like
ours, our political and social norms should be universalized
and other peoples and governments should "shape up"
to them, with diplomacy utilized for the purpose.

In these ways, our national attitudes create a climate
unconducive to the skillful employment of diplomacy.

## *The Dimension of Personal Qualities*

Closely related to attitudes are personal qualities. As
observed at the start, the qualities needed for diplomacy
are suggested by those required in everyday situations—
those of a parent in handling an obstreperous child—
patience, tact and common sense combined with firmness;
of a salesman in promoting his wares or services—tact again,
a pleasing personality with just the right mix of confidence
and courtesy, of initiative and suavity, along with an
intelligent understanding of the person he is trying to
persuade; and those of public officials of every level
engaged in the maneuvers and arm-twisting characteristic
of the political process—patience, tact, geniality, practical

judgment, perceptivity of the strengths and weaknesses of competitors and the ability to take advantage of vulnerabilities, along with a good knowledge of the game. Basic to all these activities and responsibilities—and to diplomacy—are intelligence, rationality (as opposed to dogmatism) and intuition, or a sixth sense of dealing with people. An intellectual without that sense is a fish out of water in politics.[29]

The requirement of the diplomat that he operate cross-culturally and cross-historically underlines the importance of additional qualities—those of intellectual and cultural curiosity, tolerance and empathy.

The organizational dimension of diplomacy has clearly introduced the need of other than the traditional qualities of practitioners. For it exacts an organizational sense, that is an ability to keep prime objectives in view and to guide an organization toward them, all the while retaining a sense of the political and humanistic dynamics of international politics. A part of this is the quality of leadership—of developing and inspiring subordinates, of filling the role of educator, coach and trainer of one's staff. Fused with tact, it enables the diplomat to play the role also of educator of his own government and of the host government. A subtle quality is this, indeed, as we have already noted. It requires a sense of ordonnance, of bringing together the various dimensions and resources of diplomacy into an effective political process.

Implicit are the qualities of courage and loyalty. Conditions being what they are in the world today, the diplomat must be a person of physical and moral courage, as prepared as a soldier to lay down his life for his country. He must be ready to suffer the strains of abduction and imprisonment. Always he has formed part of a nation's front line of defense: present conditions make it too evident to be questioned. His courage must be as much moral as physical. He must be willing to dissent from his government's views and take the risks of initiative when muscle-bound bureaucracies are unable to decide quickly enough what to do in situations in which time is of the essence. But courage must be disciplined by loyalty. Without that discipline, the diplomat becomes a loose cannon. Faithfulness to his government's policies and decisions is essential.

Rare is the combination of all these qualities. Hence, rare is the best type of diplomat. Hence, too, the need of a far more intensive and exacting search by governments for individuals possessing the combination and a special educational and training effort to develop it.

One is tempted to add still other qualities and indeed one must if he thinks of diplomacy not simply as a political but a civilizing process. Sir Harold Nicolson, the son of a career British diplomat and for many years on the staff of the British Foreign Office, listed the qualities of the ideal diplomat as truthfulness, precision, calm, good temper, patience, modesty, and loyalty. Other qualities and attributes, such as intelligence, knowledge, discernment, prudence, hospitality, charm, industry, courage and even tact, he considered should be taken for granted.[30] In view of our society's lack of homogeneity, its unsatisfactory educational standards, the questionable criteria for admission to our Foreign Service, and the inadequate methods of judging candidates for that Service, Nicolson's taken-for-granted category can hardly be taken for granted by ourselves.[31] It was the lack of many of these qualities which forced the resignation of Andrew Young as the U.S. Ambassador to the United Nations.[32]

Care must be taken to distinguish the qualities demanded by an international, inter-cultural political process and those which characterize the most civilized participation in that process. This is not easy. The diplomacy of some countries has reminded us that the process and its practitioners can be obstructive as well as constructive, deceptive as well as truthful, vituperative and aggressive as well as charming, dogmatic as well as intelligent, ideological as well as discerning, and our own has sometimes been imprudent and tactless.

A discussion of the personal qualities a diplomat should possess raises the question of how important the personal factor is in international politics. Over the centuries it has been highly important and it is equally so today, notwithstanding the rapidity of communication. In attestation of this are the Henry Villards, the David Bruces, the Ellsworth Bunkers and the Llewellyn Thompsons. The latter's calmness, patience and self-discipline in the face of the taunts, insults, vituperation and sarcasm of the Soviet negotiators during the negotiation of the Austrian peace treaty after World War II made that treaty possible. These qualities of this one negotiator gradually created an atmosphere conducive to agreement. They also elicited a Soviet respect for Thompson which made him influential in Moscow when subsequently serving there as U.S. Ambassador and in Washington as adviser to President Kennedy. The personal factor is still important when diplomats have the qualities to make it so.

Personal qualities imply the rules and requirements which diplomacy, in the passage of centuries, has evolved for itself. They also lay down certain standards of criticism which are applied in this and subsequent essays.

### The Dimension of Education and Training

All these dimensions emphasize the need of a broad and profound education to prepare diplomatic officers and their spouses for their tasks and of recurring periods of study throughout their careers as a means of recharging their intellectual vitality.

To represent a nation one must know well its history, culture, political philosophy and social system, and its problems, and if one is to perform acutely his intelligence and public relations functions abroad he must know those things about the country to which he is posted. As evident as this may appear, the United States has refused to admit these needs in any other than the most casual fashion. There is no Great Power so offhanded in the educational standards and training of diplomatic officers, not to add other government officials dealing with foreign affairs. Reinforcing our frontier simplicity, which incorrigibly insists upon perpetuating itself, is an aversion to elitism amounting to a phobia. These factors have not deterred the creation of military academies but have prevented the establishment of one for diplomacy.

Other countries have no such hang-up. Great Britain, France, West Germany, Austria and Switzerland, to name a few, exact the highest educational standards for their diplomatic officers, and some have established special academies for the purpose, comparable to their military academies.

In a remarkable demagogic genuflection to frontier democracy the State Department does not even require candidates for the Foreign Service to possess a college degree, much less a graduate degree, but disingenuously disengages from this hypocrisy by imposing a written examination which only college graduates can pass.

In addition to this piece of demagogy, the State Department is engaging in another, earlier noted, of exempting from the written examination those Foreign Service candidates from minority groups. This defies all realistic conception of diplomacy and invites the certainty of further disasters like Vietnam. Obviously, those responsible for this exemption, including Secretaries of State, are not keeping in mind that in its quest for respect and influence abroad—which cannot be won by unqualified people—diplomacy is an integral part of our national defense.

The superficial preparation which the State Department gives every newly commissioned Foreign Service officer is still another piece of frontier naiveté. It is called "orientation," lasts but a few weeks, and does nothing so well as to ignore diplomacy itself. Disdaining to probe deeply any dimension of diplomacy, it deals largely with a congeries of bureaucratic trivia.

The dimensions of diplomacy are so complex, and the challenges they present to diplomats and their spouses so great, that it seems obvious that only an educational and training academy focused upon these can possibly pack all that is required into an integrated curriculum.

In our case, a Foreign Service Institute, established in 1947 with the expectation it would flower into a professional academy, ranking in its field with our military academies, has never done so. Adequate funds were not provided and vision early lapsed as officers responsible for the creation of the Institute were rotated to other assignments, which has been one more calamitous price paid for the frequent rotation of diplomatic personnel.

As already suggested, the international aspect of this dimension is complemented by a domestic. Since the military and the CIA place far greater emphasis on education and training in international affairs than the State Department, a part of the Department's problem in generating a leadership role both in Washington and in the field stems from this divergence of approach. Our diplomatic establishment, thus, is constantly risking playing second fiddle within our own government as well as in the international community.

Serious, integrated education in foreign affairs and training in diplomacy should occur at the outset of officers' careers, preferably before they receive their commissions, as in the case of military officers. Novitiates could then be entrusted with more responsibility and thus find themselves, as they claim they are not, "where the action is."

Education and training, it is well to insist at the risk of repetitiousness, must be meshed with need. When a commitment is contemplated, an analysis and planning unit should automatically survey what kind of officers this commitment demands, inventory what number of this type is on hand and how many more will be needed. The facilities of the establishment must then provide the necessary education and training.

This dimension entreats us to recognize that not only our enemies or rivals can undermine us: we can undermine ourselves. We can do this as readily by an inadequate diplomacy as by wrong policies. The first step toward achieving a high quality of diplomacy is to conceptualize it. The second is to select, educate and train officers for it in a systematic, rigorous manner.

*The Management/Supervision/Logistics Dimension*

All these dimensions must be knit together and propelled toward a government's strategies. Since most of
them have become enormously complicated and inflated,
the art and science of diplomacy have been overtaken by
a sizable organizational problem. It has therefore become
difficult to keep clearly in mind that diplomacy is what
the diplomatic establishment is engaged in, that diplomacy is a political process—political *movement*—and hence
all organizational machinery and effort must be a part of
and directed to the success of that movement.

Management has acquired in some quarters a connota-
tion of constituting almost an end in itself and certainly,
in the diplomatic arena, as constituting something independent of diplomatic strategy and tactics. This is totally
fallacious. Management must be viewed as a mobilization
and propulsion of all resources needed for the formulation
and execution of strategies and tactics.

The objective of management in a diplomatic establishment is to bring to bear upon diplomacy the entire resources of the nation with maximum energy. The purpose
is to mobilize, energize, propel forward. This requires an
effective development and coordination of resources, first,
within the diplomatic establishment—including, of course,
missions and posts abroad—and, secondly, within the
entire community of government departments, along with
an integration of policy within that community. It requires
the persuasion of Congress to effect the appropriations and
other legislative action needed and to abstain from actions
blocking the strategies and tactics adopted by the Executive. It also requires checking or dulling the counter thrusts
of lobbying groups and coalitions within Congress. It
requires keeping the public quietly and systematically informed of the diplomacy being pursued. In all these
sectors, management must seize and hold the initiative.

All of this is ancillary to the political objective of concentrating the main diplomatic effort as much as possible
on that area or that subject where the greater strategic

advantage is to be obtained. At the same time, management must ensure that the highest echelons are not hypnotized by that area or subject, so that others are neglected. Diplomacy in this respect differs from war. Its victories are not won in one area alone, by bringing to bear upon it an overwhelming concentration of resources. Other nations must be made to feel that any diplomatic effort is in their interest, ultimate if not immediate, and above all that their interests and views are being kept in mind.

This emphasizes that the overseas projection must never be lost from sight. The temptation of Presidents and Secretaries of State with little or no experience in diplomacy is to view their own activity as all-important, although they are but the apex of a pyramidal diplomatic establishment which is itself of central importance. The spectacular jetting here and there of Presidents and Secretaries does not take the place of the quiet knitting together of the world community which diplomacy must achieve if it is to approach the goals of international understanding, cooperation and national security.

Our situation in the world and the responsibilities flowing from it cannot be met by either a puny organization, such as diplomats have traditionally preferred, or a large, ill-managed one. Nor can the need be overlooked of more effective management of overseas missions and posts. Thus, the old caste system separating diplomatic from administrative officers must be obliterated. Needed are diplomatic officers educated and trained in management no less than in diplomacy. This will also permit the selection from career diplomatic ranks of a permanent general manager of the diplomatic establishment, an essential ingredient in a continuing, effective practice of diplomacy as an element of national defense. Only thus can the many dimensions of diplomacy be consistently conjoined to a government's strategy and tactics.[33] Some governments achieve this by appointing in their ministries of foreign affairs officials designated "secretary general." The Soviet Union achieves it by Foreign Ministers of long tenure.

*Supervision*

Organization means supervision. Supervision means the development of people. Education and training must be conceived as integral components of supervision. This dynamic concept of the supervisory function is now lacking in American diplomacy.

Organization poses the risk of stifling an art, so that the basic challenge of supervision in a diplomatic establishment is that of solidifying the marriage of the art of diplomacy to management through education and training. For this, considerable research and creative thinking are demanded. These we have not yet undertaken. The State Department has only scudded and shuddered before the wind of this challenge in the confused, irresolute manner of a sailing vessel piloted by a succession of inexperienced or bewildered skippers.

A more positive and dynamic supervisory performance would help to solve many problems which plague our diplomatic establishment. These include a host of personal grievances of officers and their spouses, the low morale of junior officers who are not realizing that, if they are discharging their responsibilities imaginatively, they are where the action is; the cynicism of mid-career officers who have lost their hope of getting to the top; and the let-down feeling of all as they witness the dehumanized treatment of their seniors—prodded out to pasture while still in their prime, some of them possessing just that experience which can fuse initiative with discretion and action with adroitness, placing persuasion on a higher level than arm-twisting—on the level of the Jusserands and David Eugene Thompsons.[34] Supervision must employ techniques which enable a large organization to treat its personnel as human beings and to stimulate rather than suffocate their judgment, their initiative and their loyalty. Only in this way can the marriage of the art of diplomacy be effected with organization.

## Logistics

Logistics is the branch of management that deals with the procurement, maintenance and movement of people and supplies, and the provision of services such as medical and psychiatric. In a diplomatic establishment it has a sizable overseas projection.

It includes the recruitment, education, training, promotion of officers and support personnel and their assignment to the right places at the right times, matching talents and experience with global strategic and tactical plans.

Here, too, lies the function of preserving an institutional memory—the maintenance of adequate storage, retrieval and communications systems which can achieve continuity of knowledge and insight. Warnings and perceptions sent to headquarters by the diplomatic and consular listening posts over the years must somehow be kept before policy makers and officers throughout the world. One of the most imaginative tasks confronting those dealing with this managerial function is to penetrate the shell of daily tasks, daily worries, daily crises enveloping policy makers with reminders of basic, long-run perceptions and issues. This is an administrative task which cannot be performed by simple administrators. It must be performed by diplomatic officers thoroughly steeped in strategy and tactics and thoroughly trained in the dynamics of logistics.

## The International Dimension

Up to this point, we have analyzed diplomacy as the projection of a government's national policy. We have noted, however, that from an international point of view it is the means by which adjustments in national policies are made peacefully, through discussions, re-analysis of interests and exchanges of view—the kind of cross-fertilization which occurred in the tete-a-tete of Roosevelt and Jusserand—and through negotiations, and the like. As a result, accommodation takes the place of collision.

From this standpoint, diplomacy can be both a nursery and an instrument of international law and order, with diplomats serving not simply the needs of their governments but those of the community of nations.

When the breakdown of Roman authority in ancient times led to the anarchy of the European Dark Ages, the civilizing and moral influence of the learned, migratory monks played a significant role in bridging the gulf between Greek, Roman and Christian cultures on the one hand and, on the other, those of the tribal conglomerations, kingdoms and duchies which thrust up from the rubble of the Roman Empire. The erudition, ethical values and ideas of justice preserved in the monasteries and diffused by the monks contributed to an evolving consensus of values and conduct which eventually produced "Europe" and "the West" and led to a Western type of diplomacy, to international law and eventually to international organization. Without that subtle contribution, the history of Europe, the West and the world would have been very different.

So, too, with migratory diplomats and consular officers. In the best cases, with sophisticated preparation, mastery of the many-dimensioned process and sympathetic governments, they play precisely this civilizing, ethical role, contributing constructively to the evolution of the world community.

Put in another way, borrowing a perspective from the physical world, a full quarter of the oxygen we breathe is produced by the infinitesimal, free-floating aquatic plants known as phytoplankton lying on the surface of the ocean where air and water meet. Our planet is habitable only because so much of its surface consists of water and this minuscule plant is so widely distributed. So, too, with the widespread diffusion of diplomatic and consular officers of all ranks and all nations. Their multiple, quiet, subtle efforts around the globe, day in and day out, get much of the world's business rationally done, suspicions allayed, doubts removed, infinite questions answered, ideas and suggestions sown, advice imparted, negotiations inched forward, and thus contribute much of the progress made toward a world more habitable, more just and more responsive to human needs.

## NOTES AND REFERENCES

[1] Spruille Braden, *Diplomats and Demagogues* (New Rochelle: Arlington House, 1971), pp. 168-169.

[2] This convention was signed June 1, 1964, but ratification was not approved by the U. S. Senate until March 16, 1967. As a tactic to bolster its prestige, the Soviet Union delayed ratification until a year later. Some interesting examples of the initiatives and experiences of consular officers are provided by Peter Lisagor and Marguerite Higgins in their *Overtime in Heaven* (Garden City: Doubleday, 1964).

[3] While the diplomat acquires greater skills through varied roles and assignments, his substantive knowledge tends to be superficial and there is always a time lag in his taking hold of a new assignment. The question posed is whether he could not acquire such skills by training in simulated role playing.

[4] Created in 1953 to develop detailed operational plans and coordinate their implementation in our foreign relations, the OCB in 1957 was placed within the structure of the National Security Council. This is the only time the United States has had a diplomatic planning agency and it came from Eisenhower's methodical military mind which insisted on detailed plans and follow-through. The OCB difficulties are described in my *Anatomy of the State Department* (Boston: Houghton Mifflin, 1967), pp. 63ff.

[5] "Camelot" and "Skybolt" are discussed later, under "The Military Dimension."

[6] This case is analyzed in essay 18.

[7] The diplomatic missions of repressive regimes have difficulty in developing such alliances, because they

generally alienate ethnic groups, but some of them try. Such regimes sometimes send covert agents to the United States to silence—by harassment, intimidation and even assassination—the more outspoken members of alienated groups.

[8] The latest disclosure of congressional lobbying efforts by a foreign intelligence agency related to the South Korean Intelligence Agency, which made large cash gifts to members of Congress in the early 1970s in a lobbying campaign to assure continued U.S. aid to South Korea.

[9] Ethnic, economic and foreign lobbyists also bring pressures to bear upon the State Department and sometimes individual Foreign Service officers. For an example of what can befall an officer and his intelligence work, see pages 34-35. The China lobby, which supported Chiang Kai-shek, was a notable one in this respect. It worked hand-in-glove with Senator Joseph McCarthy and Congressman Richard Nixon in punishing diplomatic and consular officers who were critical of the Chiang-Kai-shek Government and reported anything favorable of the communist movement led by Mao Tse-tung. See footnote 12.

[10] The suggestion that a parliamentary system might eliminate much of the congressional pulling and hauling in American diplomacy is made later, in essay 19.

[11] A Secretary of State of the Henry Kissinger genre is not even interested in the overseas branch of the diplomatic establishment.

[12] Recent accounts of what befell our China Hands will be found in E. J. Kahn, Jr., *The China Hands* (New York: Viking, 1975) and Gary May, *China Scapegoat: the Diplomatic Ordeal of John Carter Vincent* (Washington: New Republic Books, 1979). My critique of Kahn's account will be found on pages 256-263. More extended comment on the congressional contribution to diplomacy will be found in *Anatomy of the State Department, op. cit.,* chapter 9.

[13] William Franklin Sands, *Our Jungle Diplomacy* (Chapel Hill: University of North Carolina, 1944), pp.

123ff. A different and less successful way of dealing with a dictator occurred when Spruille Braden was appointed the U.S. Ambassador to Argentina in the days of Juan Peron. See Braden's memoir, *Diplomats and Demagogues*, *op. cit.*, pp. 315ff. For Dean Acheson's terse comments, see his *Present at the Creation* (New York: Norton, 1969), pp. 187ff.

[14] "Representation" is one of the diplomat's traditional functions. He is a formal representative of his government and, as such, is viewed by many citizens of the state to which he is sent as *being* the government and country he represents. His government and country are judged very much according to the personal impression he makes. This symbolic function carries with it other functions of both substance—he is the normal agent of communication between his own foreign office and that of the state to which he is accredited, for example—and social significance. He represents his government on formal occasions. He must cultivate a wide variety of social contacts, with officials, with his fellow diplomats, with influential persons in all walks of life, and with articulate groups in the country.

[15] Carl von Clausewitz, *Principles of War* (Harrisburg: Stackpole, 1942), p. 69.

[16] *On the Manner of Negotiating with Princes*, trans. by A. F. Whyte (New York: Houghton Mifflin, 1950).

[17] See *A View from Teheran: A Diplomatist Looks at the Shah's Regime in June 1964* (Washington: Institute for the Study of Diplomacy, Georgetown University, no date but published in 1978) setting forth the text of a secret airgram sent to the State Department by the U.S. Embassy in Teheran, dated June 5, 1964.

[18] Henry S. Villard, "How to Save Money: An Open Letter to Congressman John J. Rooney," *Harper's* magazine, January 1964, pp. 20-22. The episode is also related in the author's *Affairs at State* (New York: Thomas Y. Crowell, 1965), pp. 196-197. For a more extended discussion of the initiatives which overseas officers must be ready and willing to take see chapter 4. Able diplomats can suffer acutely from this overseas dimension. The value

of David Eugene Thompson, mentioned above as an able diplomatic representative, was not recognized in his own capital. He was "disliked in Washington and deeply disliked in the Department of State." Sands, *op. cit.*, pp. 123ff.

[19] *The Fourth Floor* (New York: Random House, 1962).

[20] John Service, "Foreign Service Reporting," *Foreign Service Journal*, Vol. 00, No. 3 (March 1973), p. 24. For the complications created by communist-baiting and public hysteria see Kahn, *op. cit.*, May *op. cit.*, and O. Edmund Clubb, *The Witness and I* (New York: Columbia University Press, 1975). For other experiences in this dimension see Post Wheeler and Hallie Erminie Rives, *Dome of Many-Coloured Glass* (Garden City: Doubleday, 1955).

[21] During these seventeen years, the United States has had six different ambassadors in Moscow.

[22] Robert F. Kennedy, *Thirteen Days: A Memoir of the Cuban Missile Crisis* (New York: W. W. Norton, 1969), p. 116. Would that the succeeding Administration had been as wise in developing its policy with respect to Vietnam.

[23] George F. Kennan, *Memoirs, 1925-1950* (Boston: Little Brown, 1967), pp. 292ff.

[24] See Martin F. Herz, *David Bruce's "Long Telegram" of July 3, 1951* (Washington: Institute for the Study of Diplomacy, Georgetown University, 1978).

[25] See Charles Oscar Paullen, *Diplomatic Negotiations of American Naval Officers*, 1778-1883 (Gloucester: Peter Smith, 1967), originally published in 1912 by the Johns Hopkins University Press. Samuel Eliot Morison's *"Old Bruin": Commodore Matthew Calbraith Perry* (Boston: Little Brown, 1967) provides additional details on Perry's negotiating career as a naval officer, including his role in the opening of Japan in which his reminder to the Japanese of the force at his disposal played a significant part.

[26] See Irving L. Horowitz (ed.), *The Rise and Fall of Project Camelot* (Cambridge: Massachusetts Institute of Technology Press, 1967).

[27] Professor Neustadt's findings were published in his

*Alliance and Politics* (New York: Columbia University Press, 1970). A similar imbroglio occurred in 1979 when a U.S. military decision was made to upgrade the U.S. submarine communications facility at the Australian Northwest Cape. For the Australian Ambassador's account of this, see Alan Renouf, *The Frightened Country* (Melbourne: Macmillan, 1979); letter to author, Oct. 6, 1979.

[28] On the other hand, no little espionage and clandestine operations, including terrorism, have been directed against diplomats. See Charles W. Thayer, *Diplomat* (New York: Harper, 1959) chapters XI-XII. Since 1968, when U.S. Ambassador to Guatemala John Gordon Mein was assasinated, hardly a year has passed in which a diplomatic or consular officer of some country has not been kidnapped or murdered.

[29] On the point of rationality versus dogmatism, one might point out that Lord Bryce was an ardent devotee of democracy and human rights, but he was a rationalist, not a dogmatist. As the British Ambassador to the United States he was more philosopher than critic. He did not try to tell us how we should conduct our affairs. His influence upon American thinking was therefore considerable. His example suggests that American ambassadors could be more helpful in the cause of human rights, and in other things, if they were better equipped culturally and philosophically and possessed a greater gift of articulation.

[30] *Diplomacy* (London: Oxford University Press, 1950), 2nd ed., pp. 104-126.

[31] For further discussion of this point see Chapters 6 and 18.

[32] As the United States Ambassador to the United Nations, the Rev. Young created a series of embarrassing situations for his government. For a summary of his statements which struck many people as lacking intelligence, knowledge and tact, as well as precision, modesty and loyalty to his government's policies and eroded the President's, the Secretary of State's and the public's confidence in him, see the *Washington Post*, August 16, 1979, p. A-7. When he failed to report a meeting he had with

the representative of the Palestine Liberation Organization at the United Nations, which transgressed his government's policy, and then, when questioned about it by the State Department, failed to truthfully characterize it, his position became untenable. He resigned August 15, 1979.

[33] The concept of a general manager of our diplomatic establishment is discussed in *Anatomy of the State Department*, op. cit., pp. 246-248 and in this book on pages 63, 186, 201, 212, 235-236.

[34] So extravagant has become this prodding out to pasture that career officers are now generally given but one assignment as ambassador, at the conclusion of which they are expected to retire. This is not the same thing as selection out for inability to meet required standards of performance, which I endorse. The "prodding out" occurs because of faulty promotion procedures which produce a surplus of senior officers and the restiveness of junior and mid-career officers to rise to the top. Neither of these is adequate justification for sacrificing able and experienced officers.

## 2.

# SOME PROFESSIONAL AND POLITICAL PERSPECTIVES OF DIPLOMACY

Diplomacy, as George Santayana said of beauty, seems to be something not quite describable. "What it is and what it means," as the philosopher said of his subject, "can never be said." Few indeed have addressed the question of what diplomacy is and what it means, and fewer still have given much thought to whether it can be taught. Yet, as the United States has endeavored since World War II to match diplomatic resources to the demands of world politics, sometimes with disastrous results through a failure adequately to conceptualize diplomacy and its limits, it has become more and more urgent to do precisely this.

One of the first to try to define diplomacy was Harold Nicolson, subsequently knighted, who composed a graceful dissertation in 1939. Unfortunately, he took an overly limited definition. Instead of extracting a realistic meaning from his father's experience in the British diplomatic service or his own in the Foreign Office, he resorted to the Oxford English dictionary which said that diplomacy is the management of international relations by negotiation. Then, through emphasis on the role which writing plays in sharpening diplomacy into an instrument of precision, Nicolson wound up insisting that it is not a verbal but a written art.

Reprinted with permission from *Foreign Service Journal*, August, 1976.

This, we should have recognized, is absurd. Being a political process, diplomacy is as much oral as scriptural and indeed finds expression in a variety of modes ranging from body language to the deployment of military forces. As in local and national politics, it is essentially maneuver for political and economic advantage, including more than is involved in normal negotiation, even if one stretches that term to its outermost limits of elasticity. Nicolson's problem may have been that his book was written for the "Home University" series of a British publisher and therefore had to be oversimplified for readers of limited education.

This problem became our own, for his little book, being the only treatise in our language, in addition to being written with seductive charm, became the bible of our diplomatic establishment. Its argument that diplomacy is an art reinforced the view held by our practitioners that diplomats are born not made, and there is nothing about it which can be taught. Any attempted instruction was a waste of time and the sooner the newly commissioned officers were hustled to their first assignments the better for them and everyone else. So preparatory time was reduced from months to weeks—limited to six for the past several years. Compared to the three years demanded by the legal profession, the four by the medical and corresponding periods by other professions this should have warned us that our emphasis upon the art of diplomacy seriously undermined any claim of professional status for it.

Nor did anyone question why, if diplomacy is an art, it is the only art form deficient in teachable principles, techniques and approaches. The rudiments of every other art have been taught from time immemorial—those of sculpture to Phidias, those of painting to Michelangelo, those of music and composition to Beethoven. What is so special about the art of diplomacy?

The conventional wisdom of our establishment responded that diplomacy does not deal with physical things —marble, canvas and pigment, keyboards, sound waves and the like—but with human beings and these in cross-cultural situations demanding an inborn perceptivity and judgment. These, it maintained, could not be imparted. They were natal dispensations, conferred by the right kinds of ancestors. The developing science of psychology came more and more to contest this but we practitioners have always been leery of psychology, so any discussion of the nature and instructibility of diplomacy backed off before the question could be seriously considered whether the flowering of an inherited gift could be accelerated by suitable instruction. The point therefore seems never to have penetrated the wise old heads that instruction in an art is not necessarily intended to create but to fan and refine a genetic gift. Nor did the point register that there are different degrees of native endowment, so that appropriate assistance might enable a third-rate genius to become a second-rate; a second-rate, to enter the sacred portals of the first-rate; and the first-rate to become even more accomplished in a shorter time, which would redound to the benefit of the employing government and the tax-paying nation it represents.

In addition, an exaggerated emphasis upon the genetic ingredient subjected our diplomacy to inordinate risks of overly personalized performance. In the minds of those who rose to senior levels by gift, luck or maneuver a dangerous supposition of elitism was nurtured. Officers, when entrusted with supervisory responsibility, all too frequently conducted themselves according to their own lordly lights rather than by professional criteria, with the result that colleagues and sometimes whole missions, consular posts and our government itself were victimized by arbitrary, unethical, sometimes even cruel, behavior. In recent decades when such was available, an inspector or team of inspectors has had to be dispatched from Washington to rein in a wayward and imperious chief of mission. Not a few of our problems with Presidents, Senators, Congressmen and the public have been incubated by this conceit.

Without contesting that an art of diplomacy exists—as it does in all political processes—we should consider whether scientific ingredients are present as well. This possibility has been almost totally ignored, even by scholars who have labored at the definitional task. Practitioners have always greeted the suggestion with a snort of derision, for only the physical sciences, with their mathematical exactitude, have come to their minds. Even among scholars only one has been so bold as to assert that diplomacy is "both the art and science by which each state attempts to achieve success in its foreign policy short of forcing conclusions by armed conflict." Our own scholars have generally been content with such generalities as "the management of international relations," "the use of accredited officials for intergovernmental communication," "the business or art of conducting international intercourse" (at least there's the art ingredient), or simply "the manner in which international relations are conducted." Occasionally one has thrown in the towel completely by saying "diplomacy is what diplomats do." Relatively few have endeavored to separate out the political processes, such as discussion, negotiation, conciliation and representation. This, although an incomplete inventory, takes an analytical path.

Innumerable political science departments in our institutions of higher learning insist that a political process possesses distinguishable scientific ingredients. They also concede that diplomacy possesses these by including it in their textbooks and courses on international relations but in so casual and abstract a way as to have little connection with its arduous, complex and risky operations. It is surprising, too, that almost no *courses* on diplomacy have been offered for in-depth treatment of a political process which constitutes our principal alternative to war and on which, therefore, humanity's chances of survival depend. More astonishing, this has been the case until very recently even in schools, graduate and undergraduate, established to prepare those interested in a diplomatic career. The Fletcher School of Law and Diplomacy (diplomacy, mind you) has seriously tackled this subject only in recent years under the deanship of a colleague of ours. The Georgetown School of Foreign Service is doing so this year. But the surprise *par excellence* has been the Foreign Service Institute, supposedly established, among other things, to ready newly commissioned officers for diplomatic service. FSI has ducked not only the issue of whether diplomacy as an art can be taught but also the issue of whether instruction in diplomacy as a political process can and should be provided in its "basic officers course." In fact, the Institute has not even taught diplomatic practice, this being viewed as having some kind of Martian irrelevance to the routine, desk-bound "jobs" which are anticipated for the young officers. "They won't be involved in diplomacy for years," has been the conventional view which has guided the Institute, as though a diplomatic service is somehow not a diplomatic service until one advances to senior ranks. This, of course, reflects the Nicolson eccentricity, for it is quite true that, with few exceptions, only senior officers are likely to participate in sufficiently high-level negotiations to yield written agreements.

The consequences of this widespread abjuration of instruction in diplomacy have appeared in two major areas. Within the diplomatic establishment we have been compelled to navigate without a clear concept of our calling and what it demands. Over the years we have tacked this way and that in our recruiting and examining objectives and methods. We have swung from separate diplomatic and consular branches to a single service and back to a fragmentation into five divisions—not just two—with no basic, unifying instruction to synthesize them. We have viewed the Service less as a profession demanding preparatory professional instruction than as an aggregation of assignments, "jobs," "slots," "tracks," "cones" and classes. With professional criteria of performance and values failing to win ascendancy, promotion has become a consuming obsession. In this bewildering situation it is small wonder that almost as many different Foreign Services have emerged in the minds of officers as officers themselves, each visualized in terms of the individual's own experience and observation. The Service—indeed the entire diplomatic establishment—is a kind of Rorschach inkblot interpreted not professionally but in response to the human tendency to react emotionally to personal stimuli.

We therefore find ourselves constantly unhappy with what we have done in the name of "reform" and are forever casting about for something different without really knowing what we want. We do not know how to conceptualize specialists, including administrative officers, who, because of this uncertainty and victimization, real or imagined, hardly know how to conceptualize themselves and in desperation seek high-sounding diplomatic titles to make it clear that they truly "belong." We swing into a "global assignment policy" without first analyzing the sources of the deficiencies it is conceived to overcome and land in an Assistant Secretary's position a first-rate senior officer who lacks familiarity with the bureau's geographical region. Then, in a few months, to everybody's embarrassment, we must shift him elsewhere because he cannot produce instant "creative policies" for a region of which he is ignorant.

We pursue labor-management bargaining and the resolution of grievances without relating these to diplomacy and the qualities of mind, character and personality, or the erudition, culture, personal sacrifice and team play which diplomacy demands and therefore without a clear notion of how these new bargaining and grievance procedures must fit into the development and implementation of foreign policy. In the midst of such confusion, our Foreign Service Association, in its efforts to persuade officers of its effectiveness, has found bread-and-butter issues the easier to address. The idea of *service* has thus been further eroded.

Our lack of a sense of professional mission has become manifest in broad sectors of our foreign affairs. Without a clear understanding of diplomacy and the resources it demands, the State Department has been unable to head off rash involvements requiring diplomatic resources we do not possess, or even to formulate in convincing terms any objection to such ventures on the ground of inadequate resources. Hence, it was not the diplomatic establishment but pressure from Congress which averted a preposterous attempt to shore up an unshorable resistance to the Soviet-Cuban push in Angola. In the United Nations, unclear as to what is required of us—and judging in an almost Nicolsonesque way the prime qualification of effective U.N. diplomacy to be competence in the art of composition—we veer from one type of diplomacy to another, tacking from reason, consultation and quiet maneuver to what strikes allies and friends as impish and flambuoyant volubility, thereby amplifying opposition to us.

The other area of significant impact lies outside the diplomatic establishment. Surfeited with a discussion of foreign policy, policy making procedures and "area problems" but starved of analysis of what a national government does with policies and problems, our university graduates—and thus the more educated part of our adult population—are, like the rest of the citizenry, virtually illiterate on how governments deal with each other.

Thus it happens that when "national defense" is promoted by Presidents, Congressmen and the media it is invariably conceptualized in terms of military and economic, never diplomatic, resources. A strong "national defense posture" means a strong military, not a strong diplomatic establishment. Funds generously bestowed upon the military and intelligence agencies enable them to work with whole banks of computers while the State Department limps along with a handful and is not even certain as to how these can contribute to "diplomacy," although its officers call constantly upon the banks of other agencies to disgorge desired information. Congressmen, lacking a clear idea of the international political process, clamor to control the entire sequence of foreign affairs by legislative fiat. Confidences, on which much diplomacy rests, are scattered to the winds. Because the First Amendment guarantees freedom of speech and publication,

everything must be blabbed; diplomacy and its requirements count for nothing; all must be bugled from the
rooftops. To the consternation of friendly governments
and sources of intelligence, our diplomacy is buffeted
helplessly between Congressional hoopla and litigation.
In all this burlesque, the meaning of détente becomes so
bewildering and use of the very term such a political
liability, that the President considers himself obliged to
jettison it from his vocabulary.

Such wandering confusion is not of recent origin. While
its genesis lies beyond the limits of discussion here, its
impact had become sufficiently evident by 1970 to persuade the American Academy of Political and Social
Science to finance a two-day meeting to search for answers to five questions: what is diplomacy (i.e., how should
it be conceptualized—as an art, a science, or both)? Can
it be taught? If so, how? What resources required for
instruction are available and which need amplification and
refinement? Finally, *should* it be included in the liberal
arts curricula of our institutions of higher learning as part
of what educated citizens should know of the world in
which they live? A monograph, *Instruction in Diplomacy: The Liberal Arts Approach*, set forth the papers
circulated in advance of the meeting, the discussion of
participants, a bibliography of books on diplomacy and
the meeting's consensus that diplomacy is both an art and
a science, it can and should be taught as a liberal arts
subject and adequate materials do exist for the purpose.

Although distributed widely in the political science
community, the monograph elicited only a limited response. Nearly two centuries of neglect in this country
were not going to be ended by a single clarion call. But
several interesting developments ensued. Among them was
the creation of a permanent Committee for the Study of
Diplomacy, meetings of which have been sponsored
by American and Georgetown universities; and the School
of Continuing Education at Georgetown decided to offer
a course on diplomacy. So, in the fall of 1972, some five
months after the monograph's appearance, preparation

began for pioneering instruction on "The Dynamics of Diplomacy." Starting the following February, the course attracted an astonishingly large enrollment including two Foreign Service officers, officers from the Canadian, Italian, Soviet and several African embassies and one from the Estonian legation, an Air Force captain, several housewives and a graduate and an undergraduate student from Georgetown.

The thrust of the course was the application to diplomacy of the concepts of strategy, tactics and techniques, as well as the roles of learning, character and personality traits and skills of diplomats, thereby treating diplomacy as both science and art. After analysis of the nature of diplomacy, with some historical and comparative perspectives, the establishment of diplomatic relations was discussed in strategic and tactical terms, which brought alive the dynamics involved in the recognition of states and governments, the various shadings of diplomatic relationships which can exist and the ingenious ways in which governments get business done in the absence of such relations. The fascinating way in which the United States and the Peoples Republic of China had engineered the creation of quasi-diplomatic relations was so recent as to make unnecessary much elaboration of the point that diplomatic relations are of great variety and their construction is no routine or simple matter.

So, too, with the selection of diplomats and the *agréation* process from which comes (or fails to come) the *agrément* permitting a government to send a particular individual as its ambassador. Not only do strategies and tactics play a part in this but *agrément*, far from ending that stage of the political process, must sometimes be reinforced by additional political acts, as illustrated by the agreement of our government to receive Lord Halifax as the British ambassador in 1941. As Foreign Secretary in the Chamberlain Government, Halifax had been conspicuously associated with appeasement and was an anathema to many of FDR's New Deal colleagues. With their unfavorable reaction to Halifax's appointment finding expression in the media, FDR, to put an end to the objections, went down Chesapeake Bay to meet the envoy and his wife, who arrived on the newest and strongest battleship of the British fleet, the *King George V*, Churchill's ploy to "clothe the arrival . . . with every circumstance of importance." The tactics of these two wily politicians worked. No more was heard from the critical New Dealers. The visible Presidential imprimatur had had to be added to the invisible *agrément* to make Halifax truly acceptable and able to perform effectively.

By similarly treating the organization and functioning of embassies and their location, design and construction, as well as the privileges, immunities and roles of diplomats, these, too, came alive as dynamic factors. Even protocol, which is widely regarded as a meaningless exercise in social amenities is susceptible to tactical exploitation. In a reverse of the Halifax case, for instance, President Truman used the courtesy call of a new Czech ambassador in 1951 to tell him what Americans thought of his government's arrest, imprisonment and "trial" of an Associated Press correspondent, administering to him the rough side of his Missouri tongue. Where the President left off, Dean Acheson resumed when the envoy arrived to pay his courtesy call on the Secretary of State. This was followed by an ambush of American journalists outside Acheson's office. So unnerved was the envoy by all of this that he never ventured forth to diplomatic haunts again and six weeks later was ordered to Paris to attend a United Nations meeting, which was a face-saving tactic to cover retreat, for he never resumed his post in Washington.

Tactical exercises are also involved in the recall of diplomats, either at the request of the host government or the initiative of the sending government, the suspension and rupture of diplomatic relations and the ways by which governments continue their communication when formal relations are interrupted.

Thus the ground was cleared for a study of actual cases of diplomatic "push and shove." Just as one is fired in imagination and sharpened in analytical ability when visiting an historic site, recalling what he knows of people and events associated with it and finding every detail of the place springing forth with unsuspected meaning, so with his involvement in a specific case in which diplomats have had to maneuver. These provide sufficient detail to enable the analyst to grasp quite precisely what the situation was, the strategic and tactical problems it posed and how the diplomats resolved them.   One's perceptivity is sharpened as well as his ability to extract the significance of each detail which otherwise might have been overlooked.  The most nebulous factor of all in diplomacy—that of personal qualities and skills—is detectable.   The student thus finds that he is educating himself to an extraordinary degree in the subtleties of a political process which, by any other approach, is only general and abstract.

The cases analyzed were four.  The first was written by James J. Wadsworth on how the "Atoms for Peace" idea was negotiated painstakingly and ingeniously from 1953 to 1957, ending in the creation of the International Atomic Energy Agency—a good example of quiet, global diplomacy pursued through both multilateral and bilateral means over a long, exacting course during the Cold War.

The second, extracted from Spruille Braden's *Diplomats and Demagogues* (with supplementary assistance from Braden's colleagues and published materials in the *Foreign Relations of the United States*), dealt with the negotiation of an end to the Chaco War through multilateral diplomacy conducted almost entirely in a single capital.  With the flair of a true raconteur, Braden takes his reader through the complex maneuvers, counter-maneuvers and personal factors—friendships, learning, experience in private negotiations as a mining engineer, personal traits and skills—which he utilized in Buenos Aires over a three-year period to wind a tortuous, chicanery-bestrewn path to a peaceful settlement of a protracted war.   Like a Bayeux embroidery chronicling the Norman conquest of Britain, this account possesses fascinating detail—threats and insults, venality, stupidity, sly double-crossing and outright lying and theft of documents—in which diplomacy and the domestic politics of various governments intermingled, providing perspectives missing in the Wadsworth study.

As part of his masterful orchestration of diplomatic resources, Braden used dinner parties effectively. Knowing in advance who would sit next to his Chilean wife, whose family had standing and influence in South America, he primed her on what points to get across to her table companions, what questions to ask, what suggestions to make, what encouragements and discouragements to convey. More than once this saved his efforts from the brink of failure and of course illustrated nicely one of the contributions a wife can make to the political process.

The third case study, one of bilateral diplomacy, was provided by chapters four and five of Ellis Brigg's *Farewell to Foggy Bottom*, in which the tactics employed by a communist government to make life miserable for a Western embassy and the countermeasures employed by the embassy are recounted with Briggsian zest. The second of the two chapters focuses on how an Associated Press correspondent, accused of espionage, was jimmied loose from prison. Since that was a "protection" case, it incidentally challenges the validity of a "cone" personnel system which, unsupported by unifying instruction in diplomacy, structures "protection" as a consular function separate from strategic considerations and political and economic tactics. Unlike the Wadsworth and Braden studies, this concerned a career diplomat, which made apropos comments on the issue of career versus politically appointed officers.

A case study of our involvement in Vietnam, concentrating largely on the roles of the State Department and Embassy Saigon and supplemented by Chester L. Cooper's *The Lost Crusade*, brought the course to an end, with one of the many insights emerging being the importance to the modern diplomat of some knowledge of the military factor in foreign affairs. This is demanded not only by Great Power politics but by the necessity of the diplomatic establishment exerting a restraining influence upon Presidents who, in troubled times, are always more impressed by the visible indicia of military power and the military's "can do" zeal than by the advice of diplomats of no professional training and almost total ignorance of military resources and their limits. Presidential use of the military establishment for crucial advice, on-site investigation and appraisal and even as a source of ambassadorships repeated a message in the Vietnam situation which, as in our China experience a generation earlier, has scarcely been heard. But it came through with a bang in this study of gross diplomatic inadequacy.

A former United States ambassador to South Vietnam contributed to discussion of this case, as did others of our colleagues to other segments of the course.

Taken together, the four cases, dealing as they did with global, regional and bilateral problems, with underdeveloped as well as developed countries and a wide range of cultures and ideologies, reveal most of the basic diplomatic functions—

- gathering, evaluation and reporting of information
- forecasting of developments
- maneuvering for political or economic advantage
- advising and persuading the diplomat's own as well as other goverments on policies and tactics
- managing (or trying to manage) crises
- coordinating the various components of diplomatic missions
- working with military and intelligence organs operating outside those missions
- creating a favorable public opinion in the host society

—and the issues which they raise. Synthesized, the cases present—more adequately than a dictionary—a definition of diplomacy. They show that diplomacy is, as all politics, the art of the possible but that what is possible often depends upon the quality of diplomacy itself. They show that diplomacy is describable—that there is no impenetrable, uninstructable mystique about it. What it is and what it means can be said.

That saying is urgent indeed, both to newly commissioned diplomatic officers for professional reasons and to the general public for a more effective performance of our democracy in the world arena. We have lost the advantages of emergence from World War II as the recognized world leader, with seemingly unlimited resources and a nuclear monopoly. We must now depend more than ever before upon diplomatic skill. For this, a clear conceptualization of the political process and its resources by both the public and practitioners is imperative. It is not enough to keep repeating "no more Vietnams," "no Angolas" and similar refrains of negativism, ringing appeals for "creativity" and rhetoric about "unprecedented tasks" before us. Creativity requires learning and unprecedented tasks demand unprecedented professional efforts including a continuing analysis of what diplomacy is, how it can be made to work and what its limits are. There is no lack of materials for this. What has been lacking to date has been erudition, imagination, initiative—and and professional recognition of the challenge.

# 3.

# REFLECTIONS ON 20TH CENTURY
# DIPLOMACY

If "reading maketh a full man, conference a ready man
and writing an exact man," then the career of a diplomat
should be ideal. For no one reads more than he; no one
confers more than he; and no man writes more than he.

In addition to newspapers and magazines American,
there are newspapers and magazines local which he must
comb through, for the purpose of keeping himself and his
government informed. In addition, political tracts, company and labor union reports, and economic dissertations
of local extraction are as compulsory for his perusal as
the required reading list of a seminar. The diplomat of
the twentieth century is the beneficiary, almost *par
excellence*, of the vast and magnanimous legacy of Guten-
berg.

But this is not all. The diplomat's government is in there
pitching as well. That he may be fully informed and
prepared at all times to explain its policies (not always
consistent) and its statements (not always apt), the solici-
tous government of a twentieth century diplomat pouches
to him by sea and air, with due supplementation by cable,
a truly generous quantity of informative material. This
sympathetic interest in making its diplomats full men is
shared by all democratic governments and—no doubt—
looked upon by the airlines and shipping companies with
kindly and sympathetic interest.

Of course, no one officer—be he principal officer or

Reprinted from *The Key Reporter* (Phi Beta Kappa) Winter
1954-55.

otherwise—digests all of this. But with each officer of a mission absorbing a part, the staff as a whole disposes of the wheat of knowledge which runs through those elevators of erudition brought into existence by the inventive genius of man and known variously as periodicals and governments. Indeed, so much is this true that the foreign service officer of a twentieth century country reckons time less by the calendar than most people. He reckons it, rather, by the arrival and departure of pouches.

This means that the conference which maketh a ready diplomat is first of all conference with his staff. For this helpeth a foreign service officer to share what he knows, to fill his gaps of ignorance and to narrow the shadowy expanse which lies between knowledge real and knowledge supposed. Successful staff meetings are therefore an integral part of a diplomat's training and development.

But he must also confer—daily, too—with the people among whom he serves. The content of diplomacy these days is the content of human existence itself. Whatsoever a man weaveth that becometh a part of the fabric of diplomacy. Hence, every diplomatic and consular post is a kind of relay station, picking up and reinforcing what its own government passes along to it with its own understanding, adeptness, imagination and familiarity with local conditions added; and then relaying back to its government the viewpoints, conditions and developments of the people among whom the post is located.

This is a sizable task, particularly in these days when international affairs are not the sport of kings and aristocrats but are the compound—and sometimes the highly emotional compound—of the multiple interests of whole nations—fishermen and physicians as well as financiers, bricklayers as well as bankers, peons as well as politicians and publishers. Since this is a democratic age, the effective diplomat is not the cut-away-coat-and-striped-pants variety whose most effective pose occurs on the day he presents his credentials, or lays a wreath, or attends an official function. He is the man whose most effective work begins when he rubs shoulders with all manner of men, and comprehends their wants, their needs, their aspirations and interprets them intelligently for the enlightenment of his government.

If this means that the most effective practitioner of diplomacy these days must be a kind of ingenious curbstone mixer, I would not myself object to this deduction. The days of the Talleyrands may not be wholly over but their activities and usefulness are distinctly circumscribed. It is the rarity rather than the rule that secret maneuver and covert arrangements have any effect, for, in free countries at any rate, publicity blazes pitilessly upon all that governments do. Murder will out—so will secret arrangements—and successful diplomacy these days must evidence a sustained and profound understanding of what people want at any given time, how they propose to get what they want and how we propose to help them get it if we are to help them. Thus it is that democracy (in the free world, again) is little by little taking over the content of diplomacy, lock, stock and barrel.

The conference which maketh a ready diplomat must therefore include so systematic and ingenious a conferring with the people among whom he lives that he really knows them. This means conferring daily, conferring widely, conducting ingeniously his own opinion polls, assessing, appraising, analyzing, dissecting so that what he reports to his government makes concise good sense. This is obviously not an easy task. It requires an instinct seldom possessed by scholars. Nor is this an instinct possessed by the superficial and sophisticated. Even veteran foreign service officers have been known to go overboard in situations requiring the maximum of good judgment in analyzing trends. Something more is required than either the scholar or the sophisticated possess—a basic learning served by common sense, humility and what I might call an instinct of human kinship and understanding.

There are men who have a sixth sense of stock trading. They amass great fortunes. There are politicians who have a sixth sense of politics. They win the elections and history confers upon them the mantle of masterly political strategist. There are journalists who have a sixth sense of news. They make the scoops, write or edit the better newspapers and news magazines. There are writers and artists who have a sixth sense of feeling, of sensibility— of understanding and depicting the life they see. These are the geniuses of literature and art.

The diplomatist must have his sixth sense, too. As he walks down a street he must gather instantly what is in that street—the assorted people, their varied tastes, their condition of living, the shops and their prices, and from conversations casual and otherwise pick up the current opinions and winnow the solid views and the trends of thinking which affect his country's relations with these people. He drinks these things in through every sense— virtually through every pore. But he dare not rely only upon this. He must check these impressions and correct them by meticulous study and cross-reference. There will then emerge for his foreign office a clear impression of the life and opinions of the community in which he lives, the issues which that community regards as important, and the things which affect the policies and objectives of his own country. There is what Bagehot calls a "certain fine sensibility of nature" required for the diplomat these days; and this must include a native sense of understanding the masses of people and their affairs.

The quality which Bagehot described as possessed by Shakespeare—a "patient sympathy, a kindly fellow-feeling" —seems to be not only a "necessary constituent in the composition of manifold genius," but a constituent in the composition of a diplomat as well. It requires a "various commerce with, and experience of men." One must not only be capable of consorting with men but be of them. The diplomat these days must be of such a nature that a common man could be cut from him.

I like to think of diplomacy as an adventure in understanding. Understanding, first, of one's own people, whose highest and best interests one is endeavoring to serve. An understanding next of one's own associates. An understanding, finally, of other peoples who compose the human family.

But the understanding which constitutes the adventure of diplomacy does not end with the diplomatist himself. It embraces the understanding of the government and the people whom he serves. He must have their sympathy and support—*their* understanding—if he is to achieve really constructive results. No one works in a vacuum and least of all those who are engaged upon international affairs.

If conference maketh a ready man, there are none who should be readier to confer these days than the staffs of ministries of foreign affairs. They must be inclined to confer with their diplomatic services for knowledge and understanding. And the public must also. The adventures of the diplomatist in understanding must somehow be shared with his governmental bureaucracy and his fellow citizens.

Diplomats of all ages have had occasion to complain of the indifference and neglect of their governments and their fellow-citizens. This is not all one-sided. There have certainly been some indifference and neglect on the part of the diplomatists. Yet it is a fact that had conference with diplomatists been more of a habit of governments and people, some serious blunders in international relations might have been avoided. This kind of thing occurs in the best regulated ministries of foreign affairs and democracies—even today. So it happens, in this age of the most ingenious means of analysis and conference we have yet to solve one of the strangest problems of all times, viz. how to enable the diplomatist to meet and confer with his own fellow-citizens, and sometimes his own government, on equal terms, to convey to them what he observes and experiences and to obtain from them, in turn, a surer instinct of the emotions and thinking he is intended to represent and interpret abroad. This opens up additional paths which branch off the main boulevard of diplomacy. I do not pursue them now. But on some suitable occasion they deserve a thoughtful exploration.

Suffice it, then, to conclude this brief presentation of some aspects of diplomacy in the twentieth century on the note I should like most to emphasize—that today diplomacy must be regarded and developed as an instrument of understanding in a very broad sense, and hence the diplomatist capable of making his career an adventure in understanding must himself be a person of understanding—of a certain profoundness of learning, of reflection, of experience, as well as of instinctive humanity and character. This is the type of person, abroad as at home, who can contribute to that understanding which is the prerequisite of peace.

# 4.

# THE INITIATIVES OF DIPLOMACY

We were seated on the porch of an old house, built before the Revolution. Its hill sloped down to the Potomac, shallowed and lazied by a long drought. A canoe floated by, idling in the autumn haze. On the far side of the river, upon a lower knoll, was another old brick mansion which had served as headquarters of a Confederate general during the battle of Sharpsburg. A few minutes before, my host had remarked: "That house was nearer Sharpsburg than ours and had a better view of the countryside between. You can practically see Sharpsburg from there." I thought I had detected an apologetic tone in his voice.

This was too captivating a scene—above all on an afternoon of brilliant autumn foliage—for much serious talk, but the young man beside me, likewise a guest, was serious. He was saying as I admired the colorful scene: "I'd like to know more about diplomacy. It sounds as though it should be an interesting career. But I don't know. I am told it is no career for people of initiative. You just carry out instructions. Is that true?"

As I looked at my interrogator I could not help recalling a letter of a few years before recommending a candidate for the Foreign Service. In describing the candidate the letter writer had said: "With regard to taking orders and loyalty, Mr. W. is the type of person who will never get out of line by expressing his own dissenting opinion in any matter. Anything which pertains to the plan under which he is working or to the organization he is representing is law to Mr. W.: something not to be discussed, analyzed

Reprinted with permission from *Foreign Service Journal*, March, 1965.

or even argued. In other words, he is the perfect type for the Department of State." Often have I wondered if the author of the letter ever learned the Department had turned down Mr. W.

"Is that true?" I repeated. Hardly. There is plenty of room for individual responsibility for anyone with the courage to assume it. Even if times were normal, swiftness of communication could not deprive a good diplomatic officer of initiative. All this factor would do would be to confirm the apathetic in their apathy and place the resourceful more on their toes. But times aren't normal. You may be a consul like Michael P. E. Hoyt in Leopold-ville at the time when a nation's newly-achieved independence becomes a signal for riot, rampage and rape. Your life may be in danger. You may be sent inland to rescue threatened Americans. You may be despatched to another town to see about opening up a new consular post—the better to know what's going on, protect American citizens and advise the local leaders how far they had better not go with their orgies. In other words, you are despatched to initiate means of assuring greater initiative.

Or you may be a vice consul in Hué. You are a good deal on your own in such a place, obliged to make a lot of decisions on the spur of the moment.

In embassies, too, the times demand men of superior initiative—the ability and courage to take a fresh look at everything that goes on, to question, to analyze, to report accurately no matter whom you may be contradicting, to act decisively in a hundred daily matters Washington doesn't even know about. The experience of Ellis Briggs and his associates in Embassy Prague 1949 to 1952 shows what initiative can effect against a hostile regime.[1] It means an on-the-spot ability to trade trick for trick, strata-gem for stratagem, each necessitating immediate decisions on one's own responsibility.

In fact, no more today than ever can a government operate successfully in foreign affairs unless it can command and encourage initiative. From every failure of officers to show initiative follow apathy, ignorance and error which reduce operations to a travesty of diplomacy.

Instructions? Even specific instructions require the individual officer to fill out the steel engraving with flesh-and-blood tints of personal performance. Thought must be given to the tints required and how and when they are to be applied. A steel engraving performance will not impress another government. Nor will it gain any important objectives of one's own. An individual officer's best analysis and judgment is required to transform instructions into a successful performance.

Often an officer must decide for himself, in the light of local circumstances, how quickly to move on an instruction. Timing can be vital. To know *when* to do something is as important to success as to know *what* to do and *how* to do it. And each officer is being paid for his discretion in these things. Timing, means, manner—all these must often be left to officers' discretion.

Furthermore, if you are the diplomatic officer you ought to be, you will contest your instructions when you consider them wrong or cast in unrealistic terms. This takes guts—a quality closely related to initiative. Willard Beaulac relates an interesting example of this. In 1931 our minister to Managua received instructions from the Department to call on the President of Nicaragua and ask him to pay promptly a bill his government owed a large American company. The minister promptly reminded the Secretary of State the legation was not in the business of collecting debts of private companies and he did not plan to approach the Nicaraguan Government on the matter. He heard no further.[2]

Anyone in a diplomatic service these days has a better than even chance of serving in underdeveloped countries. Washington's thinking about those countries is done in good part by developed minds operating in the context of a developed society thousands of miles and thousands of words of confused newspaper reporting away. Centuries of differences in experience, understanding, psychology will present the humblest officer out in the rain-soaked outposts with problems more mystifying and more involved than Lord Lyons faced in the *Trent* affair.

Do you know the *Trent* affair? It happened a century

ago, but it still provides a classic example of how a diplomatic officer can best serve his government by having the guts to use his own head and move with a circumspection not necessarily existent in his own capital because, thousands of miles away, it is not as familiar as he with the local situation.

It occurred in 1861, during our Civil War. President Davis, seeking a more favorable turn in the Confederacy's foreign relations, decided to replace its agents abroad with two very gifted "special commissioners," James Mason of Virginia and John Slidell of Louisiana. The commissioners, eluding the Federal blockade of Charleston, reached Cuba and sailed for London on a British mail-packet called the *Trent*. They were intercepted by a United States sloop of war commanded by Captain Wilkes. This was done without instructions and when Wilkes removed Mason and Slidell and sailed them to an American port he acted contrary to international law. If a government agent wants to act on his own initiative he had better know his international law and diplomacy. That's the first thing to learn from this incident.

Our nation burst into wild acclaim. Among congratulations deluging Wilkes were those of the Secretary of the Navy and the House of Representatives, who did not seem to know international law either. The exultation in America was matched by vehement protest in Britain and the emotional storm brought the two nations to what appeared the brink of war. The British Government ordered its fleet to a state of readiness, began preparations to send troops to Canada, and initiated munitions and supply measures to suit. There was only a faint hope left that a break in relations, to be followed by war, could be avoided.

The British Government was represented in Washington by Lord Lyons, an experienced, understanding, skillful professional. It instructed him to demand the restoration of the prisoners and an apology, within seven days. Instead of presenting the note, Lyons on his own initiative unofficially acquainted Secretary of State Seward of its arrival and import. This was to ease the blow, permit some quiet rumination by Seward and his Government and encourage whatever processes of reason still functioned in the midst of the national clamor.

When Lyons called on Seward two days later, formally to present the note, he was met with a plea for another two days delay. Again, on his own, knowing the Lincoln Administration to be in a seriously weak condition at home for alleged failure to "press the war," Lyons acquiesced. He felt assured by this time Seward was on the side of reason and needed time to elicit support in the Cabinet for the commissioners' release. This seems clear to us today, after the event, but it was something of a gamble at the time. Seward had taken office with what had seemed considerable animosity toward Britain, and some members of his Government, prominent public figures and newspapers at home would have hotly denounced Lyons' decision had they known of it.

The two countries seemed so close to war that President Lincoln lost no time in meeting with his cabinet. The first Cabinet session was held, in fact, on Christmas morning. The chairman of the Senate Foreign Relations Committee, Charles Sumner, attended, bringing letters he had received from leading British citizens urging the United States to disavow the unauthorized action of Wilkes and to release the captives. A good example, incidentally, of how private citizens can exercise a beneficent influence. Fortunately, also, Sumner himself favored this course. But others shared the national intoxication and saw in the affair great domestic political advantages. At least one— the Secretary of the Navy—was on public record, as was the House of Representatives, as endorsing Wilkes' action. From this position it would be politically embarrassing to retreat. Moreover, the President himself seems to have been of the opinion the prisoners should be held.

An entire morning's discussion brought no conclusion. The Cabinet adjourned to the following day. The long debate on December 26 enabled Seward to win his case. It was Lyons' decision not to act promptly in the formal, literal sense of his instructions that permitted two nations to steer away from war. He obtained one of his Government's demands—the one Lyons told London was the only essential demand—release of the captives. His Government had the good judgment to take his advice to dispense with the apology.[3]

One may never be an ambassador but in the humblest diplomatic role he finds plenty of decisions to make and advice to give his government, placing him in the very same delicacy of position of Lord Lyons. And this can well occur, as I was saying, to those serving in underdeveloped areas. Those in the State Department concocting instructions and inquiries, or visiting your area for a personal look-see, may or may not have served in underdeveloped areas. You are likely to be placed in the position of making sense of questions, viewpoints, instructions which don't make sense. You must suggest modifications, or adapt instructions as you carry them out. Sometimes this takes quite a bit of initiative and responsibility as you keep in mind the essence of your government's objectives. On occasion, of course, you may feel compelled to question those objectives.

In any case, wherever you serve abroad, in underdeveloped or developed societies, Washington is thousands of miles away. Distance doesn't give as much latitude to discretion as in Lyons' day, communication being very much faster, but it still gives a lot. Fast communication can, in fact, add to your troubles and therefore exact greater initiative. The chatter of the telegraph and teletype is not always a clarifying sound and the ability of your government to reach you on the telephone requires you to be all the more alert and ready to advise. It is your local situation abroad and your local personalities which provide the missing or doubtful parts of every jigsaw puzzle Washington is daily trying to to put together. It is your initiative and resourcefulness in keeping Washington sensitive to them that makes the difference between skillful and awkward diplomacy. Sometimes you find yourself wondering if an error in Washington may not reflect an inadequacy on your part—a lack of the very initiative and resourcefulness we are talking about—in getting across thousands of miles some important part of a puzzle in proper time and proper clarity.

No, it isn't easy to tell a group of people in your distant capital, which can be certain it knows all there is to know, that perhaps it doesn't. This takes a little skill. Particularly, when you have reason to believe Washington's misapprehension is highly placed. Careers can be fouled up by this kind of thing. But this is a part of diplomacy's challenge.

Your initiative is sorely tested when an official position of Washington throws you into a state of isolation. If Washington has reached the decision to string along with a dictator, or a ruling clique, or a *coup d'état*, this can make your local situation difficult with respect to elements of the population not in the ruling group but which you consider vital to the achievement of your government's long-run objectives. You must figure out ways of bridging that local gap between your government's immediate decisions and its long-run objectives. That's your job. Nobody can do it for you. No one in your distant capital can do it or instruct you on how to do it. But you obviously must work at it with great ingenuity. You cannot undercut your Government's immediate decision. You cannot cast doubt on its authenticity. Right or wrong, the decision has been made to seek immediate, short-run results and those cannot be jeopardized. You ask how to do this? That's what we call initiative.

This constitutes the great area of difficulty to any diplomatic officer—the area in which he can get his fingers burned. The timid back off from it. They simply string along with the short-run results. It is an area in which real diplomacy is required, as much with one's associates as with foreigners—an area, in fact, we need to analyze carefully and cultivate intensively in the orientation and training of our diplomatic officers. Obviously tricky, it demands not only instincts and judgments of the finest sort but all the learning and wisdom which diplomatic experience can provide.

It is an area requiring a good deal of sympathy and in-
dulgence on the part of the Washington hierarchy, so that
initiative, if based on good judgment, receives its proper
award even if it goes awry. Here is an opportunity for an
officer's initiative to be exercised when stationed in Washington—to create this kind of attitude. It is not so widespread as to demand little or no resourcefulness in nurtur-
ing. One of the more fascinating areas for initiative. No
opportunities are lacking there.

You might find yourself in a state of isolation in your
locality by the unwillingness of elements in the population
to be seen in your company because of some decision of
your government quite apart from the local political
situation. These "unpopular" decisions are increasing in
number as the world grows smaller and what each nation
says and does is subjected to increasingly microscopic
inspection. Among the people who draw away from you
may be some intimately in touch with the political and
economic situation of the country and therefore be the
very people most able to help and guide you in your judgments. It is not always your most solid and understanding
friends who best understand the opinions and grievances of
the population and the pitch to which they may be rising.
Yet this pitch provides clues to political trends and the
durability of regimes. These clues you must keep at your
fingertips, so that Washington may decide if and when it
should shift its position. Here, the degree of initiative of
officers in the field is a crucial matter.

To get the drifts and degrees of feeling and grievance in
a local population is never easy. You must have extensive
and reliable contacts and the time to maintain them. If a
dictatorship rules the population, it has a secret police
which watches you and your contacts. You must contrive
to play a cat-and-mouse game. How do you do this with
minimal risk to your Government, yourself and your
contacts? This is a part of initiative.

As an officer acquires more finesse in diplomacy, he
finds that he must take his political soundings in manifold
ways. One learns, for example, that people of the same

calling always talk more freely to one another—military with military, lawyers with lawyers, journalists with journalists, businessmen with businessmen, labor people with labor. They have a natural inclination and pretext for keeping in touch with one another. So if your mission hasn't got a labor attaché you might find there should be one, for labor organizations thrust up from the masses and provide extensive lines of communication with the local population. So do university students, and diplomatic officers making political judgments must contrive ways of keeping in close touch with them. Routine methods, behind-the-desk attitudes will never make a first-class diplomatic or consular officer. The man who waits for instructions on how to play the game isn't in it.

The great thrust of governmental activity in international affairs has been along the whole social spectrum. You have not only a correspondingly broad spectrum to watch and act upon abroad but your whole governmental establishment at home is involved. There is almost no executive department or agency which does not share in our overseas interests. This is by no means so simple a situation that it can be covered by "instructions." You must yourself understand what is going on, what interests the various elements of your executive departments and agencies and lubricate their efforts rather than being, yourself, an individual source of friction and difficulty for them. The give-and-take that must occur between departments and agencies is on all levels and the lower levels often become better aware of the creakings and grindings than the upper. Officers lacking adequate vision and initiative can account for some of our more serious problems within our diplomatic machinery.

The give-and-take required for the transaction of your government's business abroad is also between you and your fellow Foreign Service officers. Each officer can see a situation or policy differently. He looks at them in terms of his own background, his own experience, his own education in an Henry Adams sense. When he differs from you he is more likely to be helpful to you in your own estimate of a situation than if he agrees. He will enable you to see your own problem more sharply. There is no surer way of limiting your usefulness than in holding in higher esteem officers who agree with you than those who disagree.

But differences of view must sometimes be surmounted. Suppose you are in a small mission in Africa, a third secretary in charge of economic and consular affairs. Through your contacts you begin to pick up threads of acquaintanceship in the local labor movement. These giving you insights no other colleague is acquiring, you find your initiative suggesting the necessity of supplementing inadequate representation funds by dipping into your own pocket to cultivate and multiply these contacts. Eventually you encounter an influential labor leader who, you become little by little convinced, is a communist agent. You draft an alerting message to Washington, but the principal political officer disagrees with you and refuses to transmit it. "This man is only an African nationalist," he says. What do you do? Fold up? Retreat? If you argue, *how* do you argue? *How* do you present your case? Here is a situation demanding resourcefulness and guts. If you have these qualities in ample degree, you may surmount your problem. If you haven't, you won't and not only will you find a troublesome appraisal in your personnel folder but—if you are right—your government will be caught in a disadvantageous position one fine day. Sometimes as much diplomacy is required to deal successfully with one's associates as with other governments.

Then, special emissaries might conceivably show up in your area and these are capable of leaving behind a woeful trail. I have sometimes felt in the Foreign Service like a road maintenance supervisor, whose job it was to keep in shape the highways of understanding between my government and others. Some heavy-wheeling emissary puts in an appearance and tears to pieces in a few days' time a road you have been patiently working at for months or years. So you start all over again reconstructing it. Whether you have what it takes only you can answer. No instruction from Washington can.

I remember a young Foreign Service officer serving as vice consul in Jerusalem when the British ended their mandate in Palestine and the independent State of Israel came into existence in territory Arabs claimed. Arab-Israeli hostilities flared. Blaming us for a large share of the situation, the Arabs made us feel exceedingly unpopular. Jordan—Transjordan it was called then—had gained its independence the year before. This young Foreign Service officer, aged 28, was given a dual status. At the same time he continued to serve as a vice consul in Jerusalem he was made American Representative to Transjordan. Back and forth between Jerusalem and Amman he shuttled in his car, braving bullets, and, though based in Jerusalem, his untiring initiative, ingenuity and personality won him popularity among the Arabs. This was quite some achievement. He even became a good friend of the Transjordanian King. A mere vice consul, this young officer helped greatly to bring two countries safely through a trying and hazardous period.[4] We have recently been through similarly trying experiences in Africa and Asia, not to add Latin America. We are likely to go through more.

Even junior officers, therefore, can play a great, facilitating, stimulating role in our vast diplomatic effort. They can devise and apply many lubricants which can keep our vast apparatus of international relations from grinding away numerous little bearings and developing all sorts of tragic knocks and breakdowns, the causes of which people at the top can never detect. The community of nations and the extensive, across-the-spectrum diplomacy it demands have far outstripped the capacity of the relatively few people in capitals to produce the desired results. A few people can decide we *want* to get from here to there—that's what one calls policy—but infinite are the combinations of people, moves, decisions, initiatives demanded to get from here to there.

There is one aspect of this question of initiative one should keep in mind. There is an inner initiative—an initiative of inner development—diplomacy requires. Being an art as well as a business, diplomacy is an intellectual and cultural process. This means that anyone engaged in it must study and develop. Only in this way can he constantly add to the knowledge, the insight, the experience needed to equip him to deal successfully with people of a wholly different culture and social background. The experience of others one taps through reading is as useful and illuminating as one's own, sometimes more than one's own.

There you are, my young friend. Satisfied? Then let's walk down to the river. This is season and scenery of which poets write and diplomacy itself is a kind of poetry—a poetry of initiative, a poetry of action. Initiative and action are tributes we pay to it.

## NOTES AND REFERENCES

[1] Ellis O. Briggs, *Farewell to Foggy Bottom* (New York: McKay, 1964), Chapter IV.

[2] *Career Diplomat* (New York: Macmillan, 1964), p. 25.

[3] The *Trent* affair is well described in E. D. Adams, *Great Britain and the American Civil War* (New York: Russell & Russell, n.d.), Chapter VII.

[4] This was Wells Stabler who, later in his career, became Ambassador to Spain.

# 5.

# PERSONNEL FOR A "NEW" DIPLOMACY

*PREFATORY NOTE: When Adolph A. Berle, a long-time acquaintance, arrived in Washington in 1961 with the Kennedy Administration, I talked with him about needed reforms and the usefulness of assembling a group of practitioners and knowledgeable outsiders to undertake a broad-scaled study of our diplomatic establishment and its conduct of diplomacy and to make recommendations for improvements. He passed this word along and a former Secretary of State and long-time Congressman, Christian A. Herter, was appointed to head what came to be known as the Committee on Foreign Affairs Personnel, whose report,* **Personnel for the New Diplomacy,** *was published in December 1962. The Secretary of State, Dean Rusk, being loath to request an appropriation of funds by Congress to finance the Committee, the Carnegie Endowment for International Peace stepped into the breach.*

*The Committee conceived its purposes in much too narrow terms and indeed inaccurately conceptualized diplomacy itself, treating as a "new diplomacy" what in fact is a very old diplomacy and overlooking its strategical and tactical dynamics. I felt it necessary for someone to challenge the Committee in these respects.*

One of the healthy contributions made by the report of the Herter Committee to the discussion of our diplomatic

Reprinted with permission from *Foreign Service Journal*, October, 1963.

requirements is to define the environment in which diplomacy must be practiced. Not all predecessors of the Herter Committee have taken the trouble to do this, which may account for their recommendations being insufficiently realistic and perceptive of the developing world situation since 1945. Environment obviously determines not only the tactics and techniques we must employ in diplomacy but the personal skills we must seek (and nurture) in our diplomats.

The new diplomacy the Committee concluded to have evolved from our present environment is described in the following terms:

> In pursuit of our international goals, we have developed an arsenal of instruments more varied than ever before. They include: all the tools of traditional diplomacy; international law; intelligence; political action; technical assistance and various types of foreign economic aid; military aid programs; information and psychological programs; monetary policies; trade development programs; educational exchange; cultural programs; and, more recently, measures to counter insurgency movements. Most of these fall outside the older definition of diplomacy, but all of them must be considered actual or potential elements of United States programs. Together they constitute what is here called the "new diplomacy." (p. 4)

Have any of these ever fallen outside of diplomacy? When was political action not a part of diplomacy? Is not political action the center-piece of diplomacy? Were not all the elements mentioned by the Committee a part of European diplomacy of the nineteenth and early twentieth century? Do not these elements go as far back as recorded history? One can think, for instance, of the technical and military assistance of Theodosius I who, through a combination of military power and diplomacy, overcame the Visigoths and resettled them in certain designated areas of the Roman empire, securing in return their services as soldiers. This example goes back only to the fourth century A. D., but one can without difficulty recall earlier examples, such as those afforded by Philip of Macedonia, of the melding of military elements with the diplomatic, including in the diplomatic such elements or instruments as bribery, subversion, torture, assassination, and insurgency.

Let us look at the more recent example of James Bryce, the British ambassador to this country from 1907 to 1913. Just as his study, *The American Commonwealth*, is still a classic, so his ambassadorship to the United States remains a classic, illustrative of how popular and effective a diplomatic representative can be if he is profound enough to know thoroughly his own country, the country to which he is sent, and the world in which they both function. Combining the qualities of scholar, philosopher and practical statesman, Bryce in his diplomacy effected a very skillful amalgam of political action, information and psychological programs, cultural programs, intelligence and international law.

But let us not overlook our own earliest diplomacy. During and after our Revolution, international law, intelligence and political action, not to mention insurgency and economic and military aid, were an integral part of what we were trying to do. The economic and military aid were in reverse—solicited from abroad rather than extended by ourselves—but the elements were there, fortunately for us. Furthermore, our early diplomatic representatives were information and psychological programs as well as cultural programs in themselves, which made them eminently skillful of course. For there never was a period in which it was more necessary that America be understood by Europe— not just by governments but by politicians in and out of the government, scientists, philosophers, educators. This was accomplished with eminent success by the Jeffersons, the Franklins, the Adamses of the time. Such was the quality of Jefferson, moreover, that when he was serving at Paris as the diplomatic representative of the confederated thirteen States, he was consulted by French political leaders on a variety of their domestic political questions.

Since 1900 our government has made use of private

citizens and sometimes public officials outside the diplomatic establishment to engage in programs which we now too easily associate with a new diplomacy. The work of Arthur Powell Davis comes to mind, a civil engineer who for eight years was chief engineer (1906-14) and nine years director (1914-23) of our Reclamation Service. His technical assistance to Turkestan and Panama was too real for one to conclude that this type of assistance originated with us quite newly. Grandiose programs along these lines have originated recently, of course, but the weapon—if one must speak of diplomacy in cold war terminology—has been in our arsenal for a good many years. The indigenous Indians, indeed, taught it to us, making it a part of their diplomacy in dealing with the earliest settlers on this continent.

Few Americans, including those in our diplomatic establishment, seem to be aware of just how broad were the development programs by which we endeavored to discharge our self-assumed responsibilities to underdeveloped areas inherited from our war with Spain. Largely neglected, accordingly, is the experience we gained in political, military, economic, educational, informational, psychological, social and administrative affairs, from working with the underdeveloped peoples concerned. From 1899 to 1901, the rebellion of Aguinaldo confronted the U.S. Philippine Mission with the necessity of adding counter-insurgency programs to the others. Unfortunately, indifference to off-shore responsibilities and experiences until comparatively recently, as well as our failure to require some familiarity with these responsibilities and experiences of the men and women entering our Foreign Service, has caused these experiences and their lessons to be lost. It means also that many of us, in trying to define a new diplomacy, are actually in process of discovering an old diplomacy.

I would suggest that what may be new in our present situation and therefore what may be new in the diplomacy we are endeavoring to create to meet this situation are such things as:

(1) the range or scope of elements required to be

compounded to meet not simply a situation in one or two areas of the world but in a very large number of areas, on virtually every continent, and therefore requiring considerable organization and coordination;

(2) the range of peoples and cultures involved, requiring a far greater recourse than ever before to the social and behavioral sciences;

(3) today's accelerated speed at which the world, its decisions and events revolve, requiring greater celerity of decision and maneuver, as well as greater profundity lest decisions produce only superficial improvisation from which later retreat must be contrived;

(4) the extensive participation of people, press and public opinion in the diplomatic process;

(5) the rise of a philosophy, implemented by governments, hostile to Western philosophy, life and conduct;

(6) nuclear power, with its capacity for widespread annihilation.

We must view even these elements with discriminating, historical knowledge, however. Ancient Athens also faced a hostile philosophy, subversion and the problem of the participation of popular assemblies and public opinion in the diplomatic process. Nor is the concept of diplomacy as extending to dealing with peoples (the government-to-people and people-to-people approaches) really novel. In the 1790's a French Minister, known as Citizen Genêt, had this same concept. Had he not been so imaginative in developing it he might have lasted longer. Raising troops and contracting for privateers in a neutral country are, after all, stretching the government-to-people conceptualization a little far. Nor should we forget, as far as element (2) is concerned, that the Japanese specialist and "the China hand" were part of our diplomatic effort long ago. The fact that we dropped them and have now begun once again to replace them does not make them new or area specialization new.

In suggesting what may be new elements or dimensions of our diplomacy since World War II, I mentioned first the considerable organization and coordination required of a current diplomatic establishment. This has not only been emphasized by, but has been almost an obsession of, recent analyses of the State Department and the Foreign Service. There is a heavy emphasis upon it by the Herter Committee. It seems that this emphasis has been carried so far as to require a diplomatic Copernicus to come along to suggest that the focal point of all this question of personnel for diplomacy is *personnel* for diplomacy quite as much as *organization* for diplomacy. A diplomatic establishment and its performance of the art of diplomacy revolve quite as much around the individuals who make it up as around an organizational chart.

The example of David Eugene Thompson, the United States Ambassador to Mexico in 1906-1909 is worth referring to again. His great influence in Mexico was personal. It could not have been produced by any reorganization of the State Department or the diplomatic service. His type and philosophy may not be those we need today in every country, although I suggest there are a few dictators left and we could use some influence with them, whether of the David Eugene Thompson or the Llewellyn Thompson type. The essential questions are: who are these Thompsons, where and how do we find them, and how do we preserve their talents through an extended diplomatic career? What are the conditions of service required for the cultivation and development of their talents?

The example of Jules Jusserand is also worth recalling in this connection. He became one of the confidants and advisers of a President of the United States, as Thomas Jefferson had been more than a century before of leaders of the French Government, when serving in Paris as United States Minister.

These individuals demonstrated qualities of diplomacy which resolve a government's dilemma of exercising influence without risk or charge of interference. For the influence is personal, arising from the profundity, understanding, experience, and tact of the representative.

This, I submit, is what we are trying to define as diplomacy, old and new, and the ability to perform it is what we are trying to find, train, nurture and reward by suitable conditions in our diplomatic establishment. In seeking an improvement of our diplomatic performance, then, the basic questions are: what kinds of knowledge, sagacity, perceptiveness, experience and dynamism do we need, how can we attract those people who possess them, how can we test such people more accurately both for admission and promotion purposes, and what are the conditions of service we must provide abroad as well as in Washington to nurture these qualities? To meet this challenge we must first—and accurately—analyze diplomacy, diplomatic processes and the results we want—the Theodosius, Thompson, Bryce, Jusserand results, if you will. We must then establish the criteria fitted to these results and make the criteria so widely known that people can prepare systematically and adequately as candidates. Drag-net publicity campaigns on "the Foreign Service" will not suffice. Next, we must bring to bear on selection and promotion processes the most up-to-date techniques the behavoral sciences can provide. Finally, in the field, as at headquarters, we must create the conditions which will encourage the results we want. Few, I think, would say we are doing these things successfully now. Few would say the Herter Report dealt perceptively with them.

# Part II

# THE AMERICAN CRISIS

# 6.

# ARE WE GETTING OUR SHARE
# OF THE BEST?

*PREFATORY NOTE: It is time we recognized the connection between the quality of our education and our ability to compete in the world. This connection clearly manifests itself in industry and technology. It exists, although not so clearly, in the military and diplomatic spheres. By education I mean not only formal schooling but the informal schooling one receives in family life.*

*The superiority which the Soviet Union seeks over the United States is relentlessly pursued in all sectors of human activity, from athletics and armaments to shipping and science. Within that wide range lies diplomacy, which is our principal means of safeguarding the nation's survival, promoting the values of freedom and contributing to such community needs as peace and healthy—as opposed to cut-throat—competition.*

*The State Department has overlooked these facts and has neither sounded any warnings to the American educational system or to the public generally nor undertaken any steps to redress the disadvantage which its performance is suffering due to a crumbling of the nation's educational standards. Even had that crumbling not occurred, special efforts would have been required of the Department to keep its officers abreast of the fast-paced changes which have overtaken the world since 1933 and the new and fresh diplomatic perspectives and initiatives which these changes have demanded.*

---

Reprinted with permission from *Foreign Service Journal*, November, 1962.

*As this essay suggests, one of the ingredients of high quality diplomacy is learned practitioners and one of the reasons our diplomacy is no better than it is is that our educational system is failing to provide an adequate supply of well-educated people. Over the years I became aware of how this was showing up in the performance of our Foreign Service and the State Department. I therefore requested an assignment to the Board of Examiners of the Foreign Service to explore the extent of our educational slippage. While with the Board, I volunteered for recruiting trips to American colleges and universities so as to pick the brains of faculty members and administrators concerning the problem. This essay presents the facts and conclusions which developed from that experience.*

*Adequately to represent a World Power and to constitute a dynamic instrumentality of understanding and peace in the world, each of our diplomats must know who we are as a nation, what we stand for and why (viz., our political and social philosophy), what our social problems are and how we go at them, what our achievements and failures are, along with the history of other nations and civilizations and their competing philosophies. Short of this they cannot possess the acute, profound perspectives needed to explain and defend our kind of society and promote its values of freedom in curious, often hostile and sophisticated circles around the world. This demands a good grounding in comparative philosophy, in the major political systems of the world, in world history, in sociology and in the socio-political programs and techniques employed in our diverse society. This preparation is not easy to obtain and relatively few officers commissioned in the Foreign Service and officials appointed to the State Department possess it. Nor has the State Department measured up to its responsibility to correct these deficiencies, which is one of the reasons our diplomacy is not a winning diplomacy in competition with the Soviets'.*

*The following essay, spelling out the deficiencies of candidates for the Foreign Service, received wide circulation, being picked up by* **The New York Times,** *the Associated Press and the radio news programs of the Columbia*

Broadcasting System and the National Broadcasting Company. *It is the only critique known to have been published of our educational standards in relationship to American diplomacy and of the State Department's criteria and procedures for the selection of diplomatic and consular officers.*

*The continued erosion of educational standards in this country since 1962 makes this essay as relevant today as when it appeared.*

The process of finding and selecting officers adequately equipped for our diplomatic service is a singularly exacting one which must be keyed to highly selective criteria. It has been developed by trial and error over a number of years, subjected to numerous reappraisals, exposed to various essays of experimentation. One would be justified in expecting it would bring into the Foreign Service a flow of superbly qualified young men and women, the pick of their generation—young men and women fully aware of the importance of the calling to which they aspire and at least moderately well prepared for its opportunities and obligations of representing the United States abroad.

A year of service as a Deputy Examiner engaged in interviewing candidates and a round of colleges as a part of the Department's recruiting effort have persuaded me that accomplishment falls grievously short of the goal. Of those candidates I examined a few were good, a rare one was outstanding, but the great majority were wholly unprepared for diplomatic work, and did not even have the slightest glimmer of what it was. Somehow they had acquired a feeling they might like the Foreign Service, or at any rate it would do no harm to give the examinations a whirl to see "what gives." They had no conception whatever that this is an exacting calling, involving not only considerable hazard and adventure but also a profound cultural awareness, knowledge of history and political science, some familiarity with the behavioral sciences and at least an elementary grounding in international law, international organization and diplomacy—

in other words considerable intellectual preparation, if they are adequately to represent their country abroad.

My initial surprise was to find among the candidates an abysmal ignorance of so elementary a subject as the geography of the United States. Few could even place accurately the principal rivers: one with so descriptive a name as the Ohio was not infrequently identified as being "somewhere west of the Mississippi." Few could name the principal seaports, and, of course, any requirement demanding such detailed familiarity with this country as identifying the states comprising the "wheat belt" or the "corn belt" was completely beyond the average candidate's depth.

As to elementary economics and social data, most could only guess at the population, labor force and gross national product of their country. Many did not know what constituted "gross national product." They had no clear idea as to the principal products of their country, nor as to its exports and imports. They could name a few of each, but had no notion of their relative importance and had given no thought to the role of imports in the American economy.

As with elementary geographic and economic aspects of the United States, so with historical, sociological and cultural. Americans abroad are asked a great many questions about their country. How did the United States acquire the Panama Canal? What is its status now? Who started our war with Spain (or Mexico) and what came out of it? When did our labor movement start and where does it stand now? How does a Jimmy Hoffa get control of a powerful union? What were some of the reform movements in American history? What became of them?

A good half of our candidates could answer such questions with only the thinnest recital of facts; many could not discuss them at all. Some could not recall ever having heard of the Populist movement; few knew its connection with Woodrow Wilson's "New Freedom." Asked if he knew anything about the Progressive movement, one candidate replied, "Oh, yes, that was LaFollette's movement." To the question, "Where did LaFollette come from?" he could only reply vaguely, "Somewhere out West."

I would say that the proportion of candidates who could handle current events questions reasonably well was about six out of ten. Perhaps three or four could give fairly adequate definitions of the Truman Doctrine or the Eisenhower Doctrine, even state the composition and responsibilities of SEATO and CENTO. Most of them had never heard of ANZUS.

If we explored American foreign policy we encountered baffling deficiencies. Most of them knew the origin of the Monroe Doctrine and its general content, but beyond that their knowledge rapidly petered out. The tests the Doctrine has undergone, the various interpretations placed on it, its abuses were beyond them. Naturally, we rarely ventured to ask for a discussion of whether it is still in existence, although this is a question many of them will encounter and all of them should be expected to handle with some degree of information and intelligence.

The American abroad is asked about American culture as often as about our history, our politics and our policies. An Indian dinner guest may inquire: "America is very materialistic, I understand. Is that so? What has it contributed to cultural and spiritual progress?" No more than one candidate in twenty could provide a thoughtful, well-informed response to such a question. Even sadder to relate, they were equally blank on purely factual questions. Could the candidate give his Indian guest the name of five or six American painters and tell something of their work? The names of five composers? Of two or three philosophers? Of a few poets, novelists or essayists other than the contemporaries with whom the Indian was probably familiar?

The answers were halting and feeble. Many could not name a single painter, a single composer, a single philosopher, other than contemporary. Even in the literary field knowledge was surprisingly limited. Thought-provoking questions, requiring a certain amount of relating and synthesizing—"What has been Chicago's contribution to American literature?" for example—left them gaping and stumbling. We put simpler factual questions: What was the New England school of literature in the nineteenth century? We found college graduates native to New England itself who could not answer.

Most candidates showed some slight familiarity with twentieth century writers. Asked to name some poets, they almost invariably led off with Robert Frost. Among novelists, they could produce the names of Hemingway and Faulkner, perhaps others. (One mentioned Tennessee Williams.) But under questioning this familiarity proved to be shallow; it did not survive much discussion.

Questions of a sociological nature asked us abroad and on which we should be able to throw intelligent light found candidates pitifully uninformed. Such questions concern the basis and nature of our society. They concern problems people confront abroad. They raise doubts of our fitness for leadership. What are the causes of our sizable problem of juvenile delinquency? What are the causes of our high divorce rate? Why do we permit trashy pulp magazines to exist, to be exported? Why Hollywood? To what extent are our basic civil rights effective? Rare indeed was the candidate who could cope with such questions.

As to diplomacy itself few of the candidates had any idea what it was. Nine out of ten had not even given any thought to it, it never having occurred to them to so much as look the word up in a dictionary, much less go to a library and read something about it, if only a biography or two. This was baffling indeed. I had expected to find far greater interest in a profession which candidates were considering as a career. I had expected, even, preparation, but as to this I found our universities deficient. One has to search far and wide for a course in diplomacy, particularly one in which its methods and techniques are discussed. Our universities appear to be hypnotized by the machinery and formulation of foreign policy: consideration of its execution is well-nigh non-existent.

Indeed, one conclusion that emerges from such an experience as this is that American education is letting us down. An educational system that turns out graduates lacking the simplest geographical and sociological knowledge about their country is not an adequate educational system. Universities that graduate men and women with only a smattering of knowledge of their nation's history, its governmental structure and political system, and its cultural evolution as well as of the international political system, do not merit the name of universities.

Unless the quality of our education is even more appalling than I think it is, a second conclusion must be that the State Department and the Foreign Service are no longer getting their share of the cream of college graduates.

One reason for this is that the Foreign Service is no longer the principal avenue for dedication to constructive work abroad. The spirit of service now has a score of outlets to two or three existing thirty years ago. Philanthropic and charitable organizations with overseas programs have multiplied and broadened their activities. Three thousand American companies now operate outside the United States and offer all kinds of opportunities, including negotiation of agreements with foreign governments and the development of exchange, training and technical assistance programs, in a private diplomacy very similar in content to public.

The competition of the professions is more formidable than ever. Teaching now offers many opportunities for travel and cross-cultural adventure through scholarships and fellowships, exchange programs, foundation grants, positions in overseas branches. Law schools send moot court teams to colleges to demonstrate the practice of law and attract promising undergraduates. The physical sciences have taken on new glamour; there is a widespread feeling that our country's destiny lies in the hands of the scientists. Space technology has the adventuresome appeal that diplomacy had thirty years ago and the financial rewards are much greater.

The competition is not only from this extensive area of

private and semi-public enterprise, but from other components of the Federal establishment. There are few
departments and agencies not engaged in foreign affairs in
some manner. They also have taken to offering summer
employment as a means of stimulating interest. The military services offer many opportunities which parallel the
Foreign Service, with fringe benefits our Service does not
provide.

Impairing the competitive position of the Foreign
Service is also the fact that in recent years it has become
somewhat less of a foreign service than formerly. We can
no longer offer the virtual certainty that a recruit will
spend extended periods of his life abroad, with the diversity
of life, work, travel and adventure that this means. Since
Wristonization,* officers must expect to spend sizable
periods of their careers right here at home.

The barrage of criticism directed at the Department and
the Service has discouraged some applicants. I had candidate after candidate attest to this and query me about the
criticism. It seems quite evident that we must be prepared
to discuss criticism frankly, conceding deficiencies and
mistakes where they exist, pointing convincingly to our
achievements, although these may be quiet and unobtru-
sive, presenting clearly the difficulties and problems confronting the practice of diplomacy in this age.

For this complex of reasons, we are not now achieving
the high level of quality the times require and which was
envisioned by the various committees which, in the last
fifteen years, have examined the Foreign Service and made
recommendations for its improvement. "Foreign policy,"
said the Wriston Committee in 1954, "will be dynamic or
inert, steadfast or aimless, in proportion to the character
and unity of those who serve it." Formal unity we have
achieved, but character we have neglected.

---

*"Wristonization" was the merger in 1954 of the stationary
State Department Civil Servants with the nomadic Foreign Service.
The proposal of the merger and reasons for it were set forth in
*Toward a Stronger Foreign Service*. Report of the Secretary of
State's Public Committee on Personnel, June 1954. Department
of State Publication 5458. U.S. Government Printing Office. The
chairman of the committee was Henry Wriston.

In addition, since World War II, we have achieved the establishment of a broader base for recruitment. Our candidates now come from all parts of the country, all income levels, all social environments, all occupational backgrounds, all types of schools and almost every racial and national origin. But the Department has not correspondingly extended its effort at *quality* recruitment. It has followed the letter of the recommendation that the nation's diplomatic service be more representative without recognizing the ancillary necessity of refining its competitive appeal to achieve a reservoir of suitable quality. It has not offered to college students or faculties a clear enough image of the Service and the kind of people it seeks. It has not set forth either the educational preparation needed nor, clearly and precisely enough, the personal qualifications, aptitudes and skills. It has engaged in a dragnet, come-one-come-all operation. If quality is to be combined with representativeness in our reservoir of talent, a greater effort—qualitative, in particular—is required.

To get across to our colleges, and even to our secondary schools, and the general public, a clearer image of our diplomatic service and the kind of people who can qualify is, I suggest, a fundamental responsibility of the department of foreign affairs in a democracy and it is going to take some doing. It requires, first, a clearer and deeper analysis of diplomacy. The content and techniques of our work rather than its situs abroad must now be emphasized. What is required is (1) a clearer concept among ourselves of what diplomacy is today—which is to say, the different types of diplomacy which the current environment exacts; (2) a clearer analysis of the competitive factors we are up against, including the interests of young people and why they have these interests, in order that our presentation may be sharply pitched to these interests; and (3) a more discriminating selection of the Foreign Service officers assigned to present the Service and its requirements to our educational system and the public, and the assignment of such officers for long enough periods to provide continuity of contact, experience and effort.

We must be quite clear and very determined about this.

We can no longer afford the luxury of letting the Department and the Service be represented by officers who are not sufficiently seasoned and intellectually responsive to their audiences. Let me give an example or two of what I mean. Some high school teachers who had attended one of the Department's seminars complained to me afterward that the Department's presentation was incomplete and evasive. I pointed out that naturally there were matters that could not be placed on the top of a seminar table for public discussion. That was not the kind of thing the teachers had in mind, however. They were referring instead to such instances as the reply of a senior Foreign Service officer who, when asked what kind of informational program the United States had in the area under discussion, told the questioner he would have to get his answer from USIA. No one in the seminar felt that this was satisfactory or reassuring as to the Department's familiarity with, much less coordination of, our total diplomacy.

Another example is directly related to our recruiting effort. Representatives of the Department and of another Federal agency visited a certain Eastern college for recruiting purposes. The other agency sent its deputy director; the Department's representative was a junior Foreign Service officer. Among the dozen or so students who showed up at the Department's meeting were the sons of a Foreign Service colleague. They described the Department's spokesman as timid, evasive and inadequately informed on the current crises facing the United States. By contrast, the agency representative impressed the students as mature, frank, responsive and well-informed. No more than two or three students showed any further interest in the Foreign Service, but a dozen or so filled out applications to the other agency. That other agency was the CIA. Does not this say something of the difficulties experienced by the State Department and Foreign Service in keeping effective reins on the CIA?

I would warn against any superficial or merely bureaucratic effort to improve our communication with the educational establishment and the general public. This is not something that can be handed out to officers as a kind of recruitment patter. It is not a matter of visiting more campuses or staying longer. What is needed is a clearer conceptualization of diplomacy in the twentieth century and this can come only from the minds of the officers themselves. We must take a more analytical—let us say a more scientific—interest in the over-all nature of our policymaking and diplomatic functions, and the way in which these fit into the work of other departments, other agencies, private firms, universities. We must be willing to examine our work critically, pinpointing its deficiencies as well as its excellences, its failures as well as its achievements, and ask ourselves why these deficiencies and failures occur. We must familiarize ourselves with the growing literature on foreign policy and operations and the wide range of sociological factors involved.

The Department on its side must be prepared to take steps to stimulate and make possible such an intellectual effort. This means, for one thing, that the Department and the Service must be staffed generously enough to provide time for intellectual, as contrasted with routine, day-to-day effort. Officers so hard pressed by daily demands that they can scarcely keep up with a good daily newspaper will not be able to measure up to what is required.

If this effort can be made, one consequence will be to bring us into closer relationships with our colleges and universities. The thinking of the faculties of our higher institutions of learning can help us in our search for clarification; we in turn have something to offer them. From this exchange will come a clearer understanding, on the campus and among ourselves, of the kind of work in which we are engaged and the kind of people we are seeking.

As the Wriston Committee said: "No segment of the Foreign Service machinery stands in more pressing need of modernization than its recruitment of junior officers." But no tinkering and tampering will produce this modernization. It must take place in the minds of men.

# 7.

# A NATIONAL ACADEMY OF
# FOREIGN AFFAIRS?

*PREFATORY NOTE: Because of the inadequate educational preparation of our diplomatic officers, proposals have been made intermittently for the creation of a diplomatic academy. Some of these have contemplated an educational institution comparable to the military, naval and air force academies. Others have envisaged a post-graduate institution to plumb more deeply certain areas of learning than do courses which candidates for the Foreign Service take in our colleges and universities, to fill in complete voids, such as instruction in the art and science of diplomacy, and to fill in gaps in geographical, cultural and other areas frequently encountered among candidates. The general inadequacy of our secondary educational standards produce college graduates possessing only the skimpiest knowledge of U.S. and world geography, U.S. history and U.S. government, and these therefore constitute areas of learning in need of serious reinforcement if our diplomatic and consular officers are to measure up to their representative responsibilities.*

*The latest push for the establishment of some kind of an academy was in 1963. One set of proposals then before the U.S. Senate Committee on Foreign Relations was for a National Academy of Foreign Affairs, envisaged to improve the educational preparation not only of diplo-*

matic officers but of all U.S. Government employees involved in foreign affairs. In this set was included Senate Bill 865. Other proposals were limited to a Foreign Service Academy, for the education and training of Foreign Service officers. Still another contemplated the establishment of a "Freedom Academy" to coach as many government officials and private citizens as possible in ways to counter communist strategy and tactics, including propaganda. Nothing came of any of these proposals due to the opposition of the Committee's chairman, Senator J. William Fulbright.

The issue is as much with us today as in 1963. Recent developments, such as the U.S. plunge into a triangular form of Great Power politics, render it even more pressing if we are to reduce our international fumbling to a minimum and raise our effectiveness to the maximum.

The testimony which I gave to the Committee argued the need of a National Academy of Foreign Affairs, such as proposed in Senate bill 865, since I consider it essential that all employees of the federal government involved in foreign affairs be professionally trained and form a cohesive group pointed toward the same objectives. I concentrated, however, on my experience as a Foreign Service Officer and the needs of the Foreign Service.

As to S. 865, there seem to be three basic issues involved: one, the need of such an Academy; two, the financing of such an Academy; and, three the arrangements which should be made to assure its maximum political freedom. I address myself to the first and third of these issues.

### Foreign Service Candidates Generally Unprepared

The need for such an Academy seems to be widely recognized, so widely I will take time for only a few observations from my own experience as a Foreign Service Officer. Further, to compress my observations I shall confine them to my experience as a deputy examiner of the Board of Examiners for the Foreign Service, which was my last assignment prior to my retirement. This assignment extended for some 14 months, from April 3, 1961, through May 31, 1962, during which time I participated in the oral examination of some 400 candidates for the Foreign Service. The oral examinations in which I participated took place not only in Washington, D.C. but other parts of the country. The candidates I examined came from all parts of the country, all income levels, all kinds of educational institutions, small, intermediate and large, private and public. The candidates came from varied national, racial, and social backgrounds. My observations as to their quality, therefore, are based upon a very broad cross section.

Generally speaking, nine candidates out of ten are unprepared for the Foreign Service. They have neither the knowledge nor the experience to perform adequately the arduous, complex, exacting tasks of diplomatic work as representatives of a world hard-pressed power. Rare is the candidate who knows his own country well enough to answer accurately and intelligently the simplest questions concerning it. Nine candidates out of ten cannot answer the simplest geographical, economic, political questions about their country.

As with the United States so with other areas of professional concern—international law, diplomacy, international organization, treaty obligations and arrangements, and techniques of national defense. I remember the graduate of one of our leading eastern universities and at the time of his examination a student in one of the leading law schools of the country who had never even heard of the principle of "freedom of the seas."

The average candidate is not even well abreast of current events. One comes across candidates, including some who gain admittance to the Foreign Service, who claim to keep abreast of current developments by reading a newspaper columnist long since dead.

Quite apart from the appalling gaps in formal education

is the failure of the vast majority of candidates to read on their own. Rare is the candidate who finds the time and exercises the initiative to explore subjects independently. One cannot help gathering the impression that the American student today is too much spoon fed and limits himself to professorial assignments and handouts. Even when given reading lists he doesn't read extensively.

Our diplomatic representatives are called upon to do a first-class representational job abroad and they have not had, most of them, a first-class preparation for this job. I think we must distinguish between what may be an adequate educational preparation for jobs to be performed within the United States, where a fair smattering of American history, government, geography, economic processes, social problems, and cultural patterns may suffice, and what we must consider an adequate educational preparation for a much more profound job of representing this great and complex nation abroad, a great and complex nation with great and complex responsibilities.

The educational preparation which may do for the one will not suffice for the other. The question of whether the quality of American education is high or low, good or poor, is therefore not involved. The question is whether it is good enough for the complex, exacting task of portraying and representing the nation abroad. On that, I think, the answer is clear. It is not good enough.

### *Magnitude of Task Confronting Foreign Service Officer*

One of our problems is the magnitude of the task which confronts a diplomatic officer of mastering both his own country—so as to explain it adequately—and his profession —so as to practice it adequately. A candidate strong on Americana is found to be weak on foreign affairs and vice versa. Four years of college work in which emphasis is placed upon acquiring a knowledge of the United States— its history, government, economic geography and processes, social problems, cultural development—does not provide time for the acquisition of familiarity with international law, diplomacy, international organization, and the history of other countries and areas. On the other hand, we get candidates whose interest in foreign affairs manifests itself early in their college careers so that when they carry this forward into graduate work and come to us seeking admission to our diplomatic service, they may be adequately equipped in the field of foreign affairs but they know little or nothing of their own country. It is the melding of these two essential areas that is proving to be a considerable problem for the Foreign Service and its complex demands.

We must keep in mind, also, that the drain upon competence for overseas representation is far greater now than ever before. The competition for talent, for knowledge, for maturity, for personality, and character for overseas tasks is greater than it has ever been in the history of our country. There are those who, in surveying this problem, feel there is not enough talent to go around. There are others who feel our diplomatic establishment is not competing actively, shrewdly, professionally enough to get its share of the reservoir of talent. There are agencies of our Government which employ public relations firms to assist them in their appeal to talent. So far as I am aware the State Department has never done this. Whatever the feelings on this subject, one conclusion is inescapable; we are not getting an adequate supply of well-prepared talent into our diplomatic establishment.

### Need For Training Incoming Foreign Service Officers

This means, Mr. Chairman, that a great need is to prepare men and women for our foreign affairs needs—prepare them before they enter on duty. The life of a Foreign Service Officer is so hectic, our days and nights so hard pressed, we lack any normal opportunity to improve our preparation once we have entered on duty except by experience and catch-as-catch-can reading as we go along. The proposed Academy of Foreign Affairs is to assist officers in updating their knowledge and familiarity with those affairs at some point or points in their careers following admission to the Foreign Service. My thesis is that we must assure that incoming officers have the breadth and depth of foundation on which an academy can suitably build in the ways proposed. I favor the extension of the scope of the proposed Academy to include preparation of officers for the Foreign Service prior to or immediately following their admission.

### Academy Should Be Free From Political Pressures

I am very much concerned and I know many of my colleagues are, over the very active play of political considerations which can come to a focus on such an Academy as the one proposed. We must devise ways of not only screening such an Academy from political pressures but discouraging, on its part, political deferences, those quiet, subtle genuflections of the intellect to a political climate. I must confess I have a serious and profound uneasiness on this aspect of a Foreign Service Academy. We will not only fail to advance the quality of our diplomacy but may actually set it back if we do not devise ways of assuring such an Academy complete political and intellectual freedom. Indeed, I am enough of a Jeffersonian to feel we should not only seek to devise techniques of tolerance of such freedom on the part of our Federal political establishment but should seek in positive ways to promote differences of viewpoints and approaches and analyses on the part of the Academy staff. Only originality of thought will see us through our great crisis; and originality can survive only in an environment favorable to its survival. A positive, not simply a negative screening, approach to this problem is therefore essential.

### Limiting of Permanent Staff

I have one suggestion to offer as to this. I think it might be worth considering limiting the permanent staff of such an Academy to a very small size, perhaps, not much larger than the present staff of the Foreign Service Institute, and to supplement this with visiting professors drawn from our various colleges and universities to deal with those additional areas of instruction and research we consider important.

Such professors could be contracted for sufficiently long terms to enable them to contribute knowledgeably to the Academy and engage in the research considered desirable; and at the same time, knowing they will be returning to their own institutions, the professors should be able to maintain the maximum degree of political and intellectual independence. I should think tight enough criteria could be devised to assure the successful operation of such a contract system, a further advantage of which would be to bring institutions of higher learning into closer familiarity with our diplomacy and diplomatic establishment and also to assure the representation of regional points of view in the Academy.

### Suggested Change in Method of Appointing Board of Regents and Chancellors

I would also suggest that the five members of the proposed Board of Regents to be appointed from private life by the President be appointed without the advice and consent of the Senate. I would suggest the Chancellor be appointed by the Board of Regents. Finally, I would like to go on record as favoring the inclusion of men of practical experience in diplomacy being included among the five regents to be appointed from private life, although I do not suggest that this be provided in the bill.

# 8.

# A PROPOSAL FOR THE REVISION OF
# FOREIGN SERVICE ORIENTATION

*PREFATORY NOTE: A strong push for educational reform in the diplomatic service came in 1965-66 when I was called back to the State Department as a full-time consultant. One of the long-needed reforms I promptly tackled was of the orientation course given to newly commissioned Foreign Service officers preparatory to their first assignment. This was called the Basic Officers Course and bore the caption of A—100 in the curriculum of the Foreign Service Institute.*

*I considered the reform of this course fundamental to all other reforms for, being at the point of officer in-take, it was the logical place to lay the groundwork for diplomatic careers. Here was the place to plant the seeds of a profession in officers' minds, a vision of service and the broad horizons of a commitment to the service of country and a world community crying for leadership. Here was the time and place to call to their attention the problems they faced and must somehow understand— not only the problems of their calling, but the problems of their country and of other countries, of their government and other governments, the collective problems of the world community—and the various resources—philosophic, political, economic, legal and other—which they could draw upon in their effort to serve their country and contribute to the development of a planet promotive of the values and processes of freedom. This was a concep-*

*tualization of the diplomatic profession which I had found generally missing in my Foreign Service life and the Basic Officers Course, I felt, was the place to evoke it.*

*Unfortunately, just as I reported for duty in 1965, the decision had been made to reduce the course from eight weeks to six (plus an additional four weeks for specialized consular training). This decision had been made by an old-time Foreign Service officer then serving as Director General of the Foreign Service who, far from seeing the need of moving in the direction of professionalizing the education and training of officers and lifting their vision, wanted to hustle them out to jobs with even less than eight weeks instruction. This was a blow, for I desired more, not less, time for the initial preparation of officers.*

*Faced by this adverse development I audited the Basic Officers Course the last time it was presented in an eight-week format. Having audited it earlier, when serving with the Board of Examiners of the Foreign Service in 1961-62, I thus acquired the advantage of double observation as a basis of judgment. Both times I found it so woefully inadequate as to be pitiable. As a preface to a serious and arduous calling, it was ludicrous, constituting hardly more than a superficial, high-schoolish exposure to foreign affairs, not even deserving the caption of a "course." Apart from a few general, unanalytical lectures on U.S. foreign policy and none whatever on diplomacy, it consisted in large part of trotting the participants around Washington to a number of government departments and agencies involved in foreign affairs for briefings on their objectives, programs and interests. These briefings were for the most part shallow and unilluminative of the hard problems being encountered by the United States in the shaping and execution of its foreign policies. It would have been an exhilarating experience for high school seniors but as a prologue to a diplomatic career it would have been absurd had it not borne such overtones of tragic misjudgment of the needs of a World Power. Not only did it ignore diplomacy but also international law, international organizations, the CIA's and the military's contributions to the shaping* and implementation of foreign policy, the management aspect of modern diplomacy, and even the functions officers were expected to discharge and the operating techniques by which those functions could be best performed in a world of high-powered politics. Instruction in the latter area, I was convinced, could prevent many a slippage in our diplomacy.

I drew up as professional a curriculum for an eight-week course as I could devise, desiring to simplify the expected controversy by focusing on substantive content and avoiding any additional issue, such as the length of the course. By asking for no more time than had been devoted to orientation for some years, I hoped to concentrate attention on a professional approach to this important ground-laying whatever the time allotted to it.

As my reform proposal shaped up, I consulted the Deputy Under Secretary for Political Affairs, to see what support we could count on from upper echelons and was surprised by his asking: "Why don't you go for broke for an academy?" Having been through that exercise in 1963, I had only to inquire how many votes we could count on in Congress for such a proposal and, in particular, whether he could assure the support of Senator Fulbright, for him to throw up his hands in a gesture of hopelessness.

If there was anything that did not interest me at that point it was a hopeless gesture of reform. I was after results. So we revived a long-defunct Training Advisory Committee in the State Department for the purpose of receiving and acting upon what I considered a minimal, if not modest, proposal. This Committee consisted of Deputy Assistant Secretaries, the Director General of the Foreign Service and a few other high-ranking departmental officers. To them we sent the proposal ten days in advance of a meeting to discuss and vote on it, thereby providing two weekends for perusal by those who could not find time to read it on weekdays. All ten members solemnly swore they would read the proposal before the meeting. But when the day arrived, eight of them came up to me to confide they had not had time to do so. After presenting *the proposal and joining in the discussion I withdrew and the committee vote was taken. It was eight to two against adoption. Since the two who had read the proposal confided to me later they had voted for it, it was clear that the negative vote had been an expression of stand-pat ignorance. "Oh, the little more, and how much it is! And the little less, and what worlds away!"*

*This, of course, was a heavy blow, all the heavier since it had an element of dishonesty in it. Why had not those who had failed to read the proposal said so and either abstained from voting or asked for a postponement?*

*Revealed, of course, was one of the pervading reasons why reform has been stifled in the State Department: it is so understaffed that few officers have time to read proposals of change, much less give independent thought to needed changes. Understaffing, thus, reinforces the bureaucracy's natural inclination to resist new visions, new ways, new attitudes.*

*The proposal I made in 1966 is still revolutionary. It has remained so far above the pedestrian level on which most of our diplomatic officers conceptualize what they are doing that even today it takes my breath to read it.*

*The proposal pulled no punches in its challenge not simply of the "course" but the myths, false premises and pretenses underlying it and indeed the Foreign Service itself.*

*My plea to synthesize the orientation of diplomatic and consular functions was not heeded and five years later a splitting of these into separate "tracks" or "cones" became a totally misconceived "reform" which gave rise to such grief that is is not in painful process of abandonment. No such egregious error could have occurred had diplomatic and consular functions been properly conceptualized. Whether that conceptualization, for which I pleaded in 1966, is now under way is not clear.*

*My appeal to educate officers for leadership and to employ "practical psychologists" for the purpose likewise fell on deaf ears. Senior officers also found appalling the notion that junior officers should be prepared and encour-*

aged to "take hold" early in their careers, even though I coupled with the proposal an insistence on the need of discipline and team play in the conduct of our foreign affairs. The result is that the Foreign Service today has the worst of all possible worlds—lack of junior officer ability to take hold, a lack of discipline and a lack of effective team play. On this sensitive issue I later wrote an essay setting forth the concept of initiative in diplomacy (see Chapter 4, "The Initiatives of Diplomacy") with additional comments on the Service's sad state in "Some Professional and Political Perspectives of Diplomacy" (Chapter 2).

The notion that diplomacy is a teachable art was also revolutionary and the suggestion that some theory might be involved in what everyone regarded as a practical, down-to-earth craft did as much as anything to arouse opposition to the proposed changes. The added thrust that hallowed on-the-job experience becomes nose-to-the-grindstone experience was regarded as just one more insult in a generally offensive analysis.

It had never been laid on the line before that "if our diplomatic service is to provide truly our first line of national defense, it must be an intellectual line of defense" and the idea was as objectionable as novel, if for no other reason than that it carried the implication that officers were not intellectual, or at least sufficiently so, which was in fact the case with most of them. Apart from a few offices such as the Policy Planning Council (as it was then called) and the Bureau of Intelligence and Research, to neither of which did Foreign Service officers covet assignment, a general anti-intellectual attitude pervaded —and still pervades—the diplomatic establishment. Few officers read books and a damning notation in an officer's performance appraisal could be that he does just that—"he reads books." No officer in my experience favored trying to learn anything from new methods in political science, an attitude gradually changing in recent years.

One of the myths of our Foreign Service is that it is the best in the world and this I disputed in my memorandum, *thereby adding one more unorthodox idea, if not indeed insult, to the document. The idea that tests should be administered to officers taking the Basic Course was regarded as demeaning, reducing* **officers** *to the level of* **students.** *Furthermore, it had never been done. It was viewed as a kind of Ichabod Crane notion, as fanciful as the "Legend of Sleepy Hollow" itself.*

*Such a "course" as then existed—and still exists—and the mental attitudes supporting it would not be tolerated in our military establishment and it is this very difference in mentality that leads Presidents to give greater weight to the military than to diplomatic officers in politico-military crises such as those which occurred repeatedly in our Vietnam intervention.*

*The whole thrust of this proposed reform was predicated upon a false belief that rational analysis would be persuasive. Actually, it demanded a strong leadership of top officials if it were to blast through so dense a barricade of myths, false premises and myopic conceptions as surrounded—and still surround—the subject of education and training for modern diplomacy. This leadership my proposal could not command. Vietnam and other international crises were preoccupying Rusk and his deputy, George W. Ball, and neither was sufficiently acquainted with the Department and Foreign Service to engage in much more than a pleasant rhetoric of reform. William J. Crockett, the Deputy Under Secretary of Administration, who had summoned me back to the Department, was involved in a multifaceted reform effort, and had no expendable capital to invest in this particular proposal, basic though it was to all other reform. Accordingly, it collapsed. A few of its suggestions came to be adopted but not the basic conceptualization, which the reader will find set forth in the first part of the memorandum. The memorandum, therefore, is as relevant and as much in need of action today as in 1966. As subsequent essays attest, I did not give up and kept firing away at the problem over the years.*

*One more thing I might add. This kind of experience in that year of effort convinced me I was wasting my time and the taxpayers' money. While I continued to plug away at reforms for the contracted twelve months, I omitted claiming compensation for all the days I put in. I considered this the only decent response I could make to what I came to regard as a form of hypocrisy.*

*In an unclassified memorandum to Mr. Crockett dated February 28, 1966, I set forth my proposed revision of the basic officers course, as follows:*

Every report or proposal is based upon certain premises, often undeclared. It may be helpful to declare my own.

## A. PREMISES

1. The Foreign Service of the United States is a *diplomatic* and *consular* service. It follows that an orientation of newly commissioned Foreign Service officers which does not deal in some depth with diplomacy—its nature, techniques, limitations and possibilities—would be basically defective and could not be regarded as wholly relevant to the needs of the Service or of the government the Service is intended to serve. It would seem to follow, also, that any structure of the orientation which compartmentalizes diplomatic and consular functions is unrealistic. The functions should be synthesized, just as the diplomatic and consular services were synthesized in 1924 as "the Foreign Service of the United States of America."

2. The Foreign Service of the United States is the diplomatic and consular service of a *World Power*. It follows that the pre-1939 experience—perhaps one should say pre-1945 experience—of that Service—and the experience of its individual officers who think primarily in pre-1945 terms—is of questionable relevance. We must think in terms of the needs of a nation at the summit of world leadership.

3. As one of the leading World Powers, the United States endeavors to *lead*. It follows that its diplomatic representatives, stationed at home or abroad, must contribute their maximum to this leadership. They must be chosen for leadership qualities, oriented toward leadership,

trained for leadership. The fact that this leadership must be conducted with a certain amount of subtlety means that training in the subtleties of leadership is essential. For this we need the help of practical psychologists.

4. The state of the world and demands of leadership are such that we can no longer afford the luxury of years of experience before officers assume responsibilities of initiative and leadership. This means that our orientation must be such as to enable officers, after a tour of general complement—and to some extent during that tour—to take hold and begin to influence people in their own age group. The pressures are such that "leadership" responsibilities come early to junior officers even in departmental assignments. It is clear from the President's directive of March 4, 1966 that State's responsibilities in the Federal community cannot be limited to the formal machinery of SIG or IRG.* On the contrary, this machinery will demand a good deal of initiative and resourcefulness from all levels of the State Department.

5. At the same time, a recognition of the need of discipline and organization—of team play—must be imparted. There is some risk in young officers of limited Foreign Service experience assuming too great an initiative in matters demanding considerable sagacity. There is a nice question of degree involved here and it will differ according to individuals and circumstances. In general, the better prepared officers are in substance and techniques —the more they are alerted to the depth and complexities of things—the less the risk involved in their initiative.

---

*The reference is to the Senior Interdepartmental Group, chaired by the Under (now called the Deputy) Secretary of State, and, subordinate to it, Interdepartmental Regional Groups (IRGs), chaired by Assistant Secretaries of State for geographic areas (Africa, Asia, Europe, Latin America and Near East). This system was established by President Johnson on the recommendation of General Maxwell Taylor when it became apparent that the vacuum left by the abolition of the Operations Coordinating Board had to be filled. The system, however, is for operational rather than for planning purposes. For more on this see *Anatomy of the State Department, op. cit.*, pp. 67-69.

6. Policy, we all recognize, is not enough. It must be made effective, by which one means it must gain followship. Hence, again, the need of instruction in diplomacy and its techniques.

7. I hesitate to take the space to set forth another premise, for I consider it, myself, rather evident, but so many of our colleagues question it, I am obliged to state it. Diplomacy, like any art, is basically teachable. The saying that "a diplomat is born, not made" is true only to a limited extent—the extent to which it is a truism that any artist is born, not made. But artists, including the greatest, have always had basic instruction in their media. Each artist has benefitted from a familiarity with the techniques by which other artists have achieved their effects. This does not mean that instruction alone can make great artists out of poor ones but it does mean that instruction makes better, more skilled artists. The teaching of any art cannot be simply by apprenticeship—on-the-job training—but must include theory and techniques.

8. It has always been true that only certain elements of the diplomacy of a World Power can be gained by "on the job" experience, but intellectual preparation is probably more extensively demanded today than ever before because of several factors, such as the thrust of communist ideology and the need of fully understanding it as well as the "guts" of democracy, the curiosity of other people about us and our ways of doing things, the extraordinary demands placed upon our diplomacy by the "revolution of rising expectations," the emergence of immature nations and the unending rash of military regimes, the extensiveness of research in the social and behavioral sciences which is exploding so many favored but now unsubstantiated beliefs in the minds of people, the pressure of work upon Foreign Service officers when they begin filling funded positions. The sudden opening up of former colonial areas—areas long sealed off from our policies and diplo-

macy—to the broadest possible contacts with advanced States has accentuated this intellectual-cultural demand on the diplomatic representatives of all the advanced States. Other nations demand to know more of us, demand to learn more from our experience. Our representatives must therefore know that experience—and know it intimately enough, profoundly enough, to make sense of it and communicate it. A great deal of influence and followship today is to be gained simply through information —well-informed individuals who know what they are talking about. In this broad context, on-the-job experience becomes nose-to-the-grindstone experience.

9. It follows from the foregoing that what the newly commissioned officers think about their orientation/ training is valuable in certain respects—such as whether the orientation/training is "interesting" or "dull"—but it cannot be governing. The needs of a leading World Power are the criteria by which length, content and intensity of orientation/training are to be determined.

10. Since we are the leading democratic Power, we represent to those who are hostile to democratic processes and values the major enemy. If our diplomatic service is to provide truly our first line of national defense, it must be an intellectual line of defense. Officers must be thoroughly, profoundly prepared—from the outset—to explain and defend the complex processes by which a democratic society functions, its principles, its values, its objectives. It follows that it is the Department's responsibility to assure that our diplomatic officers possess a thorough acquaintanceship with our history as a democracy, our political and other social institutions, processes and techniques by which our democracy works and the culture a democracy such as ours produces.

11. It follows—and I make this a separate premise for emphasis sake—that our diplomatic officers must be oriented with respect to not only our accomplishments

but our unsolved problems, our mistakes and failures as well as our successes. The critiques of democracy, of ourselves as a nation, of the State Department, of the Foreign Service, of our overseas performance must be set forth and analyzed. Self-analysis is the basis of improvement.

12. The necessity that our Foreign Service officers be not only natively intelligent but profoundly, analytically well-informed is directly related to Service morale. This is not only because this factor is directly related to performance but because an incoming Foreign Service officer is more than a Foreign Service officer: he is an inquisitive individual, desirous of knowing as much as possible of his country's foreign policy and diplomacy. He shares with many of his fellow citizens doubts concerning these policies and diplomacy, the adequacy of the Department and Foreign Service, the soundness of their operating procedures. To treat these matters lightly or to avoid them on his admission to the diplomatic establishment cannot satisfy his doubts or engender the respect, dedication and resourcefulness the Service needs.

13. We desire that our diplomatic officers shall be at least as well trained and prepared for diplomacy as those of any other Power. Our Foreign Service is not. My familiarity with the preparation of the British, French, German and Swiss is not profound but the little familiarity I have is to the effect that the officers of these other governments are far more thoroughly prepared than ours.

## B. CRITIQUE OF THE EXISTING ORIENTATION PROGRAM

This program has been improved in the last three years. The directorship of George Morgan and the contributions of Garrett H. Soulen and Alexander J. Davit have had notably good effects. Mr. Davit is most receptive to suggestions and ideas and it has been a pleasure to have talked with him about the course and its improvement almost daily for the seven weeks I audited the course. He has had no sensitivity as to my attendance and note taking. Perhaps this is because he has an instructional background. One can hardly overemphasize the importance of such an attitude in developing our orientation/training/education of officers. Messrs. Cortada and Stutesman are currently contributing enlivening discussion on some aspects of State Department operations. No doubt others should be mentioned in this connection and my failure to do so in no wise should be construed in any other sense than my ignorance.

The program has continued through the years to benefit from the stimulating contributions of permanent staff members, including James C. Bostain, Dr. Myron L. Koenig and Dr. Edwin M. Wright. The intellectual sparkle of these lecturers periodically brighten a program which—in spite of improvements—all too generally conforms to prosaic ruts.

The one-day indoctrination in the security programs of the Department and Service is first-class. It is conducted by a professional instructor of many years continuity in his work. This suggests the importance of specialized competence and continuity in the staffing of orientation generally.

Along with these good contributions, are others not so good—in fact, many woefully inadequate.

Basically, the conceptualization of the program is deficient. It is this conceptualization more than any other single factor that binds the program to the ground. What should be a powerful, Gulliver-type program is tied down by the multiple strings of too many nearsighted contributors and a pedestrian, vocational concept of the Foreign Service. Eight student officers out of ten sounded out by me now and three years ago view the program as "inadequate," "dull," "boring."

The student officers are not even worked hard. Classes often end at 5 p.m. and evenings are generally free. No tests are given to ascertain how much of the required or recommended reading is done or how much is absorbed in class. This is not only unscientific—so that we are all guessing about how much the student officers are absorbing or can absorb and what techniques should be employed to increase the rate of absorption—it results in a far too leisurely introduction to the Foreign Service. The first two or three days may, very appropriately, be leisurely—but certainly not the whole course. (My meaning must be clear: I am not speaking of instructors like Soulen and Davit, who work very hard to prepare for classes, to seek improvements, etc. I am speaking of the degree to which the student-officers themselves are worked.)

This leisurely pace in itself creates a false image of the Service and the Department. Anyone studying dropout cases and interviewing both the dropouts and their colleagues cannot avoid the conclusion that simply in its pace and tone A-100 is a cause of misapprehension for the young officers. It certainly creates a nonprofessional attitude toward foreign policy and diplomacy.

In other ways, A—100 is a source of officer difficulty. While the student-officer is prepared for immediate assumption of consular responsibilities—and no one can fail to be impressed with the readiness with which officers have been prepared to pick up consular duties—they are not nearly so well prepared for their general responsibilities, which are presented smatteringly and with an exaggerated emphasis upon reporting. If the true significance of reporting with reference to foreign policy and diplomacy were pointed out, this exaggeration would not be so harmful. But a realistic perspective is not provided. Reporting comes through to the student officer as "something you do," "something you can't get away from," something demanded by instructions. It receives, therefore, a pedestrian treatment.

But my criticism of the course on this point goes beyond this epitomizing of general responsibilities in terms of reporting. I refer to our attitude toward the rate or pace at which junior officers can assume general responsibilities. There is a prevailing attitude in the Service that young officers have little to contribute to such responsibilities until they have had years of seasoning. I believe this attitude enjoys a high degree of irrelevance to the present world situation. In the first place, we can no longer afford the luxury of an appreciable gap between officers' induction to active duty and their assumption of important responsibilities, under proper guidance, of course. In the second place, junior officers are so restive over this attitude of their seniors some of the best are dropping out of the Service and others suffer a serious morale problem if they do not drop out. My interviews with the latter emphasize the seriousness of this problem. While there are certain limits to what youth can do and the sensibilities of foreign peoples must assuredly be taken into account in this respect (many foreign peoples respect age, not youth and will not hospitably receive the advice of people they consider young) we must be more imaginative in perceiving the contributions which young officers can promptly make and equip them for these. I see none of this awareness in A-100. This exposure course is not geared to the early assumption of broad responsibilities. More and more, it is directed to hustling officers out to the field.

The consular segment of the program has likewise been inadequately conceptualized. It has had the advantage of meticulousness, which is not a bad quality in this nuclear age, but it has been too narrowly conceived, with too little (if, indeed, any) perspective of its political, public relations and economic importance. Even more than the general segment of A-100, the consular segment has been overly "job oriented." As one of its best lecturers observed to me: "We are running a vocational school here." Not only is this approach inadequate *per se*, but it leads to inadequate political and economic performance by consular posts, introduces a factor adverse to morale and complicates our assignments problems. Symptomatic of this "vocational" approach to consular responsibilities is the current pressure to reduce consular training to two weeks and leave the rest to be learned "on the job." This not only overlooks the recognized deficiencies of our present field supervision of junior officers (which is producing morale problems and even dropouts) but it completely overlooks the broad political and economic significance of consular work. The present training produces good consular officers in the sense I have stated already—able to perform promptly specific consular functions—but it does not produce (1) imaginative consular officers, alert to their political and economic roles and (2) a taste for consular work as a career. This is simply another way in which we are permitting A-100 to magnify our problems—and perpetuate them—rather than to help in solving them.

A-100 is now tailored to what the instructors have themselves experienced. Apart from the rare and recent Soulen or Davit, it is thus tailored to the past—a past of more than fifteen years, for the instructors, as most officers, have been considerably molded by their older colleagues and personal experience. The course is not sufficiently current, certainly not forward-looking. We are preparing officers for the 1920's—possibly the 1930's—but not for the 1960's and certainly not the 1970's.

A-100 is also tailored to do what the instructors think the officers will need to adjust well, do a good "job" in the Service, get ahead. It is not tailored to the role, needs and vision of a World Power.

Hence the program is perpetuating a good deal of the dead-end thinking that is holding back the diplomatic establishment. Take the role of coordination of foreign affairs in our federal government. This is hardly touched upon in A-100. It has taken SIG and IRG to prompt the Institute staff to give serious attention to it. The role demands cold, methodical, searching analysis, with the techniques of coordination examined fully and the merits and demerits of alternative techniques discussed. I find it hard to understand why so basic a role of the diplomatic establishment should be virtually ignored. But it is true of the treatment of many of the basic roles of the Department.

It will of course be rejoined that young officers will not be contributing to these roles for some time. But they must be prepared for them—broadly, intellectually prepared—not simply by such on-the-job experiences as they may by happenchance acquire. An individual's experiences are no longer adequate preparation for the kind of foreign policy and diplomatic performance this nation needs. The resources of many people—operators beyond one's personal acquaintanceship, along with students past and present—must be tapped. We have no right—or interest— to deny these resources to our officers. We are well aware that neither mid-career nor senior training has been available to more than a handful of officers. We must make the most of the opportunity of orienting newly commissioned officers to the insights, perspectives and experience which all available resources can yield as a *basic preparation*.

There is the important factor of attitudes in all this. We are dealing—or we should be dealing—not only with skills but with officers' attitudes. The attitudes a young officer brings to the Service will depend in no small part on his basic training. We must be sure that ambling, cursory, superficial attitudes do not get started or reinforced at this stage. On the contrary, we must be certain that candor, objectivity, curiosity, desire to rectify weaknesses and find the best ways of serving the national interest (rather than serving the officers' individual interests) get inculcated.

In some specific areas, A-100 is poorly served by departments and agencies on which it depends for presentations. In fact, not a one of these presentations can be regarded as adequate. The military is one of the less inadequate but even it does not mention, much less analyze, military diplomacy, and the complex relations it is generating at home and abroad. The CIA presentation is patently not a presentation but an evasion, which I consider a very serious deficiency. If our Foreign Service officers are not to be treated as adults—and if we cannot induce the Agency to do so—this in itself calls attention to a basic problem which such an agency presents to a democracy. If Foreign Service officers cannot be treated as responsible *diplomatic officers* we are in serious trouble as a Diplomatic Power. Every officer in the A-100 class which I audited considered the CIA presentation "false" and "silly." The State Department and Foreign Service cannot be placed in this position. This area needs prompt, high-level correction. No doubt we will have to inject into all these areas—military, CIA, Commerce, Labor, Interior and others—more analysis of our own.

I know we have tried to run the Foreign Service Institute generally and A-100 particularly on a shoestring. We use lecturers for the most part from within the Federal establishment. The chronic reply to suggestions of improvement is that these people or departments do not *have* to make this contribution and if we push too hard it will be withdrawn. I believe this puts us in a weak position. We should set high standards—and see that these are met. I believe Congress will support us in this with the needed funds. (Incidentally, I believe that we are far behind Congressional thinking as to the depth and range of training which we should provide our diplomatic officers.)

This memorandum could proceed with a presentation of other deficiencies of our present orientation of newly commissioned officers. Not to make it over long let me conclude by emphasizing that even within the limited conceptualization of the Foreign Service which now inhibits the program, it does not measure up. Too many of the basic problems of the Foreign Service come in for cursory treatment or no treatment at all. This produces another problem which aggravates all the others: too few Foreign Service officers know very much about these basic problems of the Service and the Department. Once in, most of us are preoccupied with substantive matters and, never having been drilled on basic principles, needs and problems get to viewing them through myths and legends. We tend, also, to view the Service in terms of a promotion ladder. These viewings become a basic source of morale problems, of prevalent misunderstandings of changes and adjustments made from time to time and of resistance to change. Let us not deceive ourselves as to how widely this is sensed. It is sensed by Congressmen, by the general public, whose contacts with us at home and abroad have multiplied in recent years, by journalists, by students and scholars. A very real public relations factor is involved in this deficiency. If we should stimulate greater thought of Service and Department at officers' point of entry we might conceivably lay a foundation of knowledge and insight which might ease just a little bit not only our internal problems of morale and change but our image in the minds of others.

## C. PROPOSED REVISIONS

My proposed revisions of the orientation program include the following changes designed to meet, at least in part, these deficiencies:

1. The program is extended in depth and breadth. It would no longer be a kind of "exposure" to problems but would analyze problems as well as techniques of getting at them with some degree of sharpness.

2. Since the President is constitutionally the apex of the foreign affairs establishment of the Federal Government, I proceed to his role promptly. We might wisely keep in mind the sensitivity of Presidents on this point. Some have been known to complain that the Department and Service tend to regard them as intruders in the realm of foreign policy and diplomacy. I believe that both substantively and psychologically the proposed section on the "Role and Techniques of the President in Foreign Affairs"—and the early position given it in the course—represent a healthy addition.

3. I have extended and systematized our discussion of the State Department, including in this, again, techniques by which the Department seeks to discharge its several roles.

4. I have followed this approach in my proposed treatment of the Foreign Service.

5. I have added segments on diplomacy and its techniques, on international law and international organization, as well as a concluding synthesis. The segment on international law proposes a highly condensed treatment.

Experimentation with various teaching aids will determine whether it can be so highly condensed. It is obvious, at any rate, I am not proposing to make international lawyers of Foreign Service officers or to compete with university courses on international law. The proposed treatment can be hardly more than suggestive, so that officers called on to explain—or to deal with—crises such as those in which we have taken certain initiatives (the Congo, Dominican Republic and Vietnam to name only the recent) are assisted by some slight familiarity with the elementary principles of international law.

Not unduly to lengthen my proposal, I have not spelled out in really adequate terms the techniques of diplomacy. This can be done at a later stage if the proposed addition meets with approval.

The role of private diplomacy has become so vast in international relations I believe its importance should be recognized in the orientation of incoming officers. I have therefore included a section on this. The Department, jointly with the Business Council for International Understanding, is promoting meetings and even tours of duty for Foreign Service officers with companies in recognition of the importance of this area. But, as missionaries, educators and the Staughton Lynds are constantly reminding us, the area is broader than commercial and industrial diplomacy. There is not an officer who will not encounter this area—sometimes in trying circumstances—and he should be prepared for these experiences with as full a knowledge and understanding as possible.

6. I have incorporated our training on consular affairs in the segment on international law. This has four advantages: much consular work leans upon international as well as national law; a desirable synthesis of consular with other functions of Foreign Service officers is effected; appropriate dignification of consular work is achieved; and we are provided a fresh opportunity of considering the personnel needed for more than a pack-horse presentation of this part of A-100. Throughout the course I have woven in references to consular affairs so as to further assist appropriate integration.

7. I have included a discussion of "The Population Explosion" which many of us consider of vast impact.

8. I have included a segment on "American Studies." The content of this I am leaving to the able members of the Institute's American Studies Staff.

Notwithstanding these substantial innovations, the program does not extend beyond twelve weeks, as compared with the former twelve weeks of A-100 (eight weeks of general orientation and four weeks of consular training). This has been effected by eliminating some presentations and shortening others. [Sections D and E of the Memorandum are omitted].

## F. CRITIQUE OF MY PROPOSALS

1. **Techniques of Group Leadership:** The techniques of group leadership are as important as any a Foreign Service officer requires these days. He is a member of a group as soon as he receives his commission; he is a member of a group when he reports for duty on his first assignment; and he participates in a large group—the Federal Government—when given responsibilities involving other departments and agencies. The Senior Interdepartmental Group (SIG) system will place a heavy load on Foreign Service officers in this respect. The Department's failure to recognize the importance of this and suitably train officers account for its failures in the past to exert the leadership in the Federal establishment expected of it. Its poor showing in the Operations Coordinating Board reflected this failure. I believe it could be well argued that incoming officers should be given a groundwork in this area on which subsequent courses could build.

2. **Economic and Political Theories of Communism:** While I retain in my proposed schedule the stimulating lecture of Dr. Edwin Wright on "The Universe and Mr. Marx" and devote the greater part of two days to the problem and techniques of countering subversion and insurgency, the course does not provide any analysis of the economic and political theories of communism. I

believe this to be a serious weakness. This analysis is omitted simply to keep the course to a twelve-week limit.

**3. Atomic Energy and Its Role in Foreign Affairs:** I think the American public—and our foreign friends—would be horrified to know that we build a diplomatic service on a preparation which includes no discussion of this subject. I am horrified myself. The discussion should include foreign policy relative to atomic energy and the policy-making and diplomatic roles of the Atomic Energy Commission.

**4. Vietnam:** In Vietnam we have become involved in one of our major tests of diplomatic and military resources. This will not be our last major test. Subversion, guerilla tactics and wars of national liberation will be features of our international involvement for some time to come. There are lessons to be gained from each one of these tests. Only if we are willing to study them and extract their lessons will we be able to avoid a repetition of mistakes. Why, then, should we not have a sharp, profound, objective analysis of the Vietnam problem as a case study? Newly commissioned officers are sent not only to Vietnam on first tours of duty overseas but to other areas where communist plots are constantly simmering and communist thrusts constantly attempted. Furthermore, officers are questioned about Vietnam throughout the world. It is one subject on which they should be intelligently articulate. We have the staff to do this in A-100 (that of the National Interdepartmental Seminar). We should do it.

**5. Economics:** While the course provides a good deal of discussion of economic factors in foreign policy and diplomacy this is not the same thing as an analysis of basic economics. I may be on sounder ground in this omission than the two foregoing, for this elementary grounding can be obtained by personal effort through existing textbooks. If, as I recommend, the diagnostic approach be applied to every incoming officer, an officer's gap in economics might, under the guidance of the Institute's economic staff, be filled in the course of the weeks of A-100. If not fully then, the officer should be able to complete the fill-in by self-study at his first post, possibly enriched by a correspondence course in economics provided by the Institute or some suitable academic institution.

**6. Visit to the United Nations:** This was included in A-100 three years ago and I believe it would be useful to reinstate it. The visit includes a briefing by the U.S. delegation to the U.N. as well as a visit to the U.N. itself, both of which are as valuable as visits to the various departments and agencies of the Federal Government in Washington and for the same reason.

**7. Retreat to Airlie:** When a week's retreat to Airlie was provided A-100 students, they welcomed this as a chance of living together and developing a camaraderie. It was a morale booster at the time and officers who experienced it advise it continues to be for years thereafter.

## G. ADDITIONAL RECOMMENDATIONS

1. As I have indicated above, we need the assistance of practical psychologists in developing a first-class orientation of officers. What we have tended to regard as a simple task, to be hurriedly consummated in a few weeks time, is in fact a highly complex task, in view of our international role, and it is difficult to do successfully. I recommend that this assistance be sought.

2. The serious orientation of officers as vital to the national security as Foreign Service officers should not be conducted, as it has been until now, on a shoe-string. Additional funds are needed for technical assistance in instructional techniques, for instructional materials (including films), for outside lecturers and collaborators in the development of suitable reading materials and for testing of officers.

3. Great unevenness of quality has characterized our orientation of newly commissioned officers because its supervision has been subjected to the happenstance of rotation. We need seriously to consider whether:

(a) Rotation should be tempered by such expedients as:

(1) Longer tours of service for the instructors;

(2) Staggered terms of service for the instructors, so that they do not begin tours at the same time;

(3) Making a tour as a counselor in the Junior Officer program a prerequisite for a tour of instruction in A-100 thereby making available to the orientation program the experience with officers' problems and frustrations gained in counseling;

(4) Having one of the instructors a permanent member of the instructional staff (e.g., a Foreign Service officer who, for family or other reasons, cannot accept continued service overseas. Such an officer now generally has no alternative to resignation. If he be a good officer, of sufficient seasoning and instructional ability he could be made a permanent member of the A-100 staff, thereby wedding continuity to fresh experience and thinking).

(b) We are planning instructional tours of duty with A-100 with sufficient care and forethought. In the past— i.e., in the years prior to George Morgan—we plainly have not been. But even now one is uneasy to find that Mr. Davit was not an officer selected well in advance for his present assignment but himself learned, by accident, the position was vacant and volunteered for it. Assignments to A-100 instructional positions are too important for such casual treatment. They should be made on the basis of: (a) known aptitude for instruction, (b) known amplitude of reading and thinking on the part of an officer and (c) interest and competence in instruction.

4. Further to counteract the unevenness of quality in A-100, all presentations should be on the basis of carefully prepared written material. Lecturers can then assume elementary familiarity with their subject on the part of student-officers and give more class time to analysis. Poor or hastily substituted lecturers will be supported by good written material which will diminish the damaging effects of their low-quality presentation.

5. For the same purpose and also to enrich the course,

taped (or, preferably, filmed) interviews should be prepared with outstanding practitioners of diplomacy concerning their techniques and experiences in dealing with
particularly difficult problems (such as Ambassador
Howard P. Jones, concerning his experience with Sukarno
in Indonesia; Llewellyn Thompson, his experience in dealing with the Soviets; Samuel Berger, his experience in
Korea). While I have listed such officers for speaking assignments in A-100 it is problematical that we can get them.
The richness of their experience should nonetheless be
continuously available to the orientation/training courses
of FSI.  Taping (or filming) interviews is our only technique of assuring this.

6. To prepare young officers for the kinds of situations,
difficulties and problems they encounter in the Service I
recommend the preparation of case studies of these situations, difficulties and problems.  These could be cast in
problem-solving form—"how would you conduct yourself,
or what would you do, if confronted by such-and-such a
situation or problem?" This technique permits the presentation of situations, etc. objectively, without any seeds of
discouragement or doubt as to the Service being sown.
This technique has long been employed in the military,
whose materials for officers have been prepared with the
assistance of psychologists and sociologists.  Comparable
materials dealing with Foreign Service situations, are
long overdue.  They would (1) provide a far broader guidance to the Service and its problems than is presently
achieved in A-100, (2) assure coverage of basic problems
irrespective of the happenstance of rotating instructors, (3)
reduce the number and impact—sometimes disastrous—of
presently unexpected but common problems and thereby
(4) contribute to a reduction of morale problems.

7. In our personnel records (and ADP and computer-
ization thereof) a special notation should be made of officers' educational background, aptitude for instruction,
reading habits and preference for an instructional assignment.  It is only on the basis of such information that we
can be more systematic and successful in assignments to

the A-100 instructional staff. I stress the need of noting officers' "reading habits." One of the problems we have is that the work pressures in the Service are making it impossible for officers to read anything beyond their "in box" material and hence A-100 instructors experience difficulty in holding their own in the present limited framework of A-100. If my proposed revisions are adopted the problem will be greater and our recourse to outside lecturers may have to be, at least for a while, more extensive.

8. Good officers who prove good instructors should be rewarded with systematic appropriateness. Being out of the "main stream" of assignment and promotion, they should not be left to their own devices in lining up appropriate assignments after their FSI stint. This is due not only *them*, but *the basic importance of instruction* in building the kind of a Foreign Service demanded by the times. The recent precedents of appropriating Institute staff members as ambassadors should be continued as appropriate and supplemented by suitable assignments of staff members who are of classes lower than FSO-1.

9. An outstandingly stimulating staff member (Dr. Edwin Wright) is nearing retirement. Search should be vigorously pressed for a successor of like quality. He will be hard to find. I cannot emphasize too strongly how much enrichment to A-100 is brought by such men as Dr. Wright and Dr. Koenig, even though a vocational conceptualization of the Foreign Service limits their contribution, time-wise, to a pitiful hour-and-twenty minutes and one hour respectively. With Dr. Wright's permission, his lecture should be taped for use or reference in the future.

10. A-100 is but the beginning of a career-long process of learning. This process should be actively promoted by the Foreign Service Institute. The subjects proposed to be dealt with in the first twelve weeks of an officer's service should be probed more deeply after he has had two tours abroad and is ready to absorb and relate more than on entry into the Service. During these first two tours overseas, also, the Institute should continue to

stimulate them by a suitable publication presenting special articles, reprints of articles, and references to other material which Foreign Service officers should know about. If the National Interdepartmental Seminar keeps in touch with its "graduates" through a quarterly publication, there seems no good reason why this cannot be done for graduates of A-100. There are obviously good reasons for so doing.

I close with a reminder that the Secretary has a deep personal interest in the improvement of our training of officers. He has noted that we face what he calls a "crisis of talent." In representing the Secretary at the 1963 hearings of the Senate Committee on Foreign Relations on various proposals for a Foreign Service Academy, Under Secretary Ball put the Department on record as admitting the need "to increase the effectiveness of personnel already on active service with the U.S. Government. ... (to) improve the capacity of the United States to conduct relations with other nations under the complex conditions of a complex age. ... We need a broader range of techniques and expertise even in our dealings within the free world. The State Department officer today must be far more flexible and informed than in an earlier and simpler time... he must have at least a respectable acquaintance with a wide range of disciplines and techniques. ... Today more and more of our operations abroad are conducted on a 'country team' basis. Representatives of various Federal agencies serving at a post abroad act as a unit under the guidance of the Ambassador. To train members of such country teams requires an institution of greater scope (than the Foreign Service Institute) ... a need foretold many years ago by H.G. Wells, who declared prophetically that 'History is becoming more and more a race between education and catastrophe'."

[An attachment to the memorandum presented a syllabus of the orientation course which I proposed. This is omitted.]

# 9.

# THE RUSK ENIGMA

*PREFATORY NOTE: One of the persistent problems in this country's efforts to conduct an effective diplomacy is the extremely uneven quality and lack of continuity in the men who head the State Department. Many of them come to the position with limited experience in foreign affairs and a conceptualization of diplomacy far less than global. Whole continents are beyond both their experience and their vision. Combined with this has been a lack of experience and interest in organizational management, which has become a significant dimension of modern diplomacy.*

*Beginning with Cordell Hull, who became FDR's Secretary of State in 1933, only two secretaries of state in the last forty-five years have geared the State Department organizationally to strategic and tactical needs. One of these was a general—George C. Marshall—whose military background thoroughly familiarized him with the role of organization in producing strategic and tactical results. The other was Dean Acheson who, as General Marshall's No. Two in the State Department, learned much in these respects from the General. This fact should have given Presidents and the State Department considerable food for thought, but it hasn't. Their thinking and their attitudes have scarcely changed since the following essay was written of the "enigma" of Dean Rusk. Thus, neither have secretaries of state changed. Much of what follows on Dean Rusk's limitations could be written of William P. Rogers and Cyrus Vance and some of it of Henry Kissinger, on whom comment will be found in a later essay (see below, pp. 238-244).*

Reprinted with permission from *The Nation*, March 6, 1967.

After six years in office, the Secretary of State is still an enigma to his fellow Americans. Our principal foreign policy adviser and architect of diplomacy has escaped not only notoriety but even clear characterization.

Background in part accounts for this bewildering elusiveness. In the whole stretch of Rusk's fifty-two years from birth in a Georgia parsonage, there is almost nothing that one would normally associate with preparation for his present work, and to which one could turn for clues to his competence. There is no trace of political experience; no large-scale managerial testing; no outstanding involvement in public affairs; no national recognition; not even an association with Presidents. Apart from such unfortunate predecessors as Robert Lansing and Frank L. Polk, whom almost no one remembers, Dean Rusk's record (or rather lack of record) is unique.

Nor does his parsonage extraction appear to be significant. If one could find some missionary zeal in his conduct of foreign affairs, some inclination to international crusades, such as Woodrow Wilson and John Foster Dulles exhibited, one might feel some thread with which to begin an embroidery. The overseas evils of war and colonialism, communism's threat, neutralism in the face of imminent danger, and poverty have all had strong gravitational pulls on American statesmen of evangelical disposition. Is the modest Rusk really as unevangelical as he seems? Would a probing of his attitude on Vietnam reveal any trace of hitherto undetected crusading spirit?

Rusk's former academic connection likewise offers no clear characterization. College professors are not celebrated for being practical men, but Rusk is eminently practical. Some of his critics feel he is too practical, too much of an "incher," who is thus overwhelmed by major problems before he becomes aware that they are stealing upon him and his crisis-ridden department.

Rusk gave a good account of himself as a staff officer during the last World War, both in Southeast Asia and in the Pentagon. If it is true, as is said, that he considered a permanent military career at the end of the war, he was presumably not disillusioned by his army experience. Has it had, then the effect of inducing him to yield unduly to military leadership? Does the State Department's very weak handling of the Vietnamese problem suggest this diffidence? Has Rusk been able to hold his own with McNamara, or have we been witnessing since 1961 a resumption of the pendulum swing in foreign affairs which began in World War II and was arrested only by the special resources of the Marshall-Acheson combination?

Rusk first went to the State Department in 1946, reverted to the War Department and followed Marshall back to State a year later, rising to the level of Assistant Secretary. One wonders whether he gained at the time adequate insight into the basic operating confusions of the diplomatic Establishment, or whether, swamped by the substantive problems of his particular area of specialization, he acquired only fleeting, fragmentary insights.

After he left the State Department to become president of the Rockefeller Foundation, Rusk's career was shrouded for nine years in the quiet anonymity of affluent good works. He then emerged, startlingly, in his present exalted capacity. Had he used any of these preceding nine years to prepare himself for such a role?

All these questions are intriguing, but Rusk's self-effacing nature does not permit him to help in answering them. Like General Marshall, whom he greatly admired and after whom he is said to have considered at one time patterning his own career, Rusk does not regard himself as important. Only ideas, principles, problems and correct solutions seem significant to him. Like Marshall, therefore, he preserves a jealous reticence.

The less personal question, to which we can address ourselves here, is how well Rusk has performed in his job. This is indeed a part of the enigma he presents and I can suggest some of the answers, having been in the Establishment myself. I can testify, to begin with, that while everyone wondered at the start if he could make a go of it, the Washington foreign affairs community saw him quietly, promptly and competently taking hold of the immediate demands of his job. Unlike his long-tenured predecessor, John Foster Dulles, who monopolized many decisions and no little information, Rusk was a team player. He solicited the full cooperation of his department. Moreover, his exceptional capacity for crisp, incisive analysis and for reaching decisions of military-like preciseness set a high standard to which that coopera-tion was clearly expected to ascend. He and President Kennedy worked hard and fruitfully in the early months to modernize and rejuvenate the department, to stimulate it, to bring to focus its straggling resources. They strength-ened research, restored planning to something of the vigor it had once possessed, strove to close the gap between echelons that Dulles had permitted to develop.

At the White House Rusk had a special problem. Re-sponsibilities were diffused by Presidential task forces and the brash, if well-intentioned scurrying about and thrust-ing of White House staffers. Questions and difficulties promptly arose. Was Adolph Berle, Richard Goodwin or Robert Woodward in charge of Latin American affairs? Where did Teodoro Moscoso, head of the Alliance for Progress, fit in? Was Acheson or Rusk in command of planning for the Berlin flare-up? And what was Bowles doing abroad so much of the time when Rusk needed an effective deputy at his right hand? If the White House was not sure of Rusk in that early hurly-burly, Rusk and his associates were not sure of the White House. Through it all, the Secretary kept his temper and his patience, striving doggedly for quality of performance in his own organization as the only effective answer to this broad and mystifying distribution of authority.

When the Abbé Sieyès was asked what he did during the French Revolution, he replied that he survived. His response was one that many people—looking ahead in 1961 —might have anticipated from Rusk at the end of six years. But survival has been more of a feat than anyone could have expected. In half a dozen years of repeated crises Rusk has survived not one President but two—two men of very different backgrounds, characters and values, demanding, it would seem, two different kinds of Secretaries of State. This may not have been as bad to live through as the French Revolution, but survival was no mean achievement. And Rusk has done more. He enjoys Johnson's respect—something not easily won and retained.

In the months when Lyndon Johnson was an uneasy appendage to the Executive Mansion, one saw the process in fascinating evolution. Again and again, Rusk took occasion to encourage the Vice President's interest in foreign affairs, considering this essential from a political point of view as well as from that of Johnson's personal need. The Texan had never been much concerned with events abroad and Rusk saw the benefit of overseas exposure. On his expeditions, the Vice President received cheering cables from the Secretary of State, which served two purposes: they encouraged Johnson and they warned embassies not to become disturbed by some of the more grievous demands and idiosyncracies of the Texas politician. Perhaps they also helped to keep the Vice President on the beam. The President may joke now that Mrs. Johnson is so fond of the Rusks she would never let him ditch Dean, but Johnson too has a similar sentimental attachment to a couple who had been friendly and thoughtful when times were rough.

In the hectic early days of the Kennedy administration, the quiet, analytical sorting-out process which goes on constantly in Rusk's mind made him a listener and analyst rather than an advocate, a summarizer at the end rather than a leader of debate. This caused some observers who prefer forceful and dramatic personalities to describe him, as does Arthur Schlesinger, Jr., as a kind of American Buddha. Schlesinger has even stated that Kennedy thought of replacing Rusk, but no Chief Executive in his senses would have jettisoned a Secretary of State who had the degree of Congressional respect Rusk early came to possess.

Congress is not a body that usually warms up to the head of our diplomatic Establishment, but it quickly warmed to Rusk. Not since Cordell Hull has a Secretary of State enjoyed such esteem bordering on affection. This is all the more astonishing because, unlike Hull who had spent almost a quarter century on Capitol Hill, Rusk was wholly unknown. Moreover, his college professorship and participation in the Atlantic seaboard coterie in foreign affairs were hurdles he had to surmount.

Such a man might well have foundered on Capitol Hill. Rusk, however, has a deeply rooted democratic philosophy which steers him patiently and successfully through the endless shifting and treacherous shoals of Congressional dealings. When he tells Congressmen that, far from rocking the diplomatic boat, they can be of great help to him, he believes it as profoundly as they. When he stresses the constructive uses of committee hearings, of Congressmen's travels abroad, of Congressional prying and probing all over the place, he is perfectly sincere. He even goes so far as to tell long-term members of foreign affairs and appropriations committees that having specialized in the department's operations much longer than he or any one of his associates, they know more than anybody in Washington about such things. This is indeed true, by and large, but it is rank heresy among the diplomats to concede it. If Rusk's position mystifies his career associates, it is a cheering concession to hard-working, conscientious Congressmen unaccustomed to bouquets from the Executive branch.

So it happens that a Middle West Senator ungiven to eulogy of Secretaries of State described Rusk to me as follows: "He is a sterling, distinguished public servant. The course he has followed has been honestly and realistically purposed to perpetuate the life of our country. Depending on what has been in our best interest, he has followed the commendable course of yielding when our interest so required, and remaining as firm as the Rock of Gibraltar when obduracy was needed."

But the Senator who used this language a few weeks ago has also said some very hard things of the department which Rusk heads. "In every corner of the world," he has vigorously asserted, "we are losing ground to the Communists. Our flag is trampled, our prestige and power are flouted. Our embassies are mobbed, our officials threatened or arrested at gun point." And who is responsible? The Senator continued: "As the agency responsible for our foreign relations, the State Department must stand chiefly accountable for these defeats. The harsh fact is that State is not equipped to cope with explosive conflicts our enemies are stirring." The State Department soft-pedals "grim facts," clings to "old lines," "glosses over critical matters until they turn into disasters," "forgets that we must act our role as the free world's leader, and enforce our rights if we expect to survive." State, he says, has failed to devise "a consistent plan to defeat communism's political-warfare strategy," adheres to "decision-making machinery so inefficient that it moves at caterpillar pace," and is staffed with people "not up to the tasks that confront it."

Such complaints are often heard of the State Department and its overseas Foreign Service, and I know from more than thirty-five years of study and experience in the diplomatic Establishment that they are only too well justified. Moreover, there is a serious problem of morale in the department and service under Rusk, as there was under Dulles.

It is precisely here that some of the ordinary citizen's mystification over Rusk begins. If he is as good as he is pictured by Congressmen and others, how does it happen that his organization is open to such critical indictment? If General Motors or the Department of Commerce were as severely attacked, its head would be regarded as culpable and sacked. If Rusk is not responsible for his department's performance, who—or what—is?

To say that the department is would not be very illuminating—but it is a fact. The department largely runs itself, no matter who is Secretary of State. Over the long years it has evolved its own attitudes of mind, its own premises and prejudices, its own values, its own criteria of performance, and its own procedures which both express and reinforce all these. And no secretary who lacks thorough familiarity with this state of affairs, who has not mastered the managerial techniques for operating large organizations, can possibly cope with the State Department. The indications are that Rusk is not familiar with them. He evidently does not see the vital relationship of managerial problems to foreign policy and diplomacy. This constitutes a weakness in his performance so serious that if it continues, it may well make the difference between the success and failure of American world leadership.

In this unresolved situation, the military factor in our international relationships becomes increasingly evident. Inevitably, when the contempt of diplomatic officers for training and education assures pedestrian work at the Foreign Service Institute, when their disdain for research and planning infects the department, when their reliance on daily improvisation continues unabated, the military will more and more fill the area of foreign policy and diplomacy. For the military long ago learned the value of education and training in international affairs. There are combat colonels in Vietnam today who hold Ph.D.s in international affairs. The State Department, by contrast, does not require of its officers any knowledge of international law and international organization or any systematic knowledge of the techniques of diplomacy; nor does it offer any courses in these disciplines at the Foreign Service Institute. To get even a correspondence course in international law, diplomatic officers must apply to the Naval War College.

Since the 1930's, as a consequence, the military establishment has increasingly influenced the dynamic and broadening area known as politico-military problems in world affairs. The appointment of a general as Secretary of State, another as Under Secretary, and a number of generals and admirals as ambassadors, as well as the inability of any career diplomatic officer to earn a top position in the Pentagon as a politico-military adviser, are symptoms of this disturbing trend.

This situation has deep implications for the preservation of democracy at home as well as abroad, but the department has only tinkered with it, and Rusk has in-

dulged the tinkering. His relations—personal and official—
with McNamara are excellent and some cross-fertilization
of personnel has been achieved between their two establishments. But diplomats need thorough education and
training in the politico-military area and suggestions to
that effect should not always have to come from the
military.

This problem of effective inter-agency integration of
thinking, techniques, research and other resources affects
not only diplomatic and military departments; it relates
to State's broad role in the federal government. It took
a general to establish a systematic inter-agency mechanism
for this integration: when he became President, Mr. Eisenhower quickly saw that an Operations Coordinating
Board was essential. It took another general to insist
that the vacuum be filled after Kennedy, on very poor
advice, abolished the OCB. It is now General Maxwell
Taylor who publicly calls attention to the fact that we
were politically unprepared for our Southeast Asia commitment in 1954, for our deepening involvement in that area
in the 1960's, and for the ultimate victory we are striving
for there today. I know this to be true, and one of several
reasons for my early retirement from the diplomatic service
in 1962 was to gain the freedom to say so. More and more,
the military is advising Presidents on how the State Department should be organized to function properly. Sooner
than we think, another general may be appointed to run
the department.

Dean Rusk has not given sufficient attention to correcting the prevailing attitudes of his Establishment, to re-
vamping its anarchic procedures, updating and extending
its educational training programs, vitalizing its library
facilities and demanding the money for these essential
renovations. In such areas, the department is starved for
funds. While he was Deputy Under Secretary for Administration, William J. Crockett took the revolutionary
step—revolutionary for the State Department—of employing
first-class psychologists to study the attitudes of diplomatic
officers and relate these attitudes to the Department's

operating problems. Experimentation revealed what large private firms have known for years: attitudes have a basic impact upon organizational efficiency. Crockett began experimenting with so-called "sensitivity training" to see if the deeply rooted attitudes of officers could be changed, and of course the experiments revealed that they could. But the department has resources to do this on only a very limited scale—some 100 officers a year. Out of several thousand officers this is pitifully limited, and among those treated there is constant attrition through retirement and resignation.

One of the bewildering puzzles concerns the depth of Rusk's concern for the internal well-being of his department. Before one committee of Congress—Senator Jackson's subcommittee of the Committee on Government Operations, which has been exploring for eight years the problems State encounters in formulating and coordinating foreign policy—Rusk says one thing. Before Representative Rooney's subcommittee on appropriations he takes a different tack. He tells the Jackson subcommittee: "We try to keep not just abreast of events but ahead of events"; diplomacy has undergone "a revolutionary transformation"; we live in a time when "any action taken on one important matter in one place sends a chain reaction of effect in every other important problem with which we are dealing," and we must have "officers who understand these chain reactions." All this means "more and more management," and it means the diplomatic Establishment has need of "increased staff." It means "additional ways to broaden the experience of our professional officers," more "generalists who are deeply familiar with a lot of special fields," more "understanding in depth" and "getting policy officers into a planning frame of mind. We are trying to get the word across that every officer of the department, from the junior officer all the way to the top, is responsible for his own initiative, for considering the problems in front of him and coming up with new ideas. If he happens to have an idea which is not strictly in his field of responsibility, he is encouraged to pass it along to his neighbor who does have that responsibility." In answer to a question concerning the department's success in getting its share of the national talent, Rusk replied: "There is a national shortage of talent . . . . So, that, when government moves out to recruit top talent, the competition is very keen." He emphasized his belief that "if you can build up the quality of personnel you can cut back in numbers. We try to urge our colleagues not to be timid about coming forward with ideas or suggestions, or in challenging basic assumptions or questioning a conventional interpretation of a factual situation, so we can avoid the failure of not thinking about the problem in the deepest and broadest terms." And for this, "opportunity for quiet thought is important." The department needs "far more chiefs and far fewer Indians," and to get these should "upgrade the desk officer," who is the lowest officer in the department's hierarchy. The problem of getting "accurate and relevant information" is a key one. "The ghost that haunts the policy officer or haunts the man who makes the final decision is the question as to whether, in fact, he has in his mind all of the important elements that ought to bear upon his decision, or whether there is a missing piece that he is not aware of that could have a decisive effect if it became known."

But before the Rooney subcommittee Rusk does not discuss these admirable concepts. They all cost money and his budget reflects the most niggardly thinking imaginable for a department which is on the front line of our national defense. The library is starved, research is starved, the planning staff is starved, training is starved. Far from asking for a staffing pattern which would give officers the leisure to keep "ahead of events," to acquire or preserve "understanding in depth," to seek "additional ways to broaden their experience," to "brood over" the complex problems with which the nation has entrusted them, and come up "with new ideas," the Secretary has boasted that for five years he has not asked for any personnel increases. He must know that by and large, under the conditions of the last fifteen years, officers are too hard worked to have any leisure at all. Here and there an office in the department or a section of a post overseas may be overstaffed, but it is not the pattern. Officers have, in fact, been known to faint from overwork.

If diplomacy has indeed undergone "a revolutionary transformation" it is not reflected in the Secretary's budget requests. There has been no revolutionary change in the criteria for admission of officers to the diplomatic Establishment or in testing techniques for admission, assignment or promotion of such officers. Apart from training in counterinsurgency problems begun in 1963 (which it took the imagination of the attorney general to suggest and the prestige of the President to initiate), one has looked in vain for any recognition of this revolution in the department's training program until the last year. Just recently, the department has actually introduced a science seminar and an intensive course in modern economics. It is also discussing a course in modern political science concepts and techniques, but probably won't succeed in getting it under way for lack of funds. It had to scrape up funds from private sources to start the science seminar.

These slow acknowledgments of "revolutionary transformation" in world affairs affect but a handful of officers. More than this cannot be spared by a department whose personnel has not increased during five years of expanding responsibilities. Moreover, much of the training is offered to senior officers, and these are in such surplus, due to poor planning and wholly inadequate analysis of junior-officer grumbling for promotion, that the department must now force about one-third of them into retirement, the trained and the untrained alike.

Even the introduction of computers to dispel that "ghost that haunts the policy officer" has lagged, partly from lack of funds, partly from incompetence. A department that must use obsolescent typewriters and adding machines which cost more for repairs than they are worth is not likely to invest heavily in computers. And, at least for the time being, such an investment might be dubious in any case. The people responsible for operating the few computers the department has been able to wangle have been trying for some two years to master the intricacies of printing out simple personnel data. Any broad application of computers to foreign affairs, so as to permit the storage and instant retrieval of needed information, is clearly a long way off in the State Department.

Occasionally, an event which shows the need for rapid improvement in departmental communications gets splashed on the front pages of the world's press. I remind readers of the furor in August, 1965, when the Prime Minister of Singapore, Lee Kuan Yew, stated that three years earlier the CIA had offered him a $3.3 million bribe. The State Department first denied the charge; then, when Lee produced a letter from Secretary Rusk apologizing for the incident, admitted that the Prime Minister was right. I happen to know that the department had honestly believed the charge to be false. The officers who knew of the affair had been rotated elsewhere and those responsible for Singapore and Southeast Asian matters at the time of the charge were completely in the dark. A computer would have spared the United States this, and many another, humiliation.

This brings up the long-established practice of rotating officers from job to job, country to country, continent to continent. Frequent moves make for a fascinating life, as I well know, but I long ago came to the conclusion that they make for superficial officers. Rusk, who is well aware of the practice, tells the Jackson subcommittee that the diplomatic Establishment urgently requires "more generalists who are deeply familiar with a lot of special fields." How can constantly rotating officers become "deeply familiar with a lot of special fields?" Effective training could help, but training has lagged throughout Rusk's tenure. This sluggishness is the more astonishing in view of the Secretary's own educational background. Either Rusk does not mean what he says and is only idly philosophizing along lines that he knows will please the Jackson subcommittee, or he hasn't the time to do anything about the effective management of his department, or he does not know how to delegate the task.

A choice example of how a badly managed department can leave a secretary—and the nation—in the lurch is provided by the Vietnamese problem inherited by Rusk. Since 1954, when the Geneva Agreements brought a brief respite to Southeast Asia, and the acknowledged unsteadiness of the agreements led Dulles to negotiate the formation of SEATO and to bring Vietnam within its defense perimeter, we have faced a critical need for special knowledge of the area and special skills to deal with its problems. The few resources we did have the department permitted to be dissipated by rotating officers.

For nine years after 1954 the department introduced no training in depth for officers assigned to that area. It never analyzed the new commitment; never asked itself what skills it would demand. When the department finally stirred, the move came too late for it to lead—it could only react. Such indifference is indeed disturbing; it may in large part explain why Rusk refers with such unwonted eloquence to "the ghost that haunts the man who makes the final decision."

By 1957, the department had had three years to perceive the magnitude of Vietnam and adjust to it. From then until 1963, the year in which Vietnam became a matter for Secretary Rusk himself to handle, three different desk officers in the department had been in immediate charge of South Vietnamese affairs—one for considerably less than two years. Their supervisors—directors and deputy directors of the Office of Southeast Asian Affairs—were also changed during this period: four of each came and went. Only two of the desk officers and one of the superiors had served in Vietnam and, as one might expect, these three relatively experienced men had difficulty making their knowledge prevail in the face of their colleagues' ignorance.

This travesty of diplomacy occurred not only in the

department's lower ranks but at more exalted levels as well. In the nine-year period, 1957-66, there were seven Assistant Secretaries of State for the Far East and four different Deputy Assistant Secretaries for economic matters. Of these eleven, six had had no experience in Southeast Asia, and all but one had had none in Vietnam. None had been given any special training in Vietnamese affairs before or during his tenure of office.

During this same nine-year period we had three Secretaries of State, six Under Secretaries, and four officials whose titles varied from Under Secretary to Deputy Under Secretary for Political Affairs. Three of these had had experience in Southeast Asia, only one in Vietnam. Rusk introduced one element of sanity into this vortex by arranging that Alexis Johnson, his Deputy Under Secretary for Political Affairs from 1961 to 1964, should have a year's tour of duty in Saigon as Deputy Ambassador before resuming his departmental job in 1965-66.

With the exception of ambassadors, this chaotic situation has prevailed in Saigon as well. Officers have been rotated in and out, barely able to assimilate the complexities of Vietnam before departing to some other far-off assignment. Too large a proportion of the embassy staff has consisted of junior officers unable, because of age and inexperience, to impress Vietnamese officials. Even after Rusk was nudged into giving a counterinsurgency course, the rotation frenzy canceled out much of the potential value of that project.

This is not diplomacy. Nor does it indicate a satisfactory foreign policy. For policy must take account of means and resources, as well as objectives. Although we have now gained a certain appreciation of the magnitude of the Vietnamese commitment, Rusk continues to permit the department to disperse throughout the world officers who possess some knowledge and experience in Vietnamese and Southeast Asian affairs. This practice may explain why he finds that South Vietnamese officials are not easily persuaded that we really know what we are talking about. It could also be one reason why he finds the North Vietnamese so mysteriously indisposed to negotiate. Keeping tabs on our personnel merry-go-round it just may occur to them that they should wait until we have unmistakably proved ourselves incapable of helping to build order and political stability in the South. Our own generals have been warning for a long time that force alone will not win in Vietnam. The more perceptive of them have been saying from the beginning that in this type of war the political factors are decisive. Does Rusk find himself at the head of a department which he cannot stimulate to realize this point or to act upon it?

In policy making, Rusk has been keen and adept; his analytical ability has been of the first order. In negotiations where he appears himself other governments have been impressed by his willingness to listen, his patience, his lack of evangelical fervor. An American who does not claim to have all the answers, is prepared to hear what others have to offer, and to arrive at agreements by meticulous examination of all the arguments is a welcome addition to the international community. That is why Rusk has been successful in dealing with the Soviets and is now beginning to reap some fruit from his patient efforts to build bridges to Eastern Europe.

These qualities have been Rusk's strong points in dealing with Vietnam. He has been unemotional, rational, uncrusading. He has avoided sweeping claims and generalizations. But he has also avoided the bold and revolutionary steps called for within his department to provide the human and organizational resources needed to respond to the revolution in Vietnam.

Thus, the problems of both Vietnam and departmental management have overtaken Rusk before he became aware of their awesome proportions. Unlike Vietnam, the management problem has not received any concentrated attention. The sooner it does the better, for we cannot tolerate a ramshackle diplomatic Establishment in these days when it is supposed to constitute our first line of national defense.

# 10.

# NIXON'S SEVENTH CRISIS

*PREFATORY NOTE: A prime task confronting any Administration is an effective modernization and management of the State Department and the Foreign Service. This essay reiterates the importance of drawing Secretaries of State from a reservoir of people with extensive experience in international affairs, in management and—if not in the State Department—at least with that Department.*

*When Secretaries of State appoint as their deputy individuals in their own image, as Cyrus Vance has most recently done in picking Warren Christopher, the weakness of diplomatic leadership is further amplified.*

*I would point out, however, that Elliot Richardson, whom Secretary Rogers appointed as his Number Two, belied my prediction of weakness. He proved to be the rare lawyer with a good sense of organizational management. He took hold of the State Department—as he later took hold of the Departments of Health, Education and Welfare, Defense and Justice—and got under way a most intelligent and thorough canvass of the Department from which he proposed to distill an effort to modernize the diplomatic establishment. Had he not been transferred to HEW he would have authored the one promising reform of the U.S. diplomatic establishment since the days of Philander C. Knox, who was Secretary of State under William Howard Taft. Richardson's reform effort was delegated to William B. Macomber, who was appointed Deputy Under Secretary for Management for the purpose. That development is analyzed in the next essay.*

---

Reprinted with permission from *The Nation*, February 3, 1969.

It seems that President Nixon did not relish as Secretary of State a man of great experience and skill in foreign affairs, one familiar with the State Department, the federal foreign affairs community, our foreign policies and the navigational skills which keep those policies afloat. There are such men in his party, some of them part of the Atlantic seaboard reservoir so often tapped for foreign affairs and defense appointments. But, for the first time in years, a President-elect shied away from the Eastern establishment. The indications are that Mr. Nixon did not even seek the advice of the Lovetts, McCloys, Dillons, et al.

Plainly, also, he had no inclination to resort to older precedent and appoint one of those who had challenged him for his party's nomination. "Forward together" is for national consumption, not for party politics, at least as far as foreign affairs are concerned. Instead of pursuing precedent, Mr. Nixon did something quite novel—novel, anyway, since 1925, when Calvin Coolidge appointed Frank Billings Kellogg as head of the diplomatic bureaucracy. This suggests that the slogan in foreign affairs is to be "Keep Cool with Nixon."

But another possible meaning to the appointment of William P. Rogers seems to have escaped the commentators. It is well known that Mr. Nixon has turned to this skillful lawyer during three of the six major crises which he says have beset his political career. By calling upon Rogers now for this particular position, does Mr. Nixon suggest that the diplomatic establishment has begun to loom in his mind as a seventh crisis?

Well it might. I have known the State Department and its Foreign Service for some forty years and never have I seen them in such a shambles. Policy planning in the State Department is still of a scatter-shot variety and diplomatic planning is nonexistent. There is no overall management, and therefore operations are not tied together, gaps are not filled, lapses are not anticipated, improvements are not systematically pressed. Even promotions, which should be one of the simpler operations, at least from the numerical standpoint, have been chaotic and without reference to need. Education and training are scandalously neglected, procedures fritter away experience, officers are frustrated rather than developed by conditions of service. Responsibilities, especially in the lower ranks, are vague and unchallenging. There is, in a word, no systematic control; only endless improvisation in administration, endless battling with momentary need, endless reaction to events—as in our diplomacy itself—rather than good, tight, dynamic leadership.

I hesitate to mention Vietnam in this connection, for it would seem to have been threshed down to the last grain, but several basic elements which it shares with everything else the Department does are being overlooked. One is the failure to bring to bear upon the Vietnamese experience the processes of research, analysis and planning. No systematic analysis of this involvement has been made by the State Department or any contractee of the Department. Hence, the Department has been, and still is, unable to deal profoundly with the problem of intervention, isolating the issues it presents or generalizing from the breakthroughs of technique and the constructive results which here and there ingenious diplomatic, military and aid officers have achieved. Further, there has been no attempt to systematize the errors of this venture for the instruction of future policy steerers and diplomatic pilots. From this failure, we risk not only losing in our negotiations the few precious accomplishments of intervention but of repeating our mistakes in the future. That future, as Thailand and Laos are trying to whisper in our ear, may come sooner than we think. If there is one way to insure a continuation of blunders in Southeast Asia, with their corroding effects on America's world position, this is it.

The *Pueblo* affair is another example of the State Department's chronic inability to subject its diplomacy to any kind of rigorous analysis. No methodical attention has ever been given to this type of spy operation, great though its impact is upon our diplomacy. This neglect led to the U-2 imbroglio in 1960; it will lead to others. The disjointed diplomatic agency has simply not prepared itself to cope with military and intelligence operations which affect the nation's general international efforts. Of course, diplomats would first have to be educated and trained in this area, and one of the more obscure but melancholy aspects of the U-2, Bay of Pigs and *Pueblo* affairs is that our diplomatic officers are not adequately prepared to run any phase of a modern diplomatic operation.

A part of the crisis which the diplomatic agency presents to Mr. Nixon arises from its astonishing failure to redefine diplomacy itself in up-to-date terms, so that it might have a clear idea of the kind of people it should be recruiting, the kinds of education and training it should be providing its officers, the criteria it should be following for assignments and promotions, the blend of policy, diplomacy and management it should be developing—all to effect a widespread improvement in our international performance.

Good management would encourage a contagion of know-how from the better-run to the sloppy offices, thus stimulating and bolstering the Department in areas where it is weakest. But lack of management isolates office from office, bureau from bureau. There is no means, for example, whereby the concepts and techniques of analysis and management employed by Covey T. Oliver to improve performance in Latin American relations can be transmitted to other areas. Nor is there any assurance that the gains in that bureau will be passed on to and developed by the Assistant Secretary who replaces Mr. Oliver.

In such an "anti-organization" department, morale is deplorable. In forty years of observation, I have never known State Department morale to be good, but it is now the worst that I have ever seen it.

Morale affects performance; so also do attitudes. They subtly penetrate and influence every view, every decision, every approach to a decision. They are the unspoken premises which cause men to assume they know things they do not know, understand situations they do not understand, are "managing crises" when they are only tinkering with them, disposing of problems when they are only postponing them to reappear in more aggravated form. They give rise to, or are themselves generated by clichés and myths. If Mr. Nixon wants to avoid his seventh crisis he had better put someone in a managerial position in State who knows what the prevailing attitudes are, their sources and their cures. Otherwise, both he and his Secretary of State, however shrewd and competent they may be as politician and lawyer, will be stymied.

A Middle East crisis is rising to one of its periodic crests and Messrs. Nixon and Rogers would do well to recall what lack of State Department management did to President Johnson and Dean Rusk on the last crest. For four and a half months, as that 1966-67 storm quietly gathered, the position of Assistant Secretary of State for Near Eastern Affairs remained vacant. Career diplomat Raymond Hare resigned in November, 1966, and could not be induced to remain. He was worn out; furthermore, he had given a year's notice of his departure. But no replacement had been prepared. The only one available when the time came, it was said, was Lucius D. Battle, then serving as ambassador in Cairo. But there was no seasoned successor for Battle, and one had therefore to be improvised. At the urging of Under Secretary Katzenbach who, like Mr. Rogers, had served as Attorney General and was not exactly sophisticated in the deployment of diplomatic personnel, the Department appointed as ambassador Richard Nolte, an intelligent, academic type not likely to have much influence on Nasser. Nolte's remark at the Cairo airport remains a classic. Asked by a journalist what he thought of the Middle East crisis, he replied: "What crisis?" He soon found out.

Congressional penny-pinching aggravates the short-comings of management and planning. Secretarial vacancies cannot be filled; officers become increasingly distracted by clerical duties. Supplies are so parsimoniously inventoried that even telephone directories must be scrounged. The library—unlike those at the CIA and the Pentagon— is so understaffed that it cannot meet requests for service, cannot acquire needed materials, cannot shelve promptly what it gets, cannot bind what it shelves. This is a particularly illuminating situation, for it not only exemplifies the anti-intellectual attitude of the administrators who parcel out the Department's appropriated funds but shows also how really false is a lot of the economizing. Unbound periodicals stray; they must be replaced; and back copies cost more than the original subscription numbers. Furthermore, when funds at last become available for binding, costs have increased. The State Department is a perfect demonstration, top to bottom, from people to paper clips, that penny-pinching always results in waste.

An extraordinary cynicism pervades the diplomatic establishment. Even its liberals found themselves welcoming the outcome of the Presidential election. "Nothing could possibly be worse," they said; "a change—any change —just might bring relief." They did not remember that this same hope was engendered in 1932, 1952 and 1960, and gave way to souring frustration. It is not merely change that is needed—it is reform: organizational reform, procedural reform, attitudinal reform, educational and training reform, conceptual reform. That is what confronts Mr. Nixon as he prepares for his seventh crisis.

That being so, one of Nixon's most extraordinary pre-inaugural decisions was his choice of Secretary of State. William P. Rogers is by all reports a good lawyer; he is a former Attorney General of the United States, a good negotiator in a domestic context, perhaps a good one in an international legal context, a staunch upholder of civil rights, an upright citizen, a loyal friend and counselor of the President, a cool man. These attributes are splendid, but how completely do they meet the varied diplomatic needs of the President? How sufficient are they for a successful Secretary of State?

Mr. Rogers is not totally without exposure to foreign affairs. He served in 1967 as the United States delegate on the U.N.'s fourteen-nation *ad hoc* Committee on South West Africa. Seven years earlier he headed the American delegation to the independence ceremonies for Togo, and took occasion to visit the Mali Federation (then Mali,

Guinea and Senegal) and Nigeria. He met a number of
leaders in those countries (most of whom have since been
ousted or assassinated). During the Hungarian revolution
of November, 1956, he accompanied Mr. Nixon to Austria
to investigate the plight of refugees. Another brief mission
took him abroad in 1955 as chief American delegate to a
U.N. conference on prison conditions.

That's about it and it is not very much. No continuous
professional experience; not even a sustained professional
interest.   No background whatever with respect to the
State Department or the Foreign Service. No experience
or known interest in any coordinating machinery in the
government's foreign affairs.

This lack of central involvement or even interest in his
new area of responsibility becomes the more painfully
evident when one sets Mr. Rogers' training alongside the
preparation of some of his Cabinet associates. The Secretary of Agriculture has had extensive experience with
agricultural matters.   The Secretary of Labor has been
a student of labor problems for decades, much involved in
labor-management contentions, thoughtfully coping for
years with the very challenges he will face in his Cabinet
assignment. Both Clifford M. Hardin in Agriculture and
George Shultz in Labor are seasoned experts in their fields.

In fact, Mr. Hardin seems to qualify better for the
position of Secretary of State than does Mr. Rogers. His
extensive international experience began in 1947 when he
was sent to Europe by Michigan State University to explore the broad question of what roles universities and
farm groups might play in the Marshall Plan. The following
year, in furtherance of Point Four, President Truman
included him in groups to study development possibilities
in South America. His interest in this area has continued,
and has led to his appointment as a member of the Council
on Higher Education of American Republics, which takes
him to a different country of South America each year.
In 1950, as dean of MSU's School of Agriculture, Hardin
helped found the University of the Ryukyus on Okinawa,
and that added the Pacific area to his international involve-

ment.  Four years later, he became chancellor of the University of Nebraska and introduced in that one-time bastion of Midwest isolationism a Latin American studies program and a Far Eastern Institute; he also continued Nebraska's sponsorship of the New Ataturk University in Turkey which, among other things, has brought to Lincoln more than 200 Turkish professors for advanced study. He has also been involved in educational development in sub-Sahara Africa.   This depth of familiarity with the country's overseas objectives and commitments suggested to President Kennedy that Hardin be added to the Clay committee to study the entire foreign aid program. Finally, Hardin thinks in imaginative terms. One of his pet interests is promoting "a massive, long-range innovative effort unprecedented in human history" to solve the world's food and population problem.

Compared with all this, Mr. Rogers and the man he has picked as his deputy are rank amateurs.  Neither can innovate because they do not know where to start. Neither can reform because they do not know what is wrong. Neither can appreciate the need for any "massive, long-range, innovative effort" to bring our diplomatic establishment up to date because they have yet to learn in what respects it is out of date.  As they gradually become enlightened, they will tinker, as all unprepared innovators do.  Moreover, they will by then have become overwhelmed by current crises.

Melvin Laird was smarter than Mr. Rogers.   Realizing that as Secretary of Defense he would be handicapped by his managerial inexperience, he picked an expert manager for the second spot at the Pentagon. Rogers picked a man in his own image. Mr. Richardson is also a lawyer, also an Attorney General, also inexperienced in management, also a novice in foreign affairs, in the State Department, in the Foreign Service, in diplomacy.

This, together with the fact that Laird has been deeply involved in the problems and issues of the Defense Department for fifteen years, with a fairly clear idea of how it operates—its weaknesses, its mistakes, its needs—means that Defense will continue to have an edge over State. In the light of the last eight years, I need not emphasize what this means in our foreign policies and diplomacy. There is little likelihood that a "massive, long-range, innovative effort" will tip the scales back to civilian initiative and control.

Both Mr. Rogers and Mr. Richardson may be expected to think that as lawyers and pragmatists they have much to offer American diplomacy. I wish this were so, but I fear that lawyers are poor managers and even slow to see the need for effective management. As a profession, they are given to the belief that all they need are the facts; by rigorous analysis, they can then deduce the answers. Furthermore, since they are trained to argue from briefs prepared by their staff, Mr. Rogers and Mr. Richardson will no doubt believe that they can satisfactorily counsel the President and Congress, as well as the public and officials of other governments, from the "briefs" provided by a State Department staff. If so, they are naive.

"Facts" are hard to come by in foreign affairs. Information is elusively concealed in the manner of its presentation. It is subtly permeated with the drafters' personal impressions, interpretations, hunches. A formidable husk of subjectivity surrounds every "fact." The greatest bulk of our dossiers on other peoples and their government leaders, their cultures and their needs, is comprised of what we *think* we know, and that is precisely what has bedeviled the government's handling of Vietnam. The "information" and calculations available in Washington have been treated by the Secretary of State and other Presidential advisers as reliable "facts"—and we have strayed deeper and deeper into a swamp of conjecture. Because of the man he has selected as Secretary of State and the deputy Mr. Rogers has picked for himself, this can happen to Mr. Nixon in countless situations.

As for pragmatism, we have about come to the end of that road. Within limits, it is a good approach, but relying on it almost exclusively, we have exhausted its possibilities, and our continuing faith in it is leading us into a performance of diminishing returns. Faced with the necessity to synthesize foreign and domestic resources and policies, we are required to make a more fundamental assessment of foreign affairs than we have so far attempted. For this, some philosophy is needed—something akin to the careful, systematic, basic thinking that went into the Declaration of Independence and the Constitution. And it requires, as those statements of policy and principle did not, a consideration of world responsibilities. Who is to lead in this "massive, long-range, innovative" effort?

Perhaps, someone may suggest, the number-three man in the Department, he being a career diplomat. But he also is a pragmatist. A smart operator, a man of keen insight into the reactions of foreigners, Alexis Johnson has never acquired any reputation as a thinker, a planner or a manager. And as he has shown throughout the Vietnam years—during much of which he served as a political adviser to the Secretary—he is a follower, not an innovator.

If none of these three men has what it takes to reform the Department, the situation is not yet entirely hopeless. Six other strategic positions remain to be filled: Deputy Under Secretary for Administration, Deputy Assistant Secretary for Organization and Management, Deputy Assistant Secretary for Personnel, Director General of the Foreign Service, Director of the Foreign Service Institute and Deputy Assistant Secretary of Operations.

If Mr. Rogers can be as smart as Mr. Laird, he can still bail himself out of his limitations and, by the men he selects for these positions, spare the President another major crisis. To do this he must clearly perceive three things: the necessity for superior management of the diplomatic establishment; the requirement that managers be familiar not only with management concepts but also with foreign policy and diplomacy; and the need to delegate adequate managerial powers to such men.

These six officers of the Department must create a program of management (which means, in effect, a program of reform, since the State Department now totally lacks management), and they must become a team to carry it out.

In view of Mr. Rogers' and his deputy's unfamiliarity with the State Department, the filling of this prescription is so difficult as to be unlikely. But there is a remote possibility that it will be done. Several studies of the State Department and Foreign Service of recent date are available for the launching of such a program. If the six are appointed from the career diplomatic service well in advance of vacancies, sent off to a suitable university to be trained in management concepts and techniques and to distill a program for the approval of Messrs. Nixon and Rogers, and if they are delegated adequate managerial powers, the job can be done. There is no other way to do it. If Mr. Nixon really sees the diplomatic establishment as threatening him with his seventh crisis—and whether he does or not, that, in my opinion, is the situation—he would do well to persuade his Secretary of State to take this course. It would be good politics—if Mr. Nixon gives any thought at all to 1972. And, of course, it would be a step toward insuring that there is still a nation to hold elections in 1972.

# 11.

# REFORM AT LAST?
# THE MACOMBER SPRINT

*PREFATORY NOTE: As pointed out in this essay, it was Elliot Richardson rather than the Secretary of State who perceived the need to modernize the State Department under the Nixon Administration. Richardson conducted the search for a knowledgeable and experienced person to lead the drive and got William B. Macomber installed for the purpose as Deputy Under Secretary for Administration (later recaptioned Management). As Macomber told Department officers, this effort was "of far more lasting significance than the handling of a great many of the more transitory matters which you . . . deal with on a daily basis."*

*Revealed here for the first time in public print is the basic weakness of the selection system by which the State Department picks diplomatic officers.*

*First argued in* **Anatomy of the State Department,** *the thesis is repeated that the Department needs a continuing general manager to give over-all direction and continuity of experience and leadership to that establishment, thereby giving greater consistency and more effective coordination to our moves in international politics. This would help to correct the inbalance between American and Soviet diplomacy. Unlike the Soviets, we continually change our Presidents and Secretaries of State, often selecting them from men only slightly experienced in foreign affairs.*

*The reader will observe that I return to my argument for a more modern and systematic type of education and training of diplomatic officers.*

Reprinted with permission from *The Nation*, March 16, 1970.

Once again, the State Department is off and running down the track of reform. On January 14, William B. Macomber, the new Deputy Under Secretary for Administration, revealed the strategy to an assembly of the Department's personnel that jammed a large auditorium. The premises from which the reform takes off he stated in the form of an appeal to "begin today by taking an honest look at ourselves." The self-criticism went as follows:

(*1*) In organization and management, the State Department and Foreign Service have failed to "adjust" to the new role taken by the United States since World War II.

(*2*) "We have tended to be intuitive in nature, weak in planning and unenthusiastic about management."

(*3*) As other departments of government "began legitimately to play an ever-increasing role in U.S. foreign affairs . . . the instinct of the traditional foreign policy establishment was to protect its exclusiveness . . . . We did not participate to the degree we should have in the important work of developing these new agencies. We were not organized to do so managerially, and we did not have the specialists required. We thus began to lose control of the action.' "

(*4*) "Nevertheless, Presidents have continued to look to us as their principal staff arm in forging a national policy out of the spectrum of diverse, specialized and often parochial foreign affairs interests scattered throughout our government. And Presidents have continued to expect this Department to insure that our complex and wide-ranging governmental activities abroad are coordinated and carried out in a manner consistent with the policies they have determined."

(*5*) Failing to be "systematic, competent and aggressive . . . we have not met the challenge of foreign affairs leadership as successfully as we might have. Our failure to do so has caused frustration. And it has raised a clear prospect: either we produce the improvements necessary . . . or . . . this will be done for us."

So much for "the honest look." What reforms does

Mr. Macomber propose? He offers them in four categories: personnel, organization and management, attitudes and conditions of service. They may be briefly summarized as follows:

*Personnel:* The day has passed when diplomatic officers need only a general smattering of knowledge about the more visible political, economic and social phenomena. The age of the specialist is here, and the specialist of diplomacy must be educated and trained in the "core skills." Apart from foreign languages, the Department has never paid much attention to these skills. It will now do so.

A new five-category personnel system will enable officers to specialize in political, economic/commercial, administrative, consular and such miscellaneous careers as those of scientists, doctors, nurses, security officers, building engineers (important to protect embassies and consular posts from "bugging") and permanent faculty members of the Department's training agency, the Foreign Service Institute. Most officers will be recruited for a particular speciality and will be expected to spend the bulk of their service time in it. Those demonstrating executive talent will be moved across speciality lines, thereby developing a long needed pool of foreign affairs managers.

Younger officers will be got off to "a faster and more interesting start," but older and more experienced officers will not be sacrificed. "It is our more experienced and senior officers who are our principal current assets in the immediate effort each day to protect the interests of our country and to keep the world from unleashing its megatons." At the same time, the Department needs most "those who do not already know too many reasons why too many things won't work."

The ombudsman proposed by the "Young Turks" (career officers who have been agitating for reforms for the last two and a half years) will be brought into the Department by establishing an Office of Welfare and Grievances, the director of which is to be "a senior, able and highly respected officer who will have wide authority to

investigate and advise on personnel grievances and wrongs."
He will report directly to Mr. Macomber.

*Organization and Management:* The old Policy Planning
Staff of the Department, which Secretary Rogers has
already converted into a Planning and Coordination Staff,
will not only carry on the policy planning of which the Department is in such desperate need but will work to tidy
up some of the loose ends which have dangled from top-
side decisions, including those of the National Security
Council.

The Policy and Coordinating Staff will also provide a
secretariat for the top-level interagency committee, formerly known as the Senior Interdepartmental Group, which
the Under Secretary chairs. It will perform similarly for
the subordinate interdepartmental groups over which the
assistant secretaries preside, thus producing a more effective meshing of these two echelons. These groups are seen
as the administrative tools by which the State Department can coordinate the foreign affairs of the federal
government.

There will be no Permanent Under Secretary, a career
diplomatic officer located at the Department's summit to
provide policy and management continuity from administration to administration. "A number of administrations
have resisted the idea," Macomber said, "and of course
no administration can bind a successor to accept this
device."

*Attitudes:* It being axiomatic that "changes in tables of
organization, significant as they may be, are never final
and never finally solve basic management problems," and
that "attitudes and approach that managers at all levels
bring to their jobs and instill in those about them" are far
more significant for reform, "it is important that we find
improved ways" to nurture creativity, initiative, analytical
and reflective attitudes, long-range thinking and a more
aggressive disposition to "get the jump on situations."

*Conditions of Service:* An important task of management, therefore, is to create those conditions of service
which will encourage such attitudes. This can be approached

in a variety of ways, including such personnel-organization-al devices as the Office of Welfare and Grievances and the "Open Forum Panel," instituted by Dean Rusk under pressure from young officers, which provides a channel by which officers of all levels can get suggestions to the top. Another way is to "give all our people more time to focus on new ideas, alternative solutions and imaginative tactics" by reducing the traffic of messages to and from the field. "This, along with allowing more time for creative think-ing by our Washington-based officers, is the objective of the reporting reduction operation currently under way." A "major and searching review of the role and functions of our diplomatic missions" is being initiated. Also under examination are inspection and evaluation of those missions, as well as criteria and devices for the promotion of officers and the broadening of their education, training and exper-ience through the Foreign Service Institute and assignments to "the nongovernmental foreign affairs community," which includes not only universities and foundations but business, labor and communications organizations.

These are daring words and they imply a good, hard run. No one knows the hurdles better than Macomber. He is not new to the foreign affairs community. Indeed, he is the most broadly experienced man ever to occupy the top administrative post of the Department. Further-more, he is not a Foreign Service officer.

After graduating from Yale in 1943, Mr. Macomber put in three years with the Marines, returned to Yale for a master's degree in government, took a law degree at Harvard and a master's degree in political science at Chicago. He then joined the CIA for two years, switched to the State Department in 1953 to serve on the staff of the special assistant for intelligence (presumably as CIA liaison), joined Sen. John Sherman Cooper as adminis-trative assistant, returned to State as a special assistant to the Under Secretary (Herbert Hoover, Jr.), became a special assistant to Secretary Dulles and then put in four years as assistant secretary for Congressional Relations. In that job he impressed Sen. John Kennedy who, on becoming President, decided Macomber was a Republican who should be retained. After three years as ambassador to Jordan, he returned to Washington as AID's assistant administrator for the Near East and South Asia, and in 1967 resumed his former responsibilities for State's relations on Capitol Hill.

So Macomber is well rounded, with a good deal of diplomatic, political and organizational experience. Never finding it necessary to enter the Foreign Service, he has not acquired any of the parochialisms or defense mechanisms which have done so much to limit the capabilities of intrinsically able Foreign Service officers.

What then are Macomber's chances of pulling off his sprint to reform? One must recall that the State Department not infrequently sets off on this kind of spirited exercise. Never, unfortunately, have any of its dashes lasted to the finish line.

Back in 1900, Wilbur J. Carr set off on a series of runs, the last of which ended a quarter of a century later in a piece of reform legislation known as the Rogers Act. This merged the old diplomatic and consular services into a single "Foreign Service of the United States" and prescribed a number of long overdue improvements in the selection, training, assignment and promotion of officers. On few of these did the Department or the Foreign Service carry through effectively. And that is why they reappear like awakened ghosts in Mr. Macomber's design.

Then, in 1943, Edward R. Stettinius became Under Secretary of State and initiated what FDR gleefully described as "giving hell to the State Department." As soon as Stettinius got a reorganization of the Department under way, a group of Foreign Service officers, restive for some years and now supported by clear handwriting on the wall, began running a reform race on their own. From this latter initiative came the Foreign Service Act of 1946.

Few of the objectives of either of these efforts were realized. Stettinius soon departed; his successors became too much involved in crises and international meetings to give much thought to the Department's continuing need to modernize, and the Foreign Service reformers were rotated to other assignments. To this dissipation of energy was added a failure to professionalize the standards for admission to the Service, so that a familiarity with the objectives of the 1946 act and with the establishment itself never became a part of every officer's background. Reform gradually dropped from sight and when post-war economizing overtook the diplomatic establishment, the hard-worked survivors had no time or energy to think beyond the day's requirements.

With the Kennedy administration came another sprint. This produced a "Herter Report" which recommended some personnel innovations. There the innovative spirit would have died had not the administration's third try at filling the post of Deputy Under Secretary for Administration turned up William J. Crockett, one of the relatively few creative-minded officers in the diplomatic establishment. He gave the sprint a second wind. For almost four years—from 1963 to 1967—Crockett turned in a flashy performance but, lacking the support of his superiors—and notably that of Dean Rusk—he found the goals elusive. Weary and disheartened, he retired to a less trying job in private employment.

Now, three years later, Macomber proposes another dash. The idea does not emerge from nowhere. A group of officers—a few senior, but mostly mid-career and young —have always refused to accept the departure of Crockett as conclusive. Lacking a base in the Department itself, they seized control of the private American Foreign Service Officers Association after a whirlwind campaign in 1967. They set to work defining those objectives of reform they wanted to espouse, and on the eve of the 1968 elections issued a report, "Toward a Modern Diplomacy." They also helped produce a volume of *The Annals* of the American Academy of Political and Social Science on the same subject. Copies of both were provided to various echelons of the Nixon headquarters, to Mr. Rogers when he was appointed Secretary of State, and to Elliot

Richardson when he was designated Under Secretary. Mr. Richardson's antennae were sharp enough to catch the signals and he began searching for a Deputy Under Secretary for Administration to put the Department in some sort of manageable shape.

For eight months Mr. Richardson searched so quietly that the Administration appeared to be ducking the issue. Indeed, at his press conference of August 20, Secretary Rogers threw cold water on it. Asked whether it was true that "you have a new front opening up on reorganizing the State Department," he replied with such a classic example of the Administration's technique of lowering its voice to the point of saying nothing that it is worth quoting in full.

> I don't think we have a new front. We have pretty well completed our personnel changes. We have a few staffing problems left. But on the whole the Department, I think, so far as administration is concerned, is in good shape. We have as I say—Mr. Cargo's [William I. Cargo, director of the Planning and Coordination Staff] operation still has some people— we have some places to fill. But on the whole, I think it is well staffed. And I am very proud of the people we have. I think they are unusually capable.

One of the "few staffing problems left" was filling the post of Deputy Under Secretary for Administration, and something began happening to the Secretary's tone of understated complacency when, on October 3, William B. Macomber was installed in that position.

For some reason I do not understand, some Young Turks did not relish his becoming Deputy Under Secretary. Of all the people who have taken this onerous and thankless position, Macomber showed in his January presentation that he not only has the broad background and tough-mindedness needed for a reformer but has mastered much of the reform literature. That is an intellectual feat none of his predecessors ever achieved.

In addition, he made it clear in his remarks that "This is an effort to which Secretary Rogers and Under Secretary Richardson [note the inclusion of the latter] attach great importance. They have asked me to stress today that what we accomplish in this regard will be of far more lasting significance than the handling of a great many of the more transitory matters which you and they must necessarily deal with on a daily basis." He added later in his remarks: "As Secretary Rogers says, 'let's quit talking about the problem and start solving it.' "

So Macomber seems to have taken the assignment on the basis of an understanding with his associates at the Department's summit. The spelling out of that understanding in the form of a speech to the Department's personnel was some evidence, too, of political astuteness. The understanding is now on the record. Never before has that occurred.

Nevertheless, Macomber has a far piece to go, farther than his own well-rounded design suggests. There are basic issues with which his proposals do not grapple. One of them is the proposition that U.S. foreign policy and diplomacy should remain under civilian control. This is not simply a matter of better organization and management of the State Department, or of more effective liaison with the military establishment. It is also a matter of principle, of instilling that principle into the diplomatic establishment and of training its officers to carry it out. Unless the Department can develop the determination to prevail in its own area, and to that end devise adequate educational and training programs for all its officers, it will never evolve the overwhelming leadership in the total federal community that civilian control requires.

Vietnam is not the only theatre in which the Department has lost control of foreign policy, but it is currently the most disastrous example. How did it occur that the policy of escalation was effectively challenged by civilians in the Pentagon, not by civilians in the State Department? Why did no one in State's inner circle ever question whether we had the diplomatic resources to carry off such an adventure and to guarantee its civilian direction? Who in that circle ever cautioned that foreign policy and foreign commitments must accord with diplomatic resources? Why, at the very least, did no one in State recognize its poverty of officers experienced in Southeast Asia in general and in Vietnamese affairs in particular? Why did it take the Kennedys to wake up the Department and its training organization, the Foreign Service Institute, to the need for training officers in countersubversion and nation-building diplomacy? Who even now in State is trying to determine what produced this lapse of policy, this resourceless diplomacy? If a repetition is to be avoided, the Department must know what defects in the preparation and service conditions of diplomatic officers prevented them from undertaking the hard analysis of developing policy that was essential both to challenging that policy and to relating it to available diplomatic resources. That something was missing is clear enough, and it still affects everything officers do across the whole spectrum of foreign affairs.

The same kinds of questions can be raised about a second crucial issue, that of preserving the maximum possible overtness and ethical propriety in our overseas operations. Secret organizations may well contribute to a government's operational effectiveness, but they also pose a basic threat to the principles of freedom and democracy. Hence we must keep secret operations to a minimum in foreign affairs, and we can do so only by having the most effective possible aboveboard diplomacy. This requires, again, a well-conceived policy, thoroughly indoctrinated into every diplomatic and CIA officer, and a training program that equips every diplomatic officer to perform from the start with maximum effectiveness.

Macomber is confronted by a severe scarcity of personnel. This lies beyond the perimeters of his design for reform, but is crucial to it. It does no good to plan a better educational and training system within the establishment if officers are so few that they cannot profit from it. For years, the Department's staffing pattern has been too lean to permit the development of effective educational and training programs. Dean Rusk took to boasting each year before Congressman Rooney's subcommittee on appropriations that he was not requesting personnel increases despite increasing burdens and needs. "We are just working harder," he used to say. That was demagogy and Rusk's policy of virtuous self-denial was made still more destructive by two government-wide reductions of personnel. The Nixon Administration has now decreed a third. Not only have able, experienced diplomatic officers been lost, and morale dealt a blow, but offices are understaffed to the point of making impossible the reflective, farsighted, creative thinking for which Macomber is pleading. That was one of the conditions that denied Crockett much of the momentum for reform he tried to generate.* It will deny it to Macomber as well.

From personal experience, I can testify to how devastating insufficient manpower can be. Having retired from the State Department in 1962 to work for reform on the outside, I was asked to return in 1965. One of the proposals we then formulated concerned important renovations in the orientation of young officers. We reanimated a long-dormant Advisory Training Committee to consider the proposal, setting a date for a meeting that would give its members ten days (including two weekends) to read what we had prepared. I phoned each member to convey the general idea of the proposal and to implore careful study and reflection, which each solemnly promised. On the day of the meeting, however, one after another came to me and whispered that he had not had time to read the proposal. Only two of the ten members attending the meeting had read the reform laid before them. However, no one would publicly confess his lack of preparation; the proposal was discussed in a rambling fashion and voted upon. The result? Two in favor, eight opposed.

---

*As Deputy Under Secretary for Administration 1963-67, William J. Crockett spearheaded the most searching and systematic reform effort since the days of Wilbur J. Carr, whose long and persistent reform effort is dealt with in Essay 13.

Such clinging to old notions, old attitudes, old criteria by men too busy or exhausted either to examine, think and innovate themselves or to keep abreast of others' proposals can devitalize the best intentions of reform. Not only must officers be relieved of numbing pressures on the job; they must also be given time off to stand back and look at what they are doing. Secretary Rusk liked to boast that everybody was just working harder. "Working harder" at the same old lines of policy, at the same old limited notions of diplomacy, in accordance with the same old shallow ideas of what the modern world demands. And since one of those policies had to do with Vietnam, "working harder" meant digging the nation ever deeper into disaster.

If such debacles are to be avoided, minds must be refreshed, sources of information and viewpoint amplified, routine thinking challenged. Annual leave must be taken without question—indeed, it must be required. Sabbaticals must be provided, and assignments granted to new milieus—not for just a few favored officers but for all. Much of the reform that Macomber's program envisages can be accomplished only in the minds, wills and interests of officers.

We induct into the diplomatic calling too many officers who are superficial even at the start of their careers. I recall that when I was interviewing newly commissioned officers a few years ago, I asked them if they were doing any of the reading that had been recommended in their orientation course. More than a few said No, and when I inquired further, they shocked me with this answer: "If I was good enough to get in, I'm good enough." The Department panders to this attitude instead of challenging it. It will neither put its recruits through an exacting preparation nor test their response to the orientation offered. When, at various times, I have been in a position to challenge this scandalous slackness, I have been told by those in charge that the recruits would rebel against a thorough and tested preparation. "They are fed up with courses and examinations," I was told. "They have had enough of studying. They want action. They want to get going." So the result is that the State Department introduces its officers to the most difficult calling in the world—the preservation of peace—by a superficial, slapdash "orientation."

The State Department does not call on its recruits to meet standards remotely resembling those which other occupations have set to prepare employees for modern, competitive conditions. The brokerage business, for example, looks like a relatively simple occupation—selling stocks and bonds. But consider the preparatory program which first-class firms exact of aspiring account executives —the lowest position carrying policy responsibilities. In contrast to the State Department's six-week smattering of substantive orientation (without examinations), plus four weeks of consular training, these brokerage houses put their candidates through a grueling twenty-nine weeks. Candidates must then pass the stringent examinations required by the New York Stock Exchange, the National Association of Security Dealers and the Chicago Board of Trade.

What would these brokerage firms do with candidates who "rebelled" against the hard preparatory study? They would say: "You're not for us." What does the State Department say? "Come on in anyway. You'll learn on the job." Brokerage was also once learned on the job. Is the State Department's business so much simpler, so much less important, so much less critical to the needs of society that it can still be satisfactorily learned that way?

The standard answer to this is not only that officers can "learn on the job" all they need to know but that they are so good—picked through such a rigorous examination— that they do not need professional preparation. To this I say nonsense. Mystified over the years or to how so many mediocrities got through the "rigorous" selection system, I finally requested an assignment to the Board of Examiners for the Foreign Service. To be admitted to the Foreign Service, candidates must pass a written examination and then an oral, the latter designed primarily to test personal attributes. My assignment to the board required that I participate in the oral examination of candidates who had been certified as having passed the written. I was immediately appalled by the prevailing shallowness of those examined. Wondering how they could possibly have passed the rigorous written examinations, I called for their grades. These seemed in order. Then I requested their raw scores and discovered the answer to my years of mystification. The written examination is emasculated.

The Department decides how many officers it needs each year. It has learned from experience that roughly one in five candidates will pass the orals. So, if the Department needs, say, 200 officers, it instructs the Educational Testing Service in Princeton, which both composes and grades the written examination, to pass 1,000. Come hell or high water, a thousand pass. So, when the grading is completed, ETS raises the raw scores enough to pass that many applicants. In my time with the board it meant raising raw scores as much as thirty-five points. That is, a candidate receiving thirty-five on his written examination had his score doubled to reach the passing mark if seventy.

While grading on the curve is an accepted device, the Department has let itself be blinded to the realities of what it is doing. If its oral examiners recommend, on personal traits, a candidate who in fact knows only half of what he is supposed to know, he obviously is far below par. Hence, if the Department truly wants an elite diplomatic corps, it must do something to prepare him better either before it commissions him—which I prefer—or immediately thereafter and before he begins service. This "diagnostic approach" had a brief flurry of support as a result of my "discovery," but like all reforms in the State Department, it died young. Mr. Macomber had better do something about it.

Ninety percent of Foreign Service officers need to be jolted from their anti-intellectual attitudes. All need to be reminded—continuously—that foreign affairs are difficult and complex, demanding intellectual and cultural preparation and capacity as much as common sense, political intuition and tact. These latter are important, but too often they operate so superficially as to frustrate our policies and deprive the nation of diplomatic leadership.

But it costs money to make officers come up to the mark. The Department has operated so long on a shoe-string that reform will require a substantial increase in its pitiable appropriation. Will the President and his Bureau of the Budget support a raise? Will Messrs. Rogers, Richardson and Macomber take this bit in their teeth and place their requests for increased funds in the convincing perspective of national defense?

Mr. Macomber knows Congress and its ways, but the financial aspect of reform will take much more than that—not only from Macomber and his superiors but from the White House as well. Representative Rooney has entrenched himself in his position as chairman of the House Appropriations Committee's subcommittee on the State Department as a kind of Permanent Under Secretary of State—the position that Macomber says no administration wants. He has been serving a long, long time and has acquired familiarity with the diplomatic establishment, and an influence over its affairs, that few at the summit of the State Department can rival.

All these points are relevant to the various specific proposals made by Macomber. A five-category personnel system, for instance, poses real problems of integration which can be met only by an effective set of values and objectives and a rigorous educational and training program to push it forward. Personnel planning, therefore, must be more than numbers planning; it must involve systematic development. Crockett tried hard to introduce such an educational development, comparable to the systematic requirements of the military for officer development. Had he gained the support of his superiors he might have succeeded. Lacking the support, he failed.

The proposed Office of Welfare and Grievances can be kept alert to personal inequities and blockages as well as to organizational weaknesses only if there is an adequate basic philosophy and effective training. Otherwise this idealistic experiment will become simply an in-house smoothing of the pillows. And how will the reformers offset the erosive effect of rotation? Rotation decrees that each officer shall switch jobs every three or four years, a practice that has done more than any other single factor to kill the momentum of earlier reforms. It has meant that, after an initial shake-up, things have always tended to settle back into traditional, pedestrian routines.

Just who will put all this together? Not Secretary Rogers. If no other reason existed, he is too busy. Under Secretary Richardson? He is Rogers' alter ego, and must catch all the crises Rogers is too busy to handle, and substitute for him whenever he is out of Washington. Is Macomber the man? Or Cargo, director of Policy Planning and Coordination? Who is to mesh personnel development, improved conditions of service and organizational management into substantive requirements? Where, indeed, will Vietnam be subjected to searching scrutiny? In Macomber's office as a management resource problem? Or in Cargo's office as a substantive debacle?

My guess is, that if the hard thinking is to be done that such questions as Vietnam require, Messrs. Rogers, Richardson and Macomber—and perhaps some occupants of the White House—cannot airily dismiss the concept of a permanent top manager in the State Department. True enough, no administration has yet been willing to accept the concept, but a lot of private businesses have done so, and none of them, however large, imposing or internationally involved, has on its shoulders the enormous tasks and frightening risks that fall upon the State Department.

Mr. Macomber has already appointed thirteen task forces on such problems as "career management and assignment policies," "performance appraisal and promotion policies," "personnel requirements and resources," "personnel training," "personnel prerequisites," "recruitment and employment," "stimulation of creativity," the role of the country director," the Foreign Service Institute, the "role and functions of diplomatic missions," "management evaluations systems" and "management tools." He proposed in his speech that the Secretary of State should undertake "an annual posture statement," similar to the statements issued in recent years by the Secretary of Defense. Perhaps a task force on "national defense and survival: contributions and needs of the diplomatic establishment" would turn up matters to be included in the posture statement. Perhaps another should be appointed on the "rule of law through effective diplomacy." Anyway, thirteen is an unlucky number. If only to abate the long-continued hex on reform in the diplomatic establishment, the number should be increased by at least one, and I can think of no better study than how diplomacy can contribute more effectively to the nation's survival.

## 12.

# REFORM FROM WITHIN: THE IMPORTANCE OF ATTITUDES

*PREFATORY NOTE: Reform of our diplomatic establishment has been eternally visualized in organizational terms. Far more important than the rearrangement of offices and responsibilities are the attitudes of the people comprising the organization. If these are right, a poor organization can be made to work acceptably; if they are wrong, they will ruin the best. This is why organizational reform by itself seldom takes root: the staff modifies it to its own attitudes and perceived needs and interests.*

*This essay urges that those seeking a better American diplomatic performance give thought to officers' attitudes and insists that the Department's training agency, the Foreign Service Institute, be used to instill in officers a broad understanding of the government's foreign affairs community and the positive attitudes needed to make that community function with maximum efficiency.*

*It will be noted that the synthesis of diplomatic and consular functions for which I had pleaded four years earlier as basic to greater effectiveness in our foreign affairs has not occurred but, in fact, a backward step was taken in splitting off consular functions in a separate "track" or "cone" in the Foreign Service.*

In conducting State Department personnel on a *tour d'horizon* of deficiencies and needed reforms of the Department, Deputy Under Secretary William B. Macomber, Jr., displayed an impressive knowledge of the terrain.

Reprinted with Permission from *Foreign Service Journal*, May, 1970.

He rightly pointed out that not only is skilled personnel needed, but also organizational reform, deep-seated changes in procedures, conditions of service and attitudes. He emphasized that "changes in tables of organization are never final and never finally solve basic management problems. More fundamental to management success are: first, the attitudes and approach that managers at all levels bring to their jobs and instill in those about them; and second, the management tools we are continually developing and making available throughout our organization."

As an instance of this, one might look at the Foreign Service entrance requirements. Far from constituting a management tool, they completely ignore the organizational dimension of foreign policy and diplomacy. No candidate for the Service is required to have the vaguest glimmer of it.

State's attitude is that whatever officers need to know about the foreign affairs establishment they can learn on the job. This is General Electric's and General Motors' position. They tell prospective applicants to acquire a good college education and that they will learn about the organization, its operations and problems once employed. But is not our calling more akin to a profession than to the manufacture and sale of refrigerators and automobiles, so that candidates should know at least something about it as well as having a sound general undergraduate education?

Private companies swiftly and systematically train newly employed personnel. Our attitude, on the contrary, is that knowledge of the Department, the Service and the foreign affairs community in Washington beyond the superficial exposure given in the Basic Officers Course is not really necessary. Hence, the Department neither orients the newcomer in depth nor provides to all officers special courses on organization and management at various stages of their careers. We take the same position in the orientation of novitiates as we take in entrance requirements: they need not be well prepared about problems;

they need not be forewarned; they will learn little by little, assignment by assignment, experience by experience. They will grope, make unnecessary mistakes, acquire all sorts of limited and parochial impressions and opinions, pick up all sorts of prejudices and fancies. But never mind. They will "learn." Our attitude is such that we receive applicants as amateurs in the organizational dimension of foreign policy and diplomacy, and we turn them out to their first assignments still as babes in the wood.

Twice in the last eight years I have sat through our "orientation" of newly commissioned officers. The first was on my own initiative. Horrified as an oral examiner to find how little successful candidates know about the bare bones of the organization to which they apply for admission, I felt I should find out whether this gap might be filled by our induction process. So I attended "The Basic Officers Course." That was in 1962. The gap was not filled.

Three years later I was called back as a full-time consultant to put in a year of searching inquiry into some of our basic personnel problems. One was morale. We decided to tackle this through case studies of one manifestation— the drop-out of promising young officers. This led to similar studies of young officers who had not dropped out but were considerably frustrated. These probes strongly indicated that one source of low morale centered on a total lack of preparation for the environment of our diplomatic organization.

So, again, I audited our orientation course, for, with the rotation of officers, it undergoes a perpetual tinkering; and to make any recommendation one had to be thoroughly *au courant*. Little had changed. It was improved in some areas but not in teaching the organizational environment of the nation's diplomatic corps. Both the materials and the lecturers dealt with our organization and its functioning in gingerly generalities. There was lacking a hard, realistic analysis of the problems that a diplomatic establishment presents to formulators of foreign policy and practitioners of diplomacy. At no point were the crucial organizational, operational and personnel problems frankly laid out and dissected.

Just as in diplomacy we present disagreeable matters in a way to allay their unpleasant features, so in orientation we play down the unpleasantries of our establishment. No one leveled with the young officers; consequently they shortly encountered the disagreeable on-the-job problems with bewilderment and sometimes with shock.

If it is expecting too much of government officials to tell the facts straight for fear of quotation reaching superiors or Congressmen, then at least neophytes can be required to read some of the material that is written from independent vantage points—material that tries to describe the diplomatic establishment as it is. Neither of the orientation courses that I attended had a reading list of such material. However, shortly after my second exposure, an officer took over the course and produced one. It was of recommended, not required, reading, however. No survey was undertaken or even a show of hands requested to indicate to what extent any of the reading was done.

One of the interesting points made by Mr. Macomber in his January 14 address was that various studies of the establishment over the last quarter century have been "very helpful," "reflected a great deal of thinking" and provided "much preparatory work" for reforms. If so, why have they not been made required reading by every incoming officer? Does not the attitude to which such a lapse attests, suggest that reform from within lacks a broad base of study and understanding? As a result, will not such changes as may be effected in the next few years, as have so many in the past, wither away as soon as their producers are rotated?

One positive impact this lapse does have is to convey to every incoming officer the impression that we do not have serious problems, or, if we do, they are not problems for Foreign Service officers. They are for someone else— "administrative types," for instance. As Mr. Macomber said, "Management has not been our bag." A deeply embedded attitude has made it this way and it will continue so until orientation, education and training are designed to root it out.

These lapses, of course, explain why officers must rely on their own experiences in judging the nature of the Service and the Department. Personal experience is the yardstick for identifying problems and suggesting alternative solutions. Hence the existence of as many images of the Department and Service as types of officers and experiences. These myriad conceptions, their contradictions and the confusion bred by them are a fertile source of frustration, poor morale, inadequate testimony before Congressional committees and glib replies to Presidents who ask what is wrong with the Department and are told by one of us: "You are." How much reform can such an establishment nurture and carry out for how long a time?

The Department has aggravated this situation by failing to conduct research on organizational and personnel problems, either in the Department or contracting for it to be done on the outside. There is a notable exception: when William J. Crockett was Deputy Undersecretary for Administration. Mr. Crockett tried to do something along this line.

Under Crockett's inspiration, John E. Harr, then an officer of the Department, initiated as a personal project a questionnaire addressed to FSOs to ascertain their views, attitudes and motivations with respect to their calling. The Junior Foreign Service Officers Club has also done this once with junior officers. The only examination in depth of attitudes of which I am aware, however, was that done through the case studies mentioned above and that exercise proved of short duration. Does not all this say a great deal of the seriousness of our interest in this factor which germinates many of our personnel and organizational problems?

One of our attitudes strongly inclines us to pragmatism. We depend so heavily upon information gained on the run, upon instinct and upon hunch, that we are something less than profound. Indeed, we boast that diplomats are born, not made, and we, of course, pride ourselves on being diplomats, not "organization men," planners, researchers or managers. We say that foreign policy and diplomacy are essentially political processes and hence involve simply the art of the possible. We shrug off the suggestion that diplomacy may contain scientific elements by saying, irrelevantly, that it can never be "an exact science." So we are much given to tinkering. This is why so much "reform" developed from within is just that. We call it reform but it is generally pragmatic juggling and adjusting.

Another attitude that handicaps genuine reform by ourselves is a distrust of "outsiders." We view the State Department and Foreign Service as wholly *sui generis*. So we feel little is to be gained from engaging management consultants, scholars or almost anybody outside the clan. This is why every reform that has involved a "public advisory board" has withered away as soon as its innovator disappeared. Those "modern practices in public administration" which the Foreign Service Act of 1946 extolled and which were intended to be applied sweepingly to the diplomatic establishment were applied only fragmentarily and spasmodically until William J. Crockett made his great push from 1963 to 1967. We simply do not trust those who can best advise us on "modern practices in public administration." Until this distrust is rigorously rooted out of officers through suitable educational and training devices, reform from within will never prosper.

Some of the reforms now proposed may fail to take adequate account of attitudes and wind up not as advances but retrogressions. For example, the proposed five-category personnel system. One of the categories is to be consular, separate from the political and economic staffs. Its officers, generally speaking, will be expected to serve only as consular officers—i.e., "consular specialists"— and will be assigned, judged and promoted as such. This reflects an attitude long extant in our establishment that consular work is concerned only with passports, visas, protection and welfare and can be divorced from other work. This, indeed, is how the "consular" part of our orientation for new officers is structured. The divorce has thus become embedded in our attitudes from the start of our careers.

But consular work has from time immemorial been political, informational, cultural, economic and commercial. Other nations so view it, and every other nation uses its consular posts accordingly. If for no reason other than to get our money's worth from our consular posts, we must so conduct ours. This demands consular officers of as good background and instincts in political and other areas as political officers, and with just as thorough a familiarity with our foreign policies and diplomacy. Is it conceivable that such officers will be content to serve only in consular posts? It is not to me. If they are capable in a consular position, I would expect them to want other assignments in their careers.

Such a system conjures to my mind the problems, including morale, that afflicted us prior to 1924, when we had two overseas services, diplomatic and consular. True enough, the proposal now is not to return to separate services. The categories or "tracks" are to be developed within a single service. But do we have clearly in mind the ease with which prejudice and morale mischief lurk in diplomatic passports, diplomatic immunities, tours of duty limited to capitals, and hobnobbing with the leading, "elite" personalities to be found in national capitals? These were some of the subtleties which contributed to the serious morale and operating problems we experienced before, and for some years after, the Rogers Act.* Will they not reappear in the proposed track system? They almost certainly will unless concerted and vigorous efforts are made to change attitudes and values nurtured by attitudes.

Before a reader dismisses this point, let him answer

---

*This Act, enacted in 1924, fused the separate diplomatic and consular services into a single Foreign Service.

this: what is our prevailing attitude today toward consular posts and assignments? Are they less attractive than embassies? Do we regard them as generally staffed with people of less political sensitivity, information, and judgment than those in embassies? Are they less capable of seeing the whole picture of a country and therefore viewed as making only fragmentary and superficial political assessments? Are they regarded as having less comprehension of the Department's policies and diplomacy about not only their country of assignment but to the whole range of our activity? Is this likely to increase under a track system?

Let us examine one other facet of this. To what extent do embassies bring consular officers within "the family" of officers now, even when the consular officers are posted within embassies? To what extent are they kept informed of the embassies' political, economic, informational and cultural activity and thinking so as to participate intelligently in them? To what extent do we view "consular activities" as germane to these others?

Present attitudes are an important consideration in weighing the extent to which a "category" or "track" system may reinforce a view that consular officers are somehow apart from diplomatic. This could reproduce an unhappy condition from which we were rescued by the Rogers Act. Would it not be better to broaden our conception of consular duties and correct adverse attitudes toward them than to introduce a system which may well reinforce them?

We like to believe, as Mr. Macomber said, that reforms and modernization imposed upon us from outside "will be neither as informed nor effective as those we initiate ourselves." But apart from a very few like Mr. Macomber, how well informed are we as to what needs to be done? How well informed are we as to past efforts and what went awry? To what extent, to paraphrase George Santayana, are we so unknowledgeable that we are condemned to repeat past mistakes and to innovate changes which will afflict us with evils earlier corrected? How well prepared are we to support and follow through on any of the sound changes to be made? To what extent will these be imposed upon us, not from the "outside" but by a few who perceive while the rest of us, not perceiving, will let them evaporate when the innovators vanish from the scene? These are basic questions—basic to reform—and we had better recognize that a sizable task of systematic education and training faces us.

The Foreign Service Institute must thus be envisaged in far bolder terms than heretofore. Its programs must be the keystone of any reform arch. If we do this, we must be prepared to confront the problem of numerical staffing. It is no good planning a better, more effective FSI if there are not enough officer bodies available for assignment to its courses. For years, our staffing pattern has been too tight to permit adequate programs in FSI, including correspondence courses. A disproportionate part of the time and energy of FSI staffers goes into trying to pry loose bodies from the bureaus and the Service. A staffing pattern more congenial to educational and training programs must be provided. This means more funds for an expanded staff. Are we reformers ready and willing to put that up to the Administration and Congressman Rooney? If we are and prepare our case thoroughly we may find them more than sympathetic. It is time, at any rate, we put them to the test.

# 13.

# PERSPECTIVES OF REFORM

*PREFATORY NOTE: Having observed over the years the eroding effects of the rotation system upon everything our diplomatic establishment tries to do and specifically upon Crockett's innovations from 1963 to 1967, which had withered away when, disheartened, he resigned to enter private business, I was skeptical whether Richardson and Macomber would be able to introduce any viable reforms. In search of an answer I undertook a survey of reform efforts since 1900.*

*My survey appeared in two installments, (1) "The Era of Wilbur Carr" and (2) "The Post-Carr Period," and from it emerged the basic point that enduring reform of an organization demands not only the right attitudes among those who staff it, and hence a dynamic and sustained educational effort to instill those attitudes, but also continuity of leadership. With secretaries of state coming and going as political appointees, this brought me, once more, to the thesis that the State Department needs a continuing top official—a continuing general manager—to provide continuity and consistency to its policies and operations. No private company could meet its competition without such a person and, I contend, neither can the State Department. I contested the argument that, as William B. Macomber put it, "no Administration has accepted, or is likely to accept, the notion of a 'general manager' of the State Department" by pointing out that from 1852 to 1937 the Department had in fact continuing managers in William Hunter, Alvey A. Adee and Wilbur J. Carr.*

Reprinted with permission from *Foreign Service Journal*, August, 1971.

*From presidents and secretaries of state on down, too few of those involved in the conduct of our foreign affairs know much of our diplomatic history, including the State Department's, which suggests that George Santayana's dictum that those who do not know the past are condemned to repeat it requires a supplementary dictum that those who do not know the past cannot be smart enough to perpetuate what is good in it.*

## Part I — The Era of Wilbur Carr

The first sustained effort to modernize our diplomatic establishment in this century was catalyzed within the State Department by a civil servant, Wilbur J. Carr. Born on an Ohio farm, Carr began his government career as a clerk-stenographer in 1892, landing entirely by chance in the State Department. There he served until 1937, when he was appointed Minister to Czechoslovakia—a span of 45 years.

Almost immediately upon his admission to the Department Carr became aware of the need of reform. Being a civil servant, his interests and efforts were not dissipated by rotation and changing Administrations. He learned by an ever-lengthening experience and acquired a keen sense of what could be done, when and by what means. He got to know intimately the people who could make or break the needed changes and how best to approach them.

The diplomatic-consular establishment of Carr's time was much smaller and less complicated than today's. A continuing civil servant could, in a variety of assignments, circulate through the various offices and thus pick up a detailed familiarity with the Department's work, procedures, problems, personnel and organization which is virtually impossible today. Even as a stenographer, Carr was constantly in and out of the offices of Secretaries, Assistant Secretaries and others of considerable experience, knowledge and influence. He supplemented this familiarization-through-circulation process by projects and studies of his own. He promptly undertook a compilation of United States treaties and read works on treaties and international law, as well as history and biography. In those days there was little reading material on diplomacy. Carr had no college education but he graduated from a Washington law school, by attending evening classes, and became a member of the bar. This awarded him a broader base and standing in the Department.

Seeing the consular service in dire need of reform, Carr began to tackle that intricate web of political patronage, tradition, personal favoritism, inefficiency and corruption. He worked his way up to Chief of the Consular Service, the Chief Clerkship of the Department (which corresponded to today's Deputy Under Secretaryship for Administration) and finally Assistant Secretary (for administration). Throughout this career, he quietly and persistently pressed to upgrade the performance of the consular and the diplomatic services and, finally, to fuse and upgrade the two.

The Department being small, Carr could concentrate his tactics and powers of persuasion on a few men. Even so he had his periods of discouragement. The price of progress was long-sustained, unflagging persistence. Sometimes, when change seemed too slow to be worth his great and persistent effort, he considered resigning.

One of the principal reasons for this was the difficulty of winning over to his cause successive Secretaries of State. Each new Secretary had to be educated and persuaded. Each was invariably a man of broad political experience, knew public affairs, had political connections and alliances which could be either useful or inhibiting to Carr, depending on his ambitions.

A broad sector of the government had been screened off from political patronage by the Civil Service Act of 1883. But the diplomatic and consular services were not under that Act, and thus offered possibilities for political appointees. Neither Presidents nor Secretaries of State could wholly resist Congressional pressures. Even a Chief Executive like Theodore Roosevelt, who had espoused civil service reform, resisted Carr's pressure to remove consular posts from Presidential dispensation. Carr could present his views to the top officials, but he was also exposed directly to their political sensitivities.

Two factors came to Carr's aid. One was his inclusion in small luncheons and soirées. To be identified with the State Department was a social advantage and with his emergence as a chief of the Consular Bureau Carr found himself increasingly at small get-togethers which included Representatives and Senators. Since he also began to appear on the Hill to represent the Department at appropriations hearings and in connection with his efforts to reform the consular service, his acquaintanceships began to provide him political leverage outside the Department.

The second factor to help Carr was the ferment for social regeneration that had been going on for decades and had as one of its objectives improvement of government service. Both civil service reform advocates and business groups had been insisting that the consular service be severed from political patronage and greatly improved. The Civil Service Reform League also kept a watchful eye on the nomination of ambassadors, publicizing and sometimes frustrating the appointment of large financial contributors to the party in power. Then, in 1906, some eighteen universities announced plans to prepare men interested in the diplomatic and consular services. Harvard even attempted, unsuccessfully, to establish a diplomatic, consular and colonial service school.

When Elihu Root became Secretary of State and Carr sought his collaboration in applying the merit principle to the consular service, Root was not only quick to point out the relevance of the 1883 Act but, for reasons of political tactics, insisted that the Executive Order Carr wanted should be cast in its mold. This took President Theodore Roosevelt by a flank maneuver. The Order, which he signed on June 27, 1906, committed his Administration to three principles: admission to the consular service by examination; promotion solely on the basis of ability and efficiency; and opening the examination to all, not just to designees of the President (as was the case under earlier Executive Orders). The first two principles had already appeared in earlier Executive Orders, but had been vitiated by the absence of the third.

On the whole, Carr was fortunate in his superiors. He undertook his first essay in reform when Richard Olney was Secretary of State, from 1895 to 1897, but Carr was then too junior to make much of an impression. In later years, Olney could not even recall meeting Carr. After two short-lived Secretaries came John Hay, whose long survival in diplomacy had made him the equivalent of a career diplomat. Unluckily for Carr, he was typical of a long and still-continuing tradition of the genre. He was exclusively interested in foreign policy and the day's work, and not at all in confronting in any systematic way the problems of ensuring the resources—personnel, administrative and diplomatic—needed to carry out policies. Moreover, Hay had benefited handsomely from the going system, and was not concerned about remedying its shortcomings. So Carr received no visible help from Hay, but perhaps no hindrance either, and by this time he had some steam of his own, generated by his multiplying contracts with Congressmen and outside urgers of reform, including businessmen who wanted better information, more cooperation in promotion of trade and more adequate service generally.

It was with Hay's successor, Elihu Root, that Carr picked up noticeable steam. Root was not only a cultivated man and thoroughbred statesman, but he also came to the diplomatic establishment with the great prestige of a reforming Secretary of War who had been able to carry Presidents and Congress with him in modernizing the nation's military resources.

The two men got along well. Root greatly respected the quiet, unassuming, competent civil servant who marshaled his facts meticulously and appeared at departmental meetings and Congressional committees thoroughly prepared, but Root was not the reformer at State that he had been at War and the only reforms Carr was able to engineer under Root dealt with the consular service.

The diplomatic service went untouched and the State Department virtually so.

Carr thus found himself patiently elaborating, through regulations and procedures, the advances registered in the 1906 Executive Order and a federal law enacted in the same year which brought some system to the chaotic consular service. As a result of the legislation, consular officers and posts had to be classified and graded, inspectors of posts selected, their biennial inspections funded and supervised, their reports reviewed and operational improvements suggested. Consular fees had now to be accounted for. Entrance examinations had to be devised, examiners appointed, their decisions reviewed. A promotion system had to be designed based upon "ability and efficiency." Carr, being a continuing civil servant, could see that these follow-up reforms were pushed and that all officers were imbued with their spirit and familiarized with their substance. The consular service was thus propelled on a path of more acceptable performance.

Elihu Root's successor was Philander C. Knox. Carr proposed to him that the demonstrably practicable and effective consular corps reforms be extended to the diplomatic service. This was done by Executive Order signed by President Taft on November 26, 1909. A significant thrust was this and it did not endear Carr to the free-wheeling diplomatic dukes. Once more, it was Carr who elaborated the needed regulations and procedures and provided the leadership in instilling into the diplomatic officers the spirit and criteria of the new order.

In the meanwhile, a long overdue reorganization of the ramshackle, anachronistic Department had gotten under way. Carr had no part in this, having his hands full with the consular and diplomatic services. It came from Huntington Wilson, a diplomatic officer young and impatient, in the fashion of the "Young Turks" and junior officers of today. His personality had not set well with Root, who viewed Wilson as arrogant, suspicious, overly ambitious and possibly a cut-throat type.

Wilson, who had served seven years in our Tokyo

embassy, was "horrified at the methods" of the Department and considered its "antiquated organization pitifully inadequate for the conduct of foreign relations in sorry contrast to the other great powers." One of his thoughts was to introduce geographic bureaus in the Department to be headed by men with extensive overseas experience, rather than by civil servants with whom the Department was preponderantly staffed. For personal reasons, it seems, he could extract from Root permission only to experiment with his design through the establishment of a pilot bureau—Far Eastern Affairs—with Wilson as its chief. He promptly established the pattern he had in mind for all such bureaus by ordering home from their Far East posts a diplomatic and a consular officer to serve as his assistant chiefs.

Through the chanciest fluke, Wilson, who was appointed ambassador to the Argentine in 1908, met the new Secretary of State, Mr. Knox, before departing for post. Knox asked him his views on modernization of the Department and was so impressed that he invited the young officer to serve as his number two officer and to get going with his ideas. Reorganization thereupon blossomed, in accordance with a carefully devised plan which Wilson had formulated over four years, discussed with colleagues, and demonstrated in a pilot bureau under Root. He shook up the entire Department. Among the innovations were the geographic bureaus which became the cornerstone of Departmental development and power from that time on. Organizational and operating innovations, fresh, imaginative thinking, systematic recognition of the value of overseas experience and new criteria of educational requirements and performance all now combined to provide the diplomatic-consular establishment with a new lease on life.

Wilson resigned in a tiff with the Woodrow Wilson Administration in 1913. His ideas about modern diplomacy were sound, but he was emotional, egotistical and often arrogant, which made it difficult for him to collaborate effectively with others over a sustained period.

Carr, a Republican high in the government, somehow survived the Administration of Woodrow Wilson and in 1915 was responsible for Federal legislation that embodied earlier reforms attained by Executive orders, among which were efficiency reports and entrance examinations for diplomatic officers, and new ones, such as appointments to class rather than to specific positions in overseas missions, cross-assignments between the diplomatic and consular services and transfers of departmental personnel to "the foreign service." (Thus, from Taft's Executive Order of 1909, appeared the legal term "the foreign service.")

Six years of patient persuasion and negotiation by Carr were thus rewarded. But the 1915 Act far from achieved his goals and he now headed for the landmark Rogers Act of 1924. In this nine-year effort he was assisted by the Republican electoral victories of 1918 and 1920 which brought into a pivotal position one of Carr's solid collaborators on the Hill, Congressman John Jacob Rogers.

The 1924 Act was largely the work of Secretary of State Charles Evans Hughes, Congressman Rogers and Carr. It fell to Carr again to elaborate the directives and procedures to make the Act a living document. In this he received far less than the enthusiastic cooperation of the diplomatic officers who were losing their élite, favored position. They were no longer rulers of the diplomatic roost; and, to add insult to this injury of dispossession, were being obliged not only to consort with consular "characters" but to accept a civil servant in the Department as their chief, for Carr was now made an Assistant Secretary (for administration).

Under Carr's leadership, entrance examinations for a single service were drafted, a board selected to conduct them, and a set of performance standards established for a unified overseas service. He insisted upon fair and equal treatment in assignments to the Department, in assignments abroad, in home-leave orders, in promotions and in allocations of the newly provided representation allowances. He also strove to make something of the newly provided representational allowances and of the newly provided Foreign Service School. He saw to it that instruction in that School for all new officers was made a one-year affair, a minor miracle which is still impressive forty-six years later. By this time a person of considerable political prescience and leverage, Carr got many of these moves underpinned by an Executive Order signed by President Calvin Coolidge. He was taking no chances.

Even with the support of this Order, Carr found the going hard. The diplomatic officers' resistance and tactical resourcefulness in frustrating him were considerable. Moreover they had one of their own as Under Secretary of State, Joseph C. Grew, and he was one level higher in the hierarchy than Carr. With tact, skill born of long experience and personal contacts on Capitol Hill, Carr worked with interested Congressmen to press the reforms provided by the legislation and to supplement them with the Moses-Linthicum Act of 1931. His modernization efforts were still a long way from fruition then but without his continuity of service and persistence they would have shriveled and blown away many times over. As it was, his ideas were still alive and struggling, if much circumscribed in application, by the time the next reform surge came along in 1943.

Before leaving Carr and his reforms, I must add a word concerning one other factor in his career. This was Alvey Augustus Adee. Adee was more than an official: he was a rare phenomenon in the State Department. True enough, William Hunter had provided the Department with an extraordinary underpinning of continuous experience and skill for many years, having served as Chief Clerk, except for a brief period, from 1852 to 1866 and then as Second Assistant Secretary from 1866 until his death in 1886. Adee prefaced his years in the Department with seven years as a secretary and chargé of our legation in Madrid. Returning from overseas, he entered the Department in 1877 as a clerk, in a year became chief of the Diplomatic Bureau, four years later became Third Assistant Secretary, succeeded Hunter as Second Assistant Secretary, and died in office as Assistant Secretary in 1924. This came to a total of fifty-four years in the diplomatic establishment

Adee was no reformer except in draftsmanship. He was a resourceful, farsighted diplomatic operator as well as a genuine, warm-hearted, witty, aboveboard human being. A thorough student of diplomatic practice and foreign policy, he was a continuing and sagacious adviser of Secretaries of State and Presidents. He took an interest in Carr, encouraged his efforts to broaden his cultural and political base, and, above all, imparted his remarkable insights derived from his lengthening experience in foreign affairs. No doubt more than one of the reforming Executive Orders which Carr extracted from the White House were facilitated by Adee.

The remarkable span of seventy-two years of continuous service which Hunter and Adee brought to the State Department refutes the oft-repeated legend that no Administration has accepted, or is likely to accept, the notion of a "general manager" of the Department. In a quiet way it acquired in Hunter an identifiable management focal point and, in the diplomatic field, a succeeding one in Adee. Then, from 1909, when Carr became Chief Clerk, to 1913, the Department had an effective managerial team in Huntington Wilson, Adee and Carr; from 1913 to 1924 a dual managerial team through Adee's continuity in the diplomatic and foreign policy area and Carr's in the administrative and consular. No reform movement engineered this accomplishment: it just happened that way. And our diplomatic establishment was fortunate that it did. As one reviews the foreign policies, diplomacy and establishment management of that long period, he is made aware of how much they owe to the continuity of service and the balanced, mature views and institutional memories of these men.

When Carr left the Department in 1937 to accept appointment as Minister to Czechoslovakia, the only overseas service he ever performed (and it was to prove short-lived), reform lost its one consistent continuing champion.

No other civil servant since his time has been able to match his stature and length of service. Like all officers who have taken the broad view and kept in mind the national as opposed to personal interest, Carr saw too much to be done to leave the Department with exultation over the reforms he had wrested from a reluctant government. He left, indeed, a disappointed man. Like most who have sought reform, his reach exceeded his grasp. He would have been an even more disappointed reformer had he been able to peer ahead, for henceforth, devolving upon migratory officers, reform lost all continuity.

## Part II — The Post-Carr Period*

When Wilbur J. Carr left the State Department in 1937, reform devolved upon migratory officials. The first of prominence was Under Secretary Edward R. Stettinius. Unlike Carr and Wilson, Stettinius was under no necessity of generating pressure for reform. This had slowly developed from the evidenced incompetence of the diplomatic establishment to deal with the complex international problems thrust upon the nation since 1929. Reform should have proceeded along three lines: (1) assembling knowledgeable people to identify and study the international demands upon the establishment and thus the skills, attitudes and organization it needed, (2) concrete proposals for producing such skills, attitudes and organization, and (3) ways of achieving the follow-through needed over the years. Only a part of the second was tackled.

This self-defeating shallowness lay partly in Mr. Stettinius, whose impressive appearance was not matched by his intellect. His positions in industry had resulted from paternal friends rather than from personal capacity and while his depression and war-time experience in Washington had culminated as Lend Lease Administrator he was far from what the diplomatic establishment needed for modernization. When he was named Under Secretary in

*Reprinted with permission from *Foreign Service Journal*, September, 1971.

September 1943, replacing Sumner Wells, President Roosevelt intimated that he was designated "to raise hell in the State Department." Stettinius at least did that.

He and his associates worked hard and fast for nearly fourteen months at their task of "raising hell." But they knew little about (1) the Department or the Foreign service and the linkages between the two, (2) foreign affairs especially upcoming post-war problems, and (3) the nature of diplomacy itself. The result was a focus on symptoms rather than originating deficiencies and, upon organization rather than attitudes, skills and performance. Few objectives were therefore realized. When Stettinius became Secretary in December 1944, he was promptly immersed in war and postwar business, and was out of office the following June. Many of his associates disappeared with him; and their successors became much too involved in postwar crises and international meetings to think much about what needed to be done to enable the Department to fulfill its new global responsibilities.

The time was ripe, however, for a reappraisal of the Foreign Service. Some of its more alert officers who had anticipated this desired to seize the reins of reevaluation and reform before unknowledgeable outsiders got hold of them. They had received a premonitory signal from a perceptive civil servant, Lawrence Duggan, who had persuaded Sumner Welles to introduce Labor Attachés into the Foreign Service Auxiliary; and in 1943-44 the Labor Attaché Program, which I had some part in setting up, rapidly crystallized. This democratizing move greatly amplified the Service's resources of observation, evaluation and persuasion abroad.

As these developments took place, Service reform received support from an unexpected source. A continuing dispute between the Department and the Foreign Economic Administration over the allocation of funds for commercial reporting in South America led to the establishment of an interdepartmental Joint Survey Group to review the needs and procedures of the controverted reporting. Under the chairmanship of Alan N. Steyne, an energetic, imaginative Foreign Service officer, this group began to explore related problems. On March 1, 1944, Mr. Steyne was appointed head of the Office of Foreign Service which replaced the two divisions of Foreign Service Personnel and Foreign Service Administration. He established in that office the first "planning staff" the Service had ever had. The idea of reform now acquired a tremendous boost.

The planning which Steyne envisaged necessitated the creation of several bodies: a Commission of Inquiry on the Foreign Service, composed of eminent representatives of the public, an interdepartmental committee, and a strictly departmental Steering Committee to guide the planning. In addition, three teams, each consisting of a Foreign Service officer, Budget Bureau official and representative of the public were despatched to missions abroad to review their conditions and needs.

In December 1944, Julius C. Holmes, a career Foreign Service officer, was named to Wilbur Carr's old post of Assistant Secretary for Administration. This officer had taken a leave of absence for war-time military service and at this time held the rank of general. He had given some thought to updating the Foreign Service and, before assuming office, took the prudent step of getting his principal ideas approved by Secretary Stettinius.

On December 18, 1944, a Committee on Foreign Service Legislation was created in the Department to crystallize proposals for an interim law embodying some of the more urgently needed authorizations. This was passed by Congress May 3, 1945, thus clearing the way for basic, long-term legislation. To work on this, Holmes chose as director of the Office of the Foreign Service, Monnett B. Davis, with Selden Chapin as his deputy. Both were Foreign Service officers.

On May 16, Davis was succeeded by Chapin, who appointed as his deputy Julian F. Harrington, a Foreign Service officer who had started as a clerk in the old consular service, thus bringing to the effort some of the kind of thinking that had characterized Carr's own approach to a "new foreign service." In the meantime, Julius Holmes acquired access to President Truman and got his blessing for the concept of a single unified Foreign Service and the need for basic improvements. The President also approved the elaborate committee structure developed by Alan Steyne. With this solid support from the White House, Holmes circulated a memorandum throughout the Department, inviting legislative suggestions.

Twelve studies and sub-studies, with suggested drafts of implementing legislation, emanated from Steyne's Planning Staff. James F. Byrnes succeeded Mr. Stettinius as Secretary on July 3, 1945; and six weeks later Holmes resigned to enter private business. He was succeeded by Frank J. McCarthy (not related to the Senator), a bright young aide of General Marshall during World War II, but with no experience in the diplomatic establishment. The appointment startled the in-house reformers and the Service reacted unfavorably. Mr. Byrnes added another unsettling move: he requested the Bureau of the Budget to prepare a report on State Department organization, thus reviving the Stettinius organizational reform effort.

The Bureau's report included recommendations on the Foreign Service, one of which was to merge the Department's civil service and the Foreign Service. Mr. McCarthy swung behind most of the recommendations, including this one. Responsive to an overwhelming Service opposition to such a merger and trying to adjust to a new and poorly informed Assistant Secretary, Mr. Chapin found his position increasingly difficult.

In the midst of all this the Department was inundated with over ten thousand employees from the Office of War Information, the Office of Inter-American Affairs, and the Office of Strategic Services. What to do with them demanded urgent decisions. New officials were hastily appointed in the Department to direct the programs of the dismantled agencies and the chaos which now overtook the diplomatic establishment was augmented by an unfortunate blow. Alan Steyne, who had driven himself unmercifully, had a breakdown; he went on extended leave; and when he returned was assigned to other duties. The sails of the legislative project lost considerable wind.

Suffering from bursitis, plagued by his own ignorance and the departmental confusion, and floundering badly, Mr. McCarthy resigned on October 11. His place was taken by Donald S. Russell, a long-time associate and former law partner of the Secretary, also totally unfamiliar with the diplomatic establishment; and his deputy, J. Anthony Panuch, a New York lawyer, could do little to reduce Mr. Russell's ignorance of foreign affairs. These two appointments perpetuated the insiders' loss of high-level leadership that had begun with Holmes's resignation.

Russell's initial decision was to fully support McCarthy's views on Foreign Service modernization, including merger of Departmental and Service personnel and abandonment of all legislation effort. But Chapin, by his considerable talents of persuasion, managed to get himself authorized to resume the legislative effort based on a continuance of the established Foreign Service separate from the departmental service. The new spurt was joined by Andrew B. Foster, Carl W. Strom, Edward T. Lampson, Lionel M. Summers, Marion L. Neustadt and Edmund A. Gullion. Apart from Miss Neustadt, none of this group had any background or formal training in the mass of technicalities on which reform was beginning to concentrate, such as leave, pensions, promotions, and classification of personnel. They set to work to master these. Many of the broader corridors which Steyne had inspired the Joint Survey Group to open up were abandoned.

Before Mr. Chapin could send a bill to Capitol Hill he was attacked formidably from four quarters.

"Die-hards" in the Foreign Service wanted no significant change at all, and objected particularly to proposals such as lateral entry.

The "Special Assistant to the Secretary" heading the new intelligence office wanted to be free of the proposed Board of Foreign Service Personnel in dispatching and administering his staff abroad, yet he wanted that staff in the Foreign Service and not, as proposed, in the Foreign Service Reserve.

William Benton, Assistant Secretary, whose information-al and cultural officers were viewed by FSO's as "a dubious and unassimilable group" both in the field and the Department, demanded their immediate assimilation.

Finally, William Clayton, Assistant Secretary for economic affairs, objected to the details of Chapin's bill. He resisted the proposed discrimination against specialists (who would be consigned to the Foreign Service Reserve) and vigorously attacked Chapin's concept of the proposed Director General of the Foreign Service. Clayton strongly felt that this official should not be a Foreign Service officer, a genre, he held, altogether too resistant to change.

All but the "die-hards" considered Chapin was only going through the motions of reform and really had in mind only the preservation of "the Foreign Service guild." The "die-hards," of course, considered him to be gravely jeopardizing "the guild."

The frenetic battle that raged over these issues contrasted to the quiet, long-sustained, undramatic efforts which characterized the Carr period of reform. There was a contrast in the scope of effort, also. Depression and war had revealed many inadequacies in the diplomatic establishment that Wilbur Carr had not approached and some of which, perhaps, he had not grasped. Not only new skills, but new concepts of diplomacy were now needed. A whole new vision of education and training for policy-making and diplomacy was therefore demanded. Little of these emerged. The 1946 Act failed to rise to these, although Chapin's compromises left many possibilities wide open, exploitable in time if reform could be sustained. For this, years of patient, consistent development were needed.

This, however, did not eventuate. One by one, the reformers were rotated to other assignments. Some, exhausted, deliberately sought less strenuous berths overseas to recuperate. Gradually, their thinking was dissipated, their studies were filed and forgotten. No Wilbur Carr was left to carry on. Thus, almost a quarter century later, the Young Turks found the terms of the Act so unfulfilled as to provide ample room for the reforms they wanted.

To the dissipating effects of rotation was added the failure of the reformers to professionalize the standards for admission to the Service or even to require the newly established Foreign Service Institute to incorporate in its orientation of officers a study of the Act and its objectives. Such a study could have included an analysis of the problems involved in achieving those objectives and the performance criteria which officers themselves had to measure up to in order to reach those objectives. Thus the impact of rotation could have been challenged. But there was all too prevalent a disposition to regard the Act as "a great legislative achievement" and to overlook the crucial problem of continuing implementation.

Another factor was the post-war economizing that overtook the diplomatic establishment along with the rest of the federal government. Funds were not always available for the reforms proposed. The first director of the Foreign Service Institute, for example, made manful efforts to get that agency headed in the intended direction of an academy. He undertook a number of imaginative projects. However, he found himself confronted not only by a lack of funds but, in consequence, a dearth of officers who could be spared for educational and training programs. The survivors of the economy drive were too hard worked to have much time or energy for anything beyond the day's requirements. In two years, the first of FSI's long succession of rotating directors joined the Foreign Service and left for overseas. All along its broad front, reform eroded and crumbled.

During the ensuing period in which three secretaries presided over the Department, only General Marshall proved to be an organizational innovator. In a department still functioning as a coalition of those area dukedoms which Huntington Wilson had created, the General instituted a Central (now called an Executive) Secretariat to effect an orderly presentation of problems to him and a systematic follow-through on his decisions. He also set up a Policy Planning Staff.

General Marshall's influence upon his deputy, Dean

Acheson, and the latter's fortunate succession to the General made these innovations enduring reforms. But with policy planning understood neither by their successors nor underpinned by appropriate instruction in the Foreign Service Institute, "planning" never evolved in a way to meet the nation's global requirements. As for *diplomatic planning*, any that evolved was accidental and fragmentary.

When General Walter Bedell Smith entered the Department as deputy to Dulles, he was aghast to find that, after successfully pleading on Capitol Hill the cause of more adequate education and training, there were not enough officers to make the reform possible. Nor were there enough even to carry out the 1946 Act's principle of frequent departmental assignments. He resorted to the quick expedient of fusing the Civil and Foreign Services, an idea which had long simmered in Carr's and others' minds and had been recommended in 1950 by a committee of James H. Rowe, Congressman Robert Ramspeck and Ambassador William E. DeCourcy. Thus, Wristonization came about. Being executed by bludgeoning of people rather than by long-range planning and educational preparation, it stigmatized itself as less reform than recourse to chaos.

No effort at broad-scaled reform developed for fifteen years after the 1946 act. When the Kennedy Administration began, I talked with Adolph A. Berle about needed reforms and the usefulness of creating a group of practitioners and knowledgeable outsiders to undertake a broad-scaled study of the establishment's needs and come up with recommendations for action. Mr. Berle was close to the President and occupied an influential position in the Department. He passed the suggestion on to higher echelons. Perhaps others had the same thought. In any case, the Herter Committee was born. It was a kind of Steyne "Commission of Inquiry" but without either the departmental or interdepartmental underpinning which Mr. Steyne had imaginatively engineered. No State Department official and only one Foreign Service officer was included in the twelve-man committee. It not only met infrequently but its focus was largely limited to personnel problems, which was a good deal less than what was needed.

The Committee's report, *Personnel for the New Diplomacy*, presented to Secretary Rusk and published in December 1962, betrayed a formalistic, public-administration rather than a realistic, dynamic approach to *diplomacy*. It reflected little grasp of the art and none of the science of diplomacy. It had correspondingly limited impact and generated no reform movement. Its various staff reports, however, were published by the Carnegie Endowment for International Peace (which had helped to set up and fund the Committee). The reports assisted in keeping alive the Committee's rational approach to various personnel problems and shattering myths that had bedeviled establishment thinking over the years. Some of the reports were drawn upon by the Young Turks who emerged as a spearhead of reform five years later.

In the interim, a significant in-house reform effort developed independently of the Herter Committee when the post of Deputy Under Secretary for Administration went to William J. Crockett in 1963. Mr. Crockett had had five years in the Department and, before that, six years in the Foreign Service, all in administration. Earlier, he had acquired overseas exposure as an administrative representative of the Maritime Commission in Naples, and executive officer in Beirut for the Technical Cooperation Administration. Notwithstanding this seemingly limited experience, he had picked up a good working knowledge of foreign policy and diplomacy, and being endowed with a nimble, inventive, reform-oriented mind, he gave the faltering Kennedy effort to modernize the diplomatic establishment a second wind. For almost four years—from 1963 to 1967—Crockett sprinted hard. He imported management experts, created an Office of Management Planning, brought in consultants (who were sometimes, like myself, retired reformers) and pushed along a far-flung perimeter of modernization. But his reforms were frustrated by senior officers who felt that they had done well in the Service and resisted change, by the lack of a well-thought-out-plan of reform and by the failure of his superiors to give him needed support.

Crockett tried hard to carry out the Herter Committee's recommendation of bringing into a "family of compatible services" the various overseas corps of the government. But the recommendation stalled in Congress: Messrs. Rusk and Ball would not press for it, influential senior and retired Foreign Service officers lobbied against it. Weary and disheartened by all this, Crockett retired to the rewards of private industry. Once again, rotation of officers, resignations and retirements set in and dissipated patiently assembled staffs. The effort quickly disintegrated.

A group of Foreign Service officers, mostly mid-career but with a few senior and some junior, still believed reform had to be pressed. Lacking a base in the Department, they took over the American Foreign Service Association in 1967, and converted it into an instrument of reform. One of them took a leave of absence to devote full time to the Association's effort to produce a reform movement. A year of hard work on the part of all produced a study, "Toward a Modern Diplomacy," and collaboration in a volume of *The Annals* of the American Academy of Political and Social Science on "Resources and Needs of American Diplomacy." Copies of both publications went to various echelons of the Nixon staff immediately after the 1968 election, to Secretary William P. Rogers and Under Secretary Elliot Richardson, to the press, Congressmen and a broad sector of opinion makers.

Persuaded that reform should get under way, Mr. Richardson searched for a suitable Deputy Under Secretary of Administration and on October 3, 1969, William B. Macomber, Jr., Assistant Secretary for Congressional Relations, was installed.

Mr. Macomber had an impressive preparation for reform, perhaps not the least valuable part of which was his lack of identification with the Foreign Service. He had thus escaped its parochialisms, its defense mechanisms, its fear of efficiency reports and its inclination to routine performance. More positively, he had been thoroughly seasoned in the "new diplomacy." In 18 years of experience in public affairs he had served with the Central Intelligence Agency, with State as a Special Assistant to Secretary Dulles and Under Secretary Hoover, with Senator John S. Cooper as administrative assistant and back with State as Assistant Secretary for Congressional Relations. President John F. Kennedy decided that Mr. Macomber was a Republican he should retain and named him Ambassador to Jordan. Following that tour he was Assistant Administrator in the Agency for International Development for the Near East and South Asia, and then resumed his former responsibilities for State's relations on Capitol Hill.

With this background, buttressed by substantial studies and recommendations from thirteen task forces of 250 officers, and a solicitation of suggestions from overseas missions, what are Mr. Macomber's chances of pulling off meaningful reform?

In the light of the record of earlier reform efforts, I fear the chances are dim. Mr. Macomber has the support of his Secretary. That counts for something. However, Mr. Rogers is an unknown quantity as a reformer and his fulcrum at the White House on which to rest the lever of reform is, to say the least, of dubious solidity. John N. Irwin II, the new Under Secretary, like most of those who cluster at the Department summit, is a lawyer and the *genus advocatus* is not distinguished for its interest in organizational and management problems. Former Under Secretary Elliot Richardson is a rare type of the genus. His successor will have to go a far piece to equal Mr. Richardson's comprehension of both the importance and the precepts of good management and to give Macomber the kind of aggressive support he needs.

A factor to Macomber's advantage is that the 250 officers in the Task Force groups were the most broadly representative ever to analyze the diplomatic establishment and propose reforms. He is now implementing their proposals, not his, but he is free to choose the proposals he likes.

The task force exercise has had the salutary effect of educating the participants and, through the publication of their reports, many others. Therefore, all concerned see somewhat less subjectively both problems and options. Publication of the reports, which never had a parallel except in the cases of the Wriston and Herter Committees, will help ensure that they will not be buried. They are in the public domain, and therefore invite widespread and continuing support.

But inviting support is one thing. Providing leadership is another. How much of the latter will the Secretary and his deputy encourage and along what lines? Will it stop short, for example, of making the Secretary's Committee (the Senior Interdepartmental Group) a truly coordinating and integrating device? How much leadership will the President permit? He has people at his elbow who can pooh-pooh the whole thing or even cast doubt upon it as constituting a threat to his own position in foreign affairs, which would be a tragic misinterpretation of the effort.

Neither the Secretary nor his Deputy Under Secretary for Administration enjoys the easy access to the President which enabled earlier heads of the Department and their subordinates like Wilbur Carr to carry to the political summit their advocacy of improvements. Unlike Messrs. Carr, Stettinius and Holmes, Mr. Macomber cannot himself get to the President to cultivate that understanding and reassurance of what he is about, which could generate the support he badly needs in the battles he must inevitably wage with the Bureau of the Budget and on Capitol Hill. It would be helpful if Secretary Rogers saw to it that his associate acquired such access to the President.

While Mr. Macomber has standing and contacts on the Hill, it is doubtful if he has that quiet, sustained social relationship which proved so advantageous to Wilbur Carr. Representative John J. Rooney is also a factor. While Wilbur Carr eventually came to have his Rooney in the person of Congressman Edward T. Taylor, this was late in his career. Mr. Macomber has his Mr. Rooney here and now. One Congressman can check chances of maneuver on Capitol Hill. Here is an opportunity for the American Foreign Service Association to fortify the chances of reform on Capitol Hill, but the Association has not been so strikingly successful in developing close relations with members of Congress as to offer much hope of this. Extra-establishment groups to supplement Mr. Macomber's efforts are as essential as the National Civil Service Reform League and the National Board of Trade had been to Mr. Carr. But these are hard to find and harder still to get moving. The problem of finding or germinating an outside reform "constituency" is a real one for any aspiring reformer.

Reform leadership must not only be strong at the outset: it must continue so. This requires a tempering of our rotation fetish, certainly insofar as key positions of management are concerned. Diplomatic officers will have to be educated out of their predilection for the glamor of overseas service and brought down to the firm earth of political reality here at home. They must be brought to recognize that Washington inputs are as important to their profession as anything they do abroad and to put professional interests before personal.

This requires a far more rigorous education and training of truly professional character. No reform effort can produce desired results without a greatly strengthened, more dynamic Foreign Service Institute operating on a higher intellectual and professional level than heretofore. Such an Institute could do much to temper the dissipating effects of rotation which have eroded every reform effort after Mr. Carr's time.

If the Task Force—Macomber reports, along with others, were made required study by every incoming officer (civil servants included) with a thorough discussion of the proposals injected at all levels of our educational-training program, officers would have a clearer idea of what "reform" consists of, what objectives it must seek, and what kind of performance by them it exacts. Just as

Mr. Carr personally imbued officers with the spirit and meaning of his reforms, so Macomber must seek to do this by institutional means, since he and his associates are themselves subject to rotation. Only such efforts can reverse the all-too-prevalent inclination of officers to (1) put their own careers foremost, rather than professional standards of performance; (2) become immersed in substantive duties so that their intellectual energy is diverted from the basic needs of the establishment itself; and (3) overlook the steps they themselves must take to overcome the dissipating effects of rotation.

This review plainly suggests that reform is not a one-volley affair. It is a long, sustained series of reforms. It therefore demands the strategic planning and tactical follow-through that any campaign demands. This can only come from a continuing, high-level strategist and tactician high enough in the Departmental hierarchy to be the confidant of Secretaries and possibly Presidents. This official I think of as a "general manager" of the diplomatic establishment.

Although it is said that the Department has never had a "general manager" or "permanent under secretary," one, two or three men, as we have seen, have performed this role under 19 Administrations of varied political hue. These Administrations not only accepted the principle of continuity in administrative leadership—using that term in its broad sense—but found the practice so rewarding that they retained the individuals performing the role from 1852 to 1933, irrespective of their political affiliations. Even the New Deal, from 1933 to 1937, achieved in the diplomatic establishment a greater measure of administrative unity, in the narrow sense of housekeeping, than is generally appreciated. This was accomplished by continuing in the post of Assistant Secretary (for Administration) a knowledgeable civil servant willing and able to assume this responsibility.

Reform needs such a continuing, high-ranking official, or small team of officials, who share responsibilities for the formulation and implementation of foreign policy.

We have on our hands a large diplomatic establishment, a sprawling federal community involved in foreign affairs. A military organization crowds us in our overseas efforts. This is so largely because of its superior professionalism, action-mindedness, and relative organizational efficiency. Also it has reaserch capacity, linked to planning and to operations, and a general staff mode of conducting its operations. So does the Central Intelligence Agency. Somehow the diplomatic organization must achieve a comparable level of performance in these respects. If "reform" does not get to such basic needs through the device of a continuing "general manager," it will not get very far along the road it professes to seek.

Reforms must also reach to such basic issues as the respective roles in the development and execution of foreign policy of the diplomatic establishment and the President, the military establishment, other executive departments and agencies, the Congress and the public. Anything less stops short of the sweeping nature of the review and the "reform" now needed to cope with the issues of the times in which we live.

Furthermore, demand for social reform in American society is now making itself felt, for the first time in our history, in the diplomatic establishment. If one listens understandingly to Junior Foreign Service officers and mid-careerists who have formed the "Ad Hoc Committee" he can grasp how this penetration has occurred through the gradual democratization of the Foreign Service.

The views of these officers, and the emotional ways in which they are sometimes presented, attest to the completely new milieu in which the State Department and the Foreign Service must function. This is no passing phase; it is no evanescent storm which we have only to "ride out." If Mr. Macomber and AFSA do not institute the sweeping studies and reforms needed to bring our diplomatic establishment in tune with this demand, they are in—not for reform, as they intend—but for serious trouble.

It therefore seems to me that it would be a grave mistake to view the present era of reform only in the perspective

of the AFSA and the Rogers-Richardson-Macomber proposals. These are but responses to a profound ferment of
change in American society, such as occurred in the 1820's
and 1830's, in the long period from the 1870's to Woodrow Wilson's time, and after 1929. If I am correct in this,
we are on the rim of discovering a perspective of reform
which we have been seeking for many years but have never
consciously formulated and clearly thought through.
We are being pushed to do so now and those who would
lead would be wise not to permit their grasp of immediate
changes to limit their reach for the larger ones demanded
by the times.

# 14.

# NIXISSINGER DIPLOMACY

President Nixon's call for a Washington conference of the governments of oil-consuming countries followed by almost two months Dr. Kissinger's recommendation at the Pilgrims Society dinner in London that these nations make a concerted effort to meet the energy crisis. This delay in a time of serious crisis once again draws attention to the extraordinary way in which the foreign affairs of a world power are being conducted by the present Administration. Two secretive, anti-bureaucratic officials maintain such a stranglehold on those affairs that no policy can prosper—indeed, no decisions can be reached, no action initiated—until these two get together. Since one of them, in his theatrical way, conducts diplomacy like a trouper, these occasions occur only at great intervals; hence supporting moves for decisions or suggestions floated in the course of overseas performances are much delayed. When this manifests itself in a crisis of such far-ranging implications as a boycott of the United States by oil-producing countries, diplomacy becomes a matter of concern for every citizen.

The art of diplomacy was taken over by an organizational dimension during the period of the Great Depression and the ensuing World War II. The process of understanding other governments and people, gathering and analyzing information and views, reporting, persuading,

Reprinted with permission from *The Nation*, February 9, 1974.

and acting with respect to international problems became a large multichanneled activity running through the entire bureaucracy of national government. In our case, that of a large nation with interests as complex as they are far-reaching, an impelling need arose for the most systematic mobilization possible of the people and other resources demanded for efficient conduct of far-ranging foreign affairs. The aggressive efforts of other governments, proclaiming an intention to frustrate and in the end bury us, as well as destroy the independence of other peoples, have given this pursuit the importance of a peacetime mobilization for the diplomatic defense of the nation and of such other nations threatened by invasion or subversion as our resources enable us to assist.

This requirement and the responsibilities flowing from it cannot be met by a puny organization, such as traditional diplomats prefer, or a small coterie of intimate collaborators, such as President Nixon and Secretary Kissinger prefer, or a large, ill-managed body, such as we have had since World War II with the exception of the Marshall and Acheson periods. Good management, extending to the total resources of our government, is what is needed—the systematic, imaginative running of an extensive federal Establishment by people who are trained and creative in both diplomacy and management and therefore capable of insuring conditions of service favorable to the art of international maneuver. Organization poses the risk of stifling an art, so that the basic challenge of this new dimension in the conduct of foreign affairs is to effect the marriage of an art to management.

The present incumbent of the White House and his principal adviser on foreign affairs have paid not the slightest attention to this aspect of public affairs. Indeed, they are positively averse, if not hostile to the idea. In the spring of 1968, at the University of California, Los Angeles, Kissinger stated his own view:

> Because management of the bureaucracy takes so much energy and precisely because changing course is

so difficult, many of the most important decisions [by policy makers] are taken by extra-bureaucratic means. Some of the key decisions are kept to a very small circle while the bureaucracy happily continues working away in ignorance of the fact that decisions are being made, or of the fact that a decision is being made in a particular area. One reason for keeping the decisions to small groups is that when bureaucracies are so unwieldy and when their internal morale becomes a serious problem, an unpopular decision may be fought by brutal means, such as leaks to the press or to Congressional committees. Thus, the only way secrecy can be kept is to exclude from the making of the decision all those who are theoretically charged with carrying it out. There is, thus, small wonder for the many allegations of deliberate sabotage of certain American efforts, or of great cynicism of American efforts because of inconsistent actions. In the majority of cases this was due to the ignorance of certain parts of the bureaucracy, rather than to malevolent intent. Another result is that the relevant part of the bureaucracy, because it is being excluded from the making of a particular decision, continues with great intensity sending out cables, thereby distorting the effort with the best intentions in the world. You cannot stop them from doing this because you do not tell them what is going on.

This describes precisely the conduct of foreign affairs by Nixon and Kissinger. It also describes the German conduct of foreign affairs in the time of Kaiser Wilhelm II, to the great injury of German influence. The Kaiser, too, was fearful and distrustful of his bureaucracy. He circumvented it whenever he could, surprising it as well as the rest of the world with unexpected, often dazzling moves. He neither prepared the ground for moves by utilizing his diplomatic organization nor did he successfully employ it for follow-up purposes. He calculated on quick results, but these, being at the expense of his bureaucracy and of allies and friends, were nullified at home and abroad by those whose cooperation was needed to carry them out.

These characteristics of Nixissinger diplomacy, so evident in the opening to China, the conduct of relations with the Soviet Union and the handling of the Middle East war, have cropped up afresh in U.S. efforts to deal with the international aspects of the energy crisis—and glaringly so in that segment of it relating to the Arab oil boycott.

As long as the initial phase of this crisis lasted, Kissinger was in his element. He scurried dramatically from capital to capital to obtain quick, on-the-spot evaluations of what the Arab leaders had in their minds and what the Western European leaders had in theirs, sowing seeds of wisdom and restraint among the one and exploring in the other the possibilities of concerted action. By the time he reached London he was ready to spring his proposal at the Pilgrims Society dinner. He proposed that the Foreign Ministers of oil-consuming nations put their heads together, to see how they might devise a common approach to this common and critical problem.

So far, so good. Rapid and extensive soundings had led to a sound American initiative. What then? No doubt the Secretary of State had consulted the President about this—one is assured that he had—but no other part of the executive branch seems to have been either consulted or so much as tipped off. Hence, no part was able to follow through, and when embassies in Washington tried to do so from their side, they drew blanks. Both the State Department and the Federal Energy Office confessed they knew nothing of what Kissinger had in mind.

This being duly reported by embassies to their governments, Washington's ignorance was immediately diffused around the world in a "go-slow" signal. Widespread doubt was created as to how seriously the Kissinger proposal should be taken, and well before he got back to Washington his far-reaching proposal was no longer far-reaching. Initial momentum, so essential to getting new ideas off the ground, had failed to materialize.

That is a consequence of keeping key decisions "to a very small circle" which Professor Kissinger had overlooked when living the life of an academician. His proposal could not, by any stretch of the imagination, have been viewed as "an unpopular decision" requiring secrecy in order to avoid "brutal" bureaucratic objection. It was the kind of initiative for which the bureaucracy was looking and pleading. The "sabotage" and "cynicism" came not from the Washington bureaucracy but from those very governments whose cooperation was essential if any such concerting of consuming societies was to be achieved. That, too, is an angle which the sophisticated academician overlooked. He knows a great deal about the strategies and tactics of diplomacy, but nothing whatever about the national and personal sensibilities which are involved in the success of strategic and tactical moves.

In an imaginative move, reminiscent of its reaction to the suggestion for a concert of nations to reconstruct Europe twenty-six years ago, the British Government set to work studying the Kissinger proposal the very night it was made. But there was no one at the American Embassy in London or in the American Government in Washington to work with or even to offer any guidelines for a follow-up. The British could have been helpful and were obviously eager to be, but the embers of interest began to cool. Bureaucratic cynicism of a sort set in.

The Pompidou government, on the other hand, alert for any opportunity to repay Dr. Kissinger in kind for his cavalier neglect of Paris, as he has neglected many another capital of allies and friends in recent years, moved to scotch the American initiative. It made the counter-proposal that both consumer and producer countries be brought together to work on the oil problem, and it then proceeded, as did others, to take advantage of the hiatus to press for bilateral deals with interested Arab governments.

For their part, the OPEC governments preserved their own momentum by meeting again in Geneva in a counter-move to Kissinger. This enabled them to hold wavering participants in line, reaffirm their united front, decry any similar unison of effort on the part of the consuming societies, and thus to make the Kissinger move appear to be not a natural response to the national security needs of every consuming society but a hostile thrust at the Arabs themselves.

Nor did the chirpings from Washington officials about possible military intervention in the Near East assist the United States to regain momentum. On the contrary, they were so patently ridiculous in the light of our opposition to the Anglo-French-Israeli intervention in 1956, our distaste for overseas military adventure in the wake of Vietnam, and the crumbling coalition of the West that they actually weakened Kissinger's position, making every move by Washington and the West interpretable as an act of—or preliminary to—"aggression."

Thus, in the face of a serious threat to this country, with implications running to virtually every phase of our society, prima donna diplomacy has proven effective only in denying us the momentum of a sound and hopeful initiative. Once again, for want of any conception of what organizational resources mean to diplomacy in the 20th century, Kissinger's torch of leadership has burned from dazzling splendiferousness to spluttering inefficiency. It is indeed doubtful that the move, two months later, to convoke a conference three months later, still can recapture the promise of the original initiative.

It is interesting to compare this solo, anti-bureaucratic diplomacy with the kind that got the Marshall Plan quickly aloft. Secretary Marshall also took advantage of an occasion of rhetoric to make an important suggestion which led to the plan that bears his name. He did so at the Harvard commencement in 1947. But in that case exploratory work had already been carried out by the State Department, which was thus ready for questions and primed with suggestions as soon as the trial balloon was released. There was no time lag of ignorance and mystification; no doubts as to Marshall's seriousness; no opportunity for "deliberate sabotage" or "cynicism" to seep in. Communist opposition in Western European countries and Britain never got a chance for effective maneuver. The story was, of course, different in Eastern Europe, where the Soviet Union could pull wires within the governments; and in Prague the outcome was tragic for Jan Masaryk who, as Foreign Minister, was instrumental in prompting the Czech Government to respond favorably to Marshall's proposal. A Communist coup put an end not only to that but to Masaryk himself.

This was a very different order of diplomacy from that of Nixon and Kissinger. Marshall's was a modern, organized diplomacy, with an effective management of the diplomatic establishment so as to employ fully its resources at home and abroad. By contrast, the Nixon-Kissinger brand is an 18th—or at best a 19th—century affair, secretive at home and abroad, full of drama but short of results in any area where consistent, day-by-day, methodical follow-up is demanded. The outlook for our management of the international aspects of our oil and energy crises is therefore far from bright.

# 15.

# OUR DIPLOMATIC ESTABLISHMENT: LIGHTS AND SHADOWS OF FIFTY YEARS

*PREFATORY NOTE: The earlier analysis of the successes and failures of State Department reforms suggested the usefulness of a bibliographical essay, of which none was extant, reviewing books dealing with the State Department and Foreign Service. The opportunity of doing one was sparked when an article promised the* **Foreign Service Journal** *by Secretary of State Henry Kissinger in celebration of the fiftieth anniversary of the Rogers Act of 1924 failed to materialize and an invitation to fill the gap was extended to me. It provides a supplement to the essay on "Perspectives of Reform," as well as a vehicle for a long-needed tribute to Robert F. Kelley who innovated the four-year program of Russian studies in our Foreign Service which produced the George Kennans and Charles E. ("Chip") Bohlens.*

Only since World War II has material about and from the diplomatic establishment reached both impressive proportions and analytical character. It is extraordinary that as late as 1939 about all that existed in book form on the State Department was a genial, indulgent *Inside the Department of State* by the New York Times correspondent, Bertram Hulen; sympathetic volumes in the American Secretaries of State series edited by Samuel Flagg Bemis;

Reprinted with permission from *Foreign Service Journal,* October, 1974.

and a few other independent biographies of occupants of that position such as Tyler Dennett's of John Hay and Philip C. Jessup's of Elihu Root. On the Foreign Service, materials were harder to come by. Some familiarity was required with Congressional reports and the landmark study of the old National Civil Service Reform League, published in 1919 and prophetically entitled "Report on the Foreign Service." Of individual diplomatic officers, along with Dennett's Hay, Allan Nevin's biography of Henry White and Sir Harold Nicolson's of Dwight Morrow —the one a career officer, the other a political—stood as rarities; and memoirs by the officers themselves were few and scattered, defying any systematic triangulation of American diplomacy. Illustrative of these were Henry Lane Wilson's *Diplomatic Episodes in Mexico, Belgium and Chile* (1927), Hugh R. Wilson's *Education of a Diplomat* (1938) and the choice *Diplomatically Speaking* of Lloyd C. Griscom, which, appearing in 1940, deflected at least one university student to the Foreign Service. Astride biography and memoirs lay Burton J. Hendrick's charming *Life and Letters of Walter Hines Page* (1923). But the American conduct of diplomacy was by no means unexceptionably charming, as the memoir of Post Wheeler and his wife, *Dome of Many-Coloured Glass*, published in a later, post-war epoch attests.

Most of this literature, whether written by historians, biographers or practitioners, was concerned with the unilinear progression of events and careers. There was no exploration of the strategies, tactics, techniques and skills explanatory of the process of international politics. Views of diplomacy were presented akin to what military histories, studies and memoirs would offer of the military process if they omitted the guts of battles and wars—the strategies, which determined which battles and wars should be engaged in, and the tactics, logistics, organization and personal qualities determinative of outcome. It was all insightful and fascinating but it came, in sum, to meager fare.

Such was the history of the State Department published

by Graham H. Stuart in 1949. Appearing after World War II. *The Department of State* was a kind of 19th-century anachronism, providing interesting historical perspective but too little analysis of the serious policy-making and implementing problems the Department encountered over the years and particularly after 1933 to gain a wide reading public. It was sidelight-ish rather than penetrating and criticized in many quarters as an apology.

Seven years before the appearance of Stuart's history the unilinear treatment of our diplomatic establishment started to crumble. It began with Robert Bendiner's sharply critical and not exactly unbiased exposé, *Riddle of the State Department* (1942). It continued through Harold Stein's gutsy study of the internal battles within the State Department over the Foreign Service Act of 1946 (in his *Public Administration and Policy Development: A Case Book*, 1948), Bryton Barron's emotional *Inside the State Department* (1946), James L. McCamy's *The Administration of American Foreign Affairs* (1950), Robert E. Elder's balanced but limited *The Policy Machine* (1960) and my own *Anatomy of the State Department* (1967)—spanning exactly a quarter century. The State Department was concerned. It now became the focus of analysis seeking to portray how it works and why it slips.

Little of this new literature, however, set out to explain the Department in its entirety, in its overall functioning, much of the effort being expended on it as a policy-making body. This reflected the mesmerization of academicians with decision-making, to the neglect, almost total, of what happens to decisions once made. Indeed, there continues much inclination in the academic community to consider the policy contributions of the diplomatic and consular posts as either non-existent or inconsequential, these posts being, in the academicians' remote and inadequate view, simply dispatch centers. That community has therefore lagged behind the public in general in its understanding of diplomacy and diplomatic agencies. The Department—and even more the Foreign Service—continued to be to it something like Africa before the expeditions of David Livingstone, known rather by it external coastline and the configurations of its more conspicuous policymaking rivers than by its enormous interior tributary systems and human complexities. McCamy and I tried to break through these limitations, to explore the interior, including the culture and mentality of the hinterland inhabitants.

Thereafter came the loquacious *Fires in the In-Basket* of John P. Leacacos in 1968 and John Franklin Campbell's *The Foreign Affairs Fudge Factory* three years later.

An interesting light in this new development is that practitioners themselves have joined in the analysis of performance by the State Department and Foreign Service.

Government agencies have also joined in the light-casting expeditions, with the Hoover Commission leading off in 1949, the Bureau of the Budget and the Senate Foreign Relations Committee participating later through the Brookings Institution, and the State Department itself through various committees. All of this, however, came to fairly stilted, organizationally slanted studies. No one would have gained from them any familiarity with diplomacy or of the State Department as a diplomatic organism.

It was not until Huntington Wilson's *Memoirs of an Ex-Diplomat* (1945), Willard Beaulac's *Career Ambassador* (1951) and Joseph C. Grew's *Turbulent Era* (1952) that this familiarity began to evolve through full-length memoirs from Foreign Service ranks. They were supplemented by J. Rives Childs's *American Foreign Service* (1948), the first effort of a Foreign Service officer to explain what he does, but he made the mistake of writing it while on active service. The Department so censored it that Childs tried vainly to prevent its publication. Having subsidized the venture by giving the author a leave of absence, the establishment had its way. W. Wendell Blancké fared better in 1969 by awaiting retirement to publish *The Foreign Service of the United States*. Little known but apt was a case study of the psychological and ethical problems of a vice consul in Indonesia immediately after World War II which was included in Harold Stein's casebook mentioned above.

The Service of post-war years has not been a wholly new Service or of wholly new perspectives. It has harbored many carry-overs from the earlier side-line diplomacy which had demanded little more of practitioners than a pair of ears, a pair of legs to trot to Foreign Ministries, a pen, then a typewriter, and an ability to write in decipherable English. For the most part, these survivors were dilettantes, having sought appointment to satisfy a longing for travel, hunting opportunities, socializing with notables or simply the prestige of "diplomatic status." Alexander Kirk's remark that the reason he joined the Service was because his mother wanted diplomatic facilities of travel was one of his ironic remarks which contained a germ of truth. Even the better officers are acknowledging in their memoirs published in recent years that they entered the Service not from any professional interest in foreign policy or diplomacy but because they did not know what else to do.

Along with the dilettantes were some serious practitioners and with these came a subtle change in our diplomatic establishment, our diplomatic literature and thence the public relations of the establishment. This was brought about by the altered posture of international affairs in the American mind effected by World War I, which, in turn, brought international relations courses to American universities. To this development John M. Allison referred in his notable *Ambassador from the Prairie* (1973), reporting that he took one such course pioneered at the University of Nebraska by the well-known Norman L. Hill. University students were thus graduated with a serious interest in international problems and politics and as various of these wound their way into the Service serious diplomatic practitioners began to multiply. The founding of a School of Foreign Service at Georgetown in 1919 gave further impetus to this, as did the later establishment of the Fletcher School of Law and Diplomacy.

In addition, there were two farsighted realists within the diplomatic establishment who contributed notably to this evolution. One was Robert F. Kelley, who joined the consular service in 1922 and, having been a Russian specialist at Harvard, by a series of happy accidents shortly became chief of the Division of Eastern European Affairs in the Department. Anticipating the time when the United States would have diplomatic relations with the Soviet Union, he initiated a four-year program of Russian studies abroad—in the cultural and political environment of Europe, to provide greater realism—with subsequent tours of duty as close to the Soviet Union as officers could be posted. This was the program which produced the George Kennans and Charles E. Bohlens who thereby acquired something significant—and even profound—to write about. Through the efforts of a colleague interested in professionalism in U.S. diplomacy, they got the kind of education which fitted them to recognize the significant and profound in Soviet-American relations.

The other was Prentiss Gilbert, the first and only U.S. Observer to the League of Nations. Gilbert was independent-minded, original, hostile to cliché thinking. He had had broad experience, understood international politics and, highly distrustful of the residual Wilsonian idealism in the American view of diplomacy, used his assignment in Geneva to educate and train younger colleagues on his staff in the international maneuvers which enmeshed and manipulated the League. From that realistic, farsighted effort came outstanding officers like James W. Riddleberger, Llewellyn Thompson and Jacob D. Beam.

Such are the factors which account for the emergence of a light drizzle of literature by career diplomatic officers in the 1940s and 1950s, including George Kennan's *American Diplomacy, 1900-1950* (1951). This falling weather, which gradually became a brisk shower and is now approaching a downpour, has ranged from the first full-length memoir of a long-term Foreign Service officer —Beaulac's—to Donald Dunham's collection of delightful vignettes (*Envoy Unextraordinary*, 1944), Cecil Lyon's *The Lyon's Share* (1973) and Bartley Yost's *Memoirs of a Consul* (1955). Within this range have fallen other full-length memoirs of long-termers—from Post Wheeler and his wife, Hallie Erminie Rives (a cousin of J. Rives Childs), Grew, Robert Murphy, Kennan, Bohlen, Allison—and more limited reminiscences from Ellis O. Briggs (*Farewell to Foggy Bottom*, 1964), Waldemar Gallman (*Iraq under General Nuri*, 1964), Henry S. Villard (*Affairs at State*, 1965) and Philip Bonsal's (*Cuba, Castro and the United States*, 1971) recounting special aspects or periods of diplomatic experience. The Wheeler-Rives memoir, *Dome of Many-Coloured Glass* (1955), is unique for its husband-wife collaboration, each contributing alternating chapters, and for its blazing candor. Both of them writers of distinction—he a one-time journalist and she a novelist with best sellers to her credit—their book is a kind of diplomatic *Gone With the Wind* of 860 spellbinding pages, too candid, it seems, regarding the rivalries and jealousies which wracked the Service to have been reviewable in the *Foreign Service Journal*, but it added to public enlightenment as well as literary diversion.

In addition to the expanding literature of our career practitioners, who possess more than fleeting experiences and fugitive judgments, has been a spilling downpour from political appointees and this, too, has been of great range, from such shockingly superficial and distorted memoirs as Joseph E. Davies's *Mission to Moscow* (1941), which he saw to it was made into a movie, to the solid and illuminating Carlton J. H. Hayes's *Wartime Mission in Spain, 1942-1945* (1945), Stanton Griffis's *Lying in State* (1952), Claude G. Bowers's *My Mission to Spain: Watching the Rehearsal for World War II* (1954) and *Chile Through Embassy Windows, 1939-1953* (1958), along with Chester Bowles's *Ambassador's Report* (1954), John H. Morrow's *First American Ambassador to Guinea* (1967), J. Kenneth Galbraith's *Ambassador's Journal* (1969) and Spruille Braden's *Diplomats and Demagogues* (1971)—all presenting the overseas aspect of diplomacy. Such memoirs as Roger Hilsman's *To Move a Nation* (1967) and Charles Frankel's *High on Foggy Bottom*, two years later, dealt with the Department.

From three Secretaries of State since World War II have

come meaty memoirs. Cordell Hull in two volumes (1948), James F. Byrnes in one slim volume, *Speaking Frankly* (1947) and Dean Acheson. All have dealt not only with the diplomatic establishment and its problems in Washington but its overseas involvement and problems as well, although far less than one would have hoped with the crucial organizational-management dimension and its impact upon the efficacy of embassies and consular posts in the diplomatic process.

Dean Acheson, of course, occupies a unique place in all this and so do his memoirs. Although not a careerist by mode of appointment, he was one in fact and he had the advantage of a two-year tutelage in strategic thinking and organizational management under his predecessor, General Marshall. A warmer, wittier, more humane chief we have never had and his *Present at the Creation* (1969) stands alone in its sharp definition of policy decisions and executory moves in terms of strategies, tactics, techniques and personal qualities—a model of sharp memoir writing and a rebuke to those who think of diplomacy as simply an art and not one of the social sciences.

Our diplomacy of aid—and economic diplomacy in general—has received little attention. No memoir of our informational and cultural diplomacy exists, so far as I am aware, except John Mecklin's *Mission in Torment* (1965) describing our Saigon Mission. Of the memoirs and studies of our Southeast Asian fiasco, relatively few have focused on our diplomatic performance. Of these, three of the more sharply illuminating are Chester L. Cooper's *The Lost Crusade: America In Vietnam* (1970), Edward G. Lansdale's *In the Midst of Wars* (1972) and David Halberstam's *The Best and the Brightest* (1972).

Some additional features of this period have been the appearance of the novel on diplomacy (including that analysis of our Southeast Asian diplomacy in the guise of a novel, *The Ugly American*, which appeared in 1958, two years after Graham Greene's *The Quiet American*, both focused on Ed Lansdale, whose memoir was earlier mentioned); the first full-length portrayal of a State Department civil servant (Katharine Crane's *Mr. Carr of State: Forty-seven Years in the Department of State*, 1960); the appearance in 1967 of Max Savelle's pioneering and exhaustive study of *The Origins of American Diplomacy: The International History of Anglo-America, 1492-1763*; studies of the diplomatic roles of the President and Secretary of State; books on negotiating with communist regimes; and serious efforts to grapple with diplomacy as a political science.

Among the latter, several pioneering and landmark studies have attested to our growing interest in our planetary relations. These have included the one solid historical study of our diplomatic service, Warren F. Ilchman's *Professional Diplomacy in the United States, 1779-1939: A Study in Administrative History* (1961) which is more than its subtitle suggests; Graham H. Stuart's unique *American Diplomatic and Consular Practice* (rev. 1952), which is a political science approach to diplomacy and consular work; and Charles W. Thayer's *Diplomat* (1959), the first effort of a Foreign Service officer to essay a political science analysis of his calling. Coming eleven years after Rives Child's more limited study, it is truly a notable attempt to conceptualize diplomacy in modern terms. It has not supplanted but it is far more realistic and up-to-date than Harold Nicolson's *Diplomacy*.

John E. Harr's *The Professional Diplomat* (1969) has an excellent opening chapter on the declared subject before getting into organizational problems and the Crockett reforms. It provides material post-Ilchman, as do studies emanating from the Herter Committee in the early 1960s and the book on which Frederick C. Mosher and Harr collaborated concerning the effort to introduce systems analysis into the diplomatic establishment (*Programming Systems and Foreign Affairs Leadership*, 1970). The extraordinary surge of American interest has thus assaulted much of the periphery of diplomacy excepting the one segment on which Acheson alone has ventured. More works could be cited but the limitations of space compel an invitation to be extended to the avid reader to repair to the bibliographies of Robert B. Harmon (*The Art and Practice of Diplomacy: A Selected and Annotated Guide*, 1971), Richard Fyfe Boyce and Katherine Randall Boyce (*American Foreign Service Authors. A Bibliography*, 1973), and Elmer Plischke (in my *Instruction in Diplomacy: The Liberal Arts Approach*, 1972). The fact that bibliographies have at last become available is a sign of the change which has overtaken us.

Mention of that volume on *Instruction in Diplomacy* merits a few words of amplification, for it, too, is a landmark, which I do not hesitate to say, for I was only the editor and one contributor, it being the product of many minds. It evolved from a two-day meeting in Philadelphia sponsored by the American Academy of Political and Social Science to bring together scholars and practitioners for a concerted effort to analyze diplomacy, define it in accurate terms and examine whether it should be taught as an integral part of the liberal arts program of our institutions of higher learning. No such effort had ever been undertaken before and it raised the question sharply whether diplomacy is indeed susceptible to a scientific approach. The consensus was that it certainly is.

The *Foreign Service Journal* itself has reflected these changes in attitude. If its pages are not so copious as one would have expected and hoped, they at least have reflected growing skepticism, un-ease and willingness to question. I have no doubt that if Wheeler and Rives were to publish *Dome of Many-Coloured Glass* today, the *Journal* would review it.

Anyone must ask how much of this downpour has sunk into general consciousness or indeed into his own and how much has run off the surface, outstripping the time and capacity of both public and practitioner to absorb it? I have no doubt that it has run off a good part of the diplomatic community. Our failure to professionalize our calling and therefore to require some familiarity with its literature for admission and the shocking failure to utilize to this end the introductory "orientation" of newly commissioned officers at the Foreign Service Institute has produced a hardly literate Foreign Service. Apart from this is the fact that officers, once on duty, are too driven in their daily tasks to do much reading and the funding of sabbaticals has hardly been high on the list of departmental budget priorities so that a "year off" to catch up a bit has reached only a pitiful fraction of the total corps.

As far as the academic community is concerned, I am constantly astonished at professional meetings of political scientists to find how little of this literature has been absorbed. The product of a prestigious graduate school in foreign affairs who is now teaching university courses in international relations asked me the other day: "What do diplomats *do?*" An answer to this has been available for some time if one will read such books as those mentioned above, but academic minds are too channeled to other fields than diplomacy. Diplomacy being rarely taught in our institutions of higher learning except in unilinear form by history departments means that there is little learning, higher or any other, about diplomacy.

Perhaps, in the next fifty years, this will change and the *Foreign Service Journal* on that occasion will have more to celebrate than an amplitude of materials explicatory of our calling. Perhaps by then we may even have professionalized our diplomacy and our political officers will see it as primarily political action with political reporting and analysis assuming their proper place as supplementary to action rather than as now their principal functions.

# 16.

# THE OVERSEAS PROJECTION: REFLECTIONS ON CHINA AND OTHER HANDS

The epitaph which John Keats proposed for himself, in despair, at the close of his short life—"here lies one whose name was writ in water"—is one which many American diplomats have considered peculiarly apt for them. Not only have their careers and accomplishments been writ across water; but, despite their involvement in an important, fascinating, and exciting occupation, seemingly in it: no one for a long time paid much attention to them. From this watery erasure they have been little by little rescued in the last quarter century as their country, swept into the endless typhoon of international politics, acquired crucial and worldwide responsibilities. Among the increasing number of books by and about American diplomatic officers and diplomacy itself are recent ones writ not in water but in witch hunt and war. E. J. Kahn, Jr. on *The China Hands* and Harold J. Noble on the tribulations of Embassy Seoul during the North Korean invasion are exemplary of these. And no one need be reminded of the persistent newspaper reports which add other accounts in blood.

Two hundred and sixty years ago, the acute Francois de Callières concluded his treatise on diplomacy by noting that disappointments in life await everyone, but "in no profession are disappointments so amply outweighed by such rich opportunities as in the practice of diplomacy." Opportunities to do what? To serve one's country and,

---

This essay-review originally appeared in the *Virginia Quarterly Review*, Spring 1976 (Vol. 52, No. 2), under the title: "American Diplomacy: Water, Witch Hunt, War and Blood."

if his government is so oriented, to serve the combined causes of truth, international understanding, and peace. Thus, in the end, to serve civilization itself.

This may seem quite enough and so, it appears, thought some of our diplomatic officers of a generation ago, who devoted themselves to Chinese affairs. But there are responsibilities so closely intertwined with opportunities as to be inseparable from them and thus affect and even determine the nature of the opportunities themselves—to conduct oneself with skill, discretion, and an uncommon amount of common sense not only in a wholly different culture and sometimes historical period, thousands of miles away from one's own headquarters, but with respect to those very headquarters, so as to win the respect and confidence of two different governments—the host and one's own. This is not easy. Learning, political instinct, wisdom, and finesse, are required—sophistication, in a word—and they are as much the name of the game as opportunity.

I will avoid the temptation to excoriate the scurrilous and un-American witch hunt to which the McCarran-McCarthy-Hurley-Nixon-Chambers-Budenz crowd resorted in pursuing a perfectly legitimate question as to the reporting, conduct, and philosophic beliefs of American diplomatic representatives. Kahn has done so with a brilliance which will grip every reader from his first to his last page.

But neither will I succumb to the tempting conclusion to which the victims (and their defenders, including Kahn) have surrendered that this is all there is to their experience. Two myths were engendered by the witch hunt. One was that the China Hands and confederates in the State Department lost China and did so because, as Communists or Communist sympathizers, they secretly wanted this to occur and contributed whatever they could to bring it about. That was nonsense, without one iota of truth to blemish it. The other myth is pithily put by Professor John K. Fairbank in his dust-cover comment on Kahn's book, *viz.* the China Hands were hounded out of the diplomatic service "because China's revolution proceeded as they correctly foresaw it would." On this premise, Kahn's book, Fairbank says, "has the story." It hasn't. Persecuted, treated atrociously by some so-called "loyalty security boards," deserted by all but an exceptional colleague, and hounded out of the Foreign Service some of the China Hands were; others escaped first-degree burns and survived but were forever mutilated in their careers; while still others went on to scale the heights. What accounts for these differences? The Kahns, Fairbanks, *et al.* are diverting us from the answer, which exacts a refined analysis of what diplomacy is, how well the China Hands performed in that arduous and risky calling, and how effectively the State Department and Presidents assisted them. The period was not simply one of McCarthyism; it was a period of gross diplomatic inadequacy with respect to China.

By taking one of the victims as an example, John S. Service, on whom Kahn focuses much of his attention, perhaps I may make my meaning clear in limited space. Service I do not know, but by all accounts he is one of the most decent, self-effacing, considerate, and—insofar as China is concerned—learned and perceptive of humans. But he had serious limitations, and the State Department did nothing whatever to detect and stimulate or assist him in overcoming them. President Roosevelt added to his burdens and risks by appointing a blundering, egocentric dunce of a general as his special representative and then as ambassador in Chungking. All of this was during a war, and it all exposed Service—and his government— to extraordinarily complex demands.

Like another victim, John Paton Davies, Jr., Service had been born and reared in China, the son of missionaries. He had spent little time in this country and knew little of it. Washington was less familiar to him than Kunming, Peking, Shanghai, Chungking, or Yenan. He knew little or nothing about it until, after a decade of service in China, he was assigned to the State Department and promptly committed a grievous error which set the FBI and the

McCarran-McCarthy-Hurley wolves on his trail. He never received the slightest professional introduction to diplomacy nor even a briefing on the Foreign Service, the State Department, and the foreign affairs community of which Congress is a part. During his decade in China, continuing virtually a lifelong expatriation, Service was from twenty-six to thirty-six years of age. Twenty-six to thirty is not exactly a ripe age for involvement in one of the more hellish of American foreign policy situations. Furthermore, in that decade, he was not on the embassy staff, advised and tutored by seasoned colleagues, but served as a young, free-wheeling political adviser to General Stilwell.

Far more knowledgeable and perceptive of China than of his own country, Service contributed to Washington an extraordinary reporting—brilliant at times—of conditions, developments, and likely outcomes, but nothing in Kahn's study indicates that he took the most elementary precautions to ensure that his reporting was "getting through" in Washington. Kahn does not tell us, for instance, whether Service used any of the familiar devices by which Foreign Service officers keep their Departmental colleagues posted on what they are doing, their problems, the complexities of judgment with which they are confronted and thus encourage, in return, information on the drifts of Departmental and White House thinking and moves, political cross-currents, comments "up the line" on what he is doing, and the like. Coming into our diplomatic establishment as he did, an untutored, unprofessional expatriate, he may never have known that such devices or practices existed or appreciated the wisdom of using them. It would have been a miracle if all of this appalling slackness had not resulted in serious trouble.

Moreover, conditions being what they were in China, Service sometimes reported in haste, often on impulse. This can induce the most perceptive reporting and also the riskiest. At times, as Kahn says of one memorandum to Washington, his reporting and policy advice found expression in an "emotional" document, and Service conceded it was composed in "some haste and heat." A diplomatic officer who does not retain his "cool" is in for trouble. That particular memorandum, as things turned out, proved critical to Service's fortunes. A diplomat is not simply a reporter, nor precisely a political scientist, as the Kahns and Fairbanks would have us believe. He is a political operator, a government adviser and persuader as well, and this is what makes his calling so exacting and at times so hazardous. If he considers his government's policy wrong, as Service did, he must exercise all the greater care in choosing his rhetoric.

Service's use of the term "democracy" in describing Mao Tse-tung's Communist movement poignantly suggests this lack of care. Time and again he insisted that the "widespread popular support" which the Communists had achieved "must be considered a practical indication that the policies and method of the Chinese Communists have a democratic character." "Democratic"? In what sense? In the sense in which an ordinary American would construe it, this would be considered naive at best, betraying a complete misconception—or nonconception—of Communist philosophy. So, too, with language indicating that Chinese Communist policy toward the United States was "and will remain one of extending cooperation regardless of American action." Kahn relates the experience of another career officer who served in China at the time, John Carter Vincent (who was also hounded out of the Foreign Service) when interrogated by a congressional committee later. He was asked what he knew about Mao and Communism. Vincent, who had served for years in China and wound up there as the Number Two officer in Embassy Chunking, responded that he had never met Mao, had never read anything by or about him, and was virtually illiterate on the subject of Communism generally. Kahn tells this with great glee, as though the officer scored a coup to the committee's embarrassment. It was, in fact, no coup at all and can only be viewed as an extraordinary confession of unprofessionalism reflecting embarrassingly upon both the officer and the Department.

Another indiscreet and imprecise practice indulged in

by Service was in the use of "fascist" and "nazi" in referring to Chiang Kai-shek's regime. There was no advantage
and only considerable emotional risks in resorting to Western terms to describe an Oriental authoritarian regime.
Not only had these become terms of opprobrium and
therefore emotionally loaded but there were significant
differences between the Western and Asian regimes.

"Representation," a diplomat has written, "is the
term used to describe a diplomat's efforts to demonstrate
through his personality, manners, hospitality, and erudition the admirable qualities of his country and thus of
the advantage of maintaining close friendly relations with
it." What of the advantage to all concerned of maintaining close friendly relations with visiting congressmen?
This is dictated by not only common sense but considerations of national security, not to say the political instinct
of self-preservation.

Unfortunately, Kahn's narrative is a mixture of fact and
fancy and cannot be wholly relied upon for inferences as
to the conduct of the China Hands. For instance, he
purports to relate what happened in Chungking when
Congressman Walter H. Judd showed up there on a visit
toward the end of 1944. Judd had been a medical missionary in China, considered he knew all there was to be
known about the country, and was an endless monologist
when he got started. Kahn writes: "When he [Judd]
turned up, a State Department functionary detailed to
look after him begged all the American officials on the
scene to be nice to him, but the more the diplomats
thought about it the madder they got. One night when a
few of them were supposed to have dinner with him they
stood him up; convening instead in a room just above
*his* room, they sang in what they hoped was a carrying
voice, 'Poor Jud is dead.' "

It seems that these were not "diplomats" but OWI
officers, Judd was not accompanied by a State Department
escort and it was the OWI chief who asked his staff to be
polite to Judd. The Congressman was not stood up but,
after listening for a long while to his well-known views on

China, some of the staff excused themselves and there-upon did their convening and singing in the room above. Had these indeed been Foreign Service officers—China Hands—this would have been a shocking instance of skewed conduct.

Macomber has a whole chapter in his *Angels' Game* on the diplomat's relations with Congress. It contains nothing novel or esoteric, just plain sense, none of which some of the OWI Hands seemed to have possessed, at least in this instance. Such deliberate antagonism of an influential Chiang supporter in the Congress could only fortify any suspicion that he might have had that American representatives in China were a heedless, reckless, undisciplined lot. It was just this suspicion which came to permeate Washington and made it difficult for colleagues of the China Hands to come to their defense when the walls caved in.

Diplomacy has always been, at least in modern times, a profession of professions, a calling of callings—of politics and political science, of military science, law, journalism, economics, history, philosophy, public relations, and almost anything else one can think of (a calling of the Renaissance man). So Harold Noble's preparation was remarkably apt. Born and reared in Korea, he got his doctorate in this country, spent some years in university teaching on the West Coast, served in the U.S. Marine Corps during World War II, became a migratory journalist in Asia and shifted to government service with the U.S. occupation authorities in Japan and Korea, where he wound up as political adviser to Lt. Gen. John H. Hodges in Korea. He was attached to the U.S. delegation to the U.N. General Assembly meeting in 1948 and then, at Ambassador John Muccio's request, joined Muccio's embassy in Seoul as first secretary.

The record which Noble kept of the embassy's experience during the North Korean invasion provided the material for *Embassy at War*, a first-class account greatly enriched by the extensive notes of Frank Baldwin. Noble's Korean background, as the Chinese background of such

China Hands as Service and Davies, gave him a command of the indigenous language and insights possessed by no other member of the embassy staff and, together with his family's relationship with Syngman Rhee—Noble's father had taught Rhee—brought the American mission a ready and invaluable entrée to the irascible President. His record, therefore, throws revealing light on what well-qualified first secretaries can do as negotiators and persuaders of heads of state that ambassadors sometimes cannot and demonstrates the absurdity of Sir Harold Nicolson's contention that diplomacy is a written rather than a verbal art.

William Macomber only gently contests that absurdity, but his book is a thoroughly modern discussion, moving through the thickets of verbal and written diplomacy with an almost augustan dignity. As Horace observed, a classic must be interesting as well as instructive and Macomber, who is a first-class diplomatic operator, could have made his *opus* a *magnum* had he kept this in mind and reduced his abstractions to the living world, as Charles W. Thayer did in *Diplomat*. He does not so much as obliquely refer to the China Hands although their experiences and tribulations are poignantly apropos of many of his generalities.

These various studies are of a piece, attesting how times have changed and how impossible it is for the careers, accomplishments, and failures of American diplomats and diplomacy itself ever again to be writ in water, least of all when the only available water is of tears of regret.

## 17.

# OF TRIBES AND TRIBULATIONS
# IN SOUTHERN AFRICA

One of the problems which all governments face with respect to Africa is that the arbitrary boundaries which empire builders carved out of the African continent in the 19th century had no relation to tribal distribution. Hence, the proliferation of putative nation states in recent years on that continent has generated not a system of nation states but an ethnic wonderland.

While some tribes were divided between colonial tracts, as was the ancient Kingdom of Congo between French, Belgian and Portuguese holdings, others were bunched together in uneasy colonial units. Nigeria consists of no less than 200 tribes, each with its own roots, history, culture and language or dialect, greatly complicating communication, governance, education and nation-building within that state. When one of its tribes—the Ibo—became such a target of discrimination and persecution as to threaten genocide, it tried to withdraw from the Nigerian union and form an independent Biafra. To have allowed the Ibos to do this would have been to invite others to do so, hence Biafra was mercilessly beaten into submission, its population decimated in the process. Virtually every African state is an affirmation of this uneasy tribal alliance and a negation of that common history, culture,

Reprinted with permission from *Foreign Service Journal*, December 1978 (Vol. 55, No. 12).

language, loyalty and aspiration which characterize nation-hood.

Tribal rivalries and fears can reach atrocious levels, as in Uganda, raising up leaders who, like Attila the Hun 1500 years ago, behave more like beasts than humans. Idi Amin is of the Kakwa tribe and his Attilian terror has been vented upon the other tribes of that unhappy land, principally the luckless Lango. As an army officer pursuing a military career, Amin found that his principal rival was Shaban Opalato, a Lango, and, when he decided to seize power, the president he had to depose was Milton Obote, also a Lango. Of the thousands Amin has seized, tortured, mutilated, burned alive, cast into rivers for crocodiles to feed upon and otherwise disposed of since his coup, many have been Lango. Some two-thirds of the Langi and Acholi soldiers in the Uganda army have been murdered and even their widows and children have been butchered. Amin's objective has not been merely to seize power through primitive tribal savagery but to maintain that power for life.

The dictators of the newly independent black African countries are soldiers waging war—tribal war—upon rival tribes and tribal leaders within their borders in an effort to hold together by force the disparate parts of their inherited tracts. Hence, their behavior, so bizarre and incomprehensible to Americans, including the Andrew Youngs who try to understand Africa by superimposing upon it their civil rights experience in the United States, is not only tolerated by other African leaders but accepted as normal. They have the same tribal emotions, fears, rivalries and problems at home as Amin and while Amin is an exaggerated and monstrous case, he is still understandable and acceptable as a tribal phenomenon. This explains why Africans will not condemn him and his behavior at meetings of the Organization of African Unity or the United Nations. Whatever the U.N. Charter or U.N. declarations and treaties may say about human rights, tribal standards hold among Africans. Tribal rights and interests take precedence.

It is in this perspective that one must view the Rhodesian problem. That land, also, is a tribal patchwork, although not to the degree of some others like Nigeria and Zaire. It is Joshua Nkomo's thirst for power as a member of the minority Matebele tribe that leads him to reject all suggestions of a free election to determine the composition of a Rhodesian government. He knows he would be outvoted every time by the dominant Shonas to which belong the black leaders who have joined Ian Smith's government in an Interim Agreement to hold an election. All talk of "one man, one vote" and "black majority rule" is as irrelevant to the guerrilla fighter based in the bush of Zambia as it would have been to Fidel Castro in the sierras of Cuba. Nkomo wants, as Castro wanted, power and he knows he cannot obtain it without imposing by force the rule of a minority tribe upon a majority. His guerrillas are not "Rhodesian" blacks simply rebelling against white rule and willing to set up a "one man, one vote," "black majority" regime but Matebeles willing to do battle for tribal dictatorship.

This is also true of Robert Mugabe who leads the guerrillas based upon Mozambique. For while he is a Shona, Mugabe belongs to a small subdivision of the tribe and he has never had the support of its major subdivisions. Hence, he too would be outvoted in any election. He wants no part of the "one man, one vote" or "black majority rule" which have become the stated objectives—or shibboleths—of American and British policy.

These are, therefore, not "black nationalists" seeking the liberation of Rhodesia from white domination but black tribalists vying for tribal or personal dominance of a new Zimbabwe. Neither of the guerrilla leaders, nor the two together, comprise any "national liberation movement" which the Soviets profess to be supporting around the world but are efforts of tribal leaders or would-be leaders which the Soviets, Cubans and Chinese are exploiting for their own interests, among which is the humiliation of the West which has done so much to elevate living standards and political standards and processes in Africa as elsewhere in the world. What is going on is a power play and no one can dress it up otherwise.

This is why, as Julius Nyerere complains, it has been impossible to fuse the forces of the two rebel movements. Nyerere has publicly wrung his hands over this but he knows the reason as well as anyone. Being tribally consti- tuted and engaged in a winner-take-all thrust for power, neither of the rebel forces is going to join hands with the other, any more than it is going to join hands with the moderate leaders in Salisbury on the basis of one man, one vote. It has therefore been obvious to all but the blind that a bloody civil war between the two "liberation" rivals will follow any collapse of the Interim Government.

This situation—and what has happened in other black African states—confronts the Shona and white populations of Rhodesia-Zimbabwe with a grim prospect, especially since the west has refused to provide them weapons with which to defend themselves against the Soviet-Cuban- Chinese-equipped guerrillas. Our reluctance to support the Interim Agreement has derived from a hope against hope of winning Nkomo and Mugabe over to "one man, one vote" and "black majority rule" and a desire to avoid any act which would precipitate an escalation of the con- flict. This is a delaying tactic to gain time for the medi- atory effort, on the slim chance something might happen to overcome the tribal factor, or at least postpone the day of holocaust. One might question whether the available guerrillas could absorb any marked increase of Soviet and Chinese arms, but there has always existed the possi- bility of Cuban troops intervening as they have done in Angola and Ethiopia.

An objective of victory presupposes that a tactic of delay is related to a positive strategy which the tactic will serve, but so far as one can ascertain there is no such US or western strategy, only a Micawber-like hope that "something will turn up." We are thus as paralyzed in Rhodesia as were the British and French vis-à-vis the Axis in the Spanish civil war. In the interests of promoting détente and avoiding an escalation of the Spanish conflict, the British and French governments abstained from intervention while the Nazi and Fascist governments exploited this, intervening to their heart's content and thereby ensuring the victory of Franco and contributing to the slide to World War II.

What applies to our approach to Rhodesia applies to our approach to southern Africa generally. The absence of a positive, clearly defined objective has deprived the United States of a well thought out, dynamic system of tactics and wise deployment of personnel resources. With the region belatedly recognized as a critical one in the waning years of the Ford administration, the present administration came to power determined to reverse the tide that had set in against us, but its first move was to appoint an ambassador to the U.N. totally bereft of international experience and therefore unable to contribute to our strategic and tactical thinking. He was able to establish an emotional rapport with African leaders but, possessing only naive ideas of what our policies should be, relying for advice on a hand-picked assistant secretary of state for international organization affairs, as devoid as he of any practical knowledge of Africa and international politics and beset by an inclination to shoot glibly from the lip, he and his diplomatic efforts have been faulted by successive errors of judgment and faux pas, eroding respect for U.S. diplomacy throughout the world.

The administration then proceeded to ease out an assistant secretary for African affairs familiar with the continent and its leaders, to create the appearance of a break with the Ford-Kissinger policy, and appointed as his replacement an individual with only the most superficial acquaintanceship with Africa. Appointments were made to the national security and policy planning staffs of African "experts" who were not experts at all. When an astute, knowledgeable, experienced director of the State Department's office of southern African affairs was elevated to deputy assistant secretary, his replacement was lifted from Belgrade; he lasted but a short time and was transferred to the Foreign Service Institute; and this crucial office at this time of writing is without a director. In the midst of these changes, as the Rhodesian crisis intensified, the experienced and able Rhodesian desk officer in the department was replaced by one with no prior background in Rhodesian affairs. All of this would make anyone wonder if we know what we are doing. It certainly ensured that the initiative in Africa would continue to be with the Communist triad.

Beneath these obvious inadequacies lie more subtle and profound ones. The Foreign Service Institute long ago abandoned the efforts of President Kennedy and Governor Mennen Williams to upgrade our African expertise, with the result that too many officers and their spouses in our African embassies and consular posts are finding their assignments boring and depressing. African cities and towns can indeed be dirty, usual social and cultural amenities lacking, and tribes dominant in capitals aloof and even hostile. Instead of being stimulated by this cultural challenge, officers are resisting assignments to Africa and the bureau of African affairs is finding it difficult to achieve a suitably high level of competence and performance in our missions. Faced by this the department and ambassadors, even some of the best, are doing virtually nothing to provide the needed cultural leadership. Since attitudes of officers and their spouses are readily sensed by people abroad, our political efforts are seriously handicapped and will continue to be until a more sophisticated cultural and psychological leadership is provided.

The department has also been remiss in not reviving the imaginative innovation of Mennen Williams in the early 1960s of an advisory committee on Africa. When we face serious and bloody crises, surely it is wise to mobilize all possible intellectual and cultural resources.

Our powerful rival, the Soviet Union, engages in no such slap-happy diplomacy and reliance upon amateurs. It has a driving strategy, to which every tactical move and personnel resource is related. Furthermore, being itself a state of ethnic diversity held together by oppression, it sympathetically encourages black Africa's propensity for oppression. For these reasons, black African leaders are seeing the Soviet Union as a model and leader rather than the United States or any other Western country except perhaps France, whose astute diplomacy has generated an extraordinary influence with almost all of its former equatorial colonies. In considering our options, we would do well to study that accomplishment.

Along with these factors there has continued a public and emotional badgering of South Africa whose help we have equally consistently, albeit more quietly, solicited in efforts to find a solution to the Rhodesian problem. This has represented anything but skillful diplomacy and has certainly not been in our strategic interest. It has not promoted change and compromise in South Africa but stiffened attitudes, playing into the hands of South African hardliners, and raising false expectations in other parts of the continent. It has been a wretched substitute for the international political art and science of maneuver and persuasion.

Just as important, it has played into the hands of communist propaganda. While South Africa does indeed have a racist-authoritarian regime, it is restrained by parliamentary values and a relatively free press. On any objective list ranking the "badness" of regimes it would not be anywhere near the top. It would obviously fall below the Soviet regime which has caused as many as seventy to eighty million deaths in forced labor camps and prisons and at the hands of secret agents since 1917. It obviously ranks far below the fanatic Khmer Rouge regime which has decimated the population of Cambodia. On the African continent, South Africa is not in the same class with Ethiopia, Sudan, Uganda, Burundi, Guinea, Angola, Mozambique and Equatorial Guinea, to mention the worst. No United Nations or Organization of African Unity resolution has condemned any of these states or imposed sanctions upon them.

We insist upon the ending of apartheid but African experience surely suggests that this ending could only be the beginning, not of one-man, one-vote or black majority rule, but another monstrosity—that of tribal dictatorship with all the oppression, discrimination, corruption and chaos this would produce. Is this what we want? If not, how is it to be avoided? We have the moral right and indeed the obligation to make plain our abhorrence of South Africa's violations of human decency. But, on our part, we need to have the decency to stop posturing as the savior of mankind—the one great moral leader with the answer to all the problems of human rights in the world and to start thinking through and ahead in the light of what has happened already in Africa and in the light of our overall national interests.

It is time for our African policy to reach out for reason, balance and perspective instead of following the tom-tom beating of emotional and often racist and ideological drums. It is time to take a vigorous diplomatic offensive with a policy which asserts our own analysis, values, perspectives and strategic interests. It is time to bring to bear upon our southern Africa efforts our best professional resources and our most subtle and sagacious maneuvering in the African tribal thicket.

# 18.

# ONE DAY IN THE LIFE OF
# SIMAS KUDIRKA AND THE
# STATE DEPARTMENT

The day was November 23, 1970. The place was off the Gay Head Bluff of Martha's Vineyard, in territorial waters of the United States. A U.S. Coast Guard cutter, the *Vigilant*, was moored alongside a Soviet ship, the *Sovetskaya Litva*, for an exchange of views concerning Soviet fishing practices which were depleting marine stocks in the Atlantic off New England. Similar meetings with Soviet fishing fleets had been held off both our coasts pursuant to fishing agreements between the two countries. The groundwork for this particular discussion off Gay Head had been laid by the American Embassy in Moscow. It was no impromptu event.

Simas Kudirka, a Lithuanian crew member of the *Sovetskaya Litva*, alerted a visiting party from the cutter of his intention to defect and later got himself to the cutter where his presence was accidentally discovered by one of a Soviet party paying a return visit. A Soviet spokesman for the party—apparently a KGB agent—conveyed to the Coast Guard skipper (whom I will hereafter call "the skipper") his awareness of the defection, but made no request for Kudirka's return, apparently in defer-

---

Reprinted with permission from *Foreign Service Journal*, September 1979 (Vol. 56, No. 9).

ence to well-known U.S. policy on political asylum and the fact that the ships were in U.S. territorial waters. However, he intimated that the Soviet side would be appreciative if Kurdirka's return were volunteered by the Americans.

In a series of radio-telephone conversations with superiors in Boston, the skipper received orders from the admiral in charge of the Coast Guard district to return Kudirka if so requested by the Soviet vessel. Horrified by this and well aware of what punishment Kudirka would be meted out if this were done, and with the defector emotionally pleading for asylum, the skipper stalled for time. From the admiral's chief of staff came a strong intimation that the skipper might find it expedient to elicit from the Soviet captain a formal request for Kudirka's return, as this would "make the record look good."

Two hours later, the admiral repeated his order. The agonized skipper, having received a formal request for Kudirka's return—a request which KGB agents aboard the *Sovetskaya Litva*, by this time aware of the American confusion and indecision, seemed to have pressed that ship's reluctant captain to make—now obeyed. He permitted Soviet crewmen to board and search the cutter, locate and seize the hapless defector, savagely subdue him, wrap him in a blanket, bind him with yards of cordage and remove him. The ships were now unmoored, the skipper having taken this precaution in the event of a reversal of the admiral's order, and the Lithuanian was returned to the Soviet vessel on a lifeboat—ironic term—generously supplied by the cutter.

The denial of asylum being completely at variance with long-established U.S. policy, the ensuing furor raised in question what policy and operational controls the State Department had exercised. The following sets forth the State Department's role in the affair:

1:15 — Coast Guard headquarters in Washington received a telephone call from its Boston chief of staff (the admiral being ill at home, although in telephonic communication with his chief of staff) advising that the cutter officers had been signaled by Kudirka of an intention to defect. So inadequate were communication lines and practices between Coast Guard and State—notwithstanding the presence for some years of Soviet fishing fleets and earlier discussions off our coasts—that an hour and a half were consumed in a search for the proper office in State to alert. Logically, it turned out to be the Office of Soviet Affairs.

2:45 — In that office a senior Foreign Service officer heading the "Bilateral Political Relations" section (hereafter called "section chief") was notified by the Coast Guard of the prospective defection. He promised to call back advice as soon as he had a copy of the Boston message, which was provided him within a half hour by the Department's Operations Center.

3:15 — The section chief, as promised, called the Coast Guard. Mindful of attempts by the Soviet Government to fake defections in the past so as to gain intelligence information or to create embarrassments for the United States, he advised that "the possible defector should not be encouraged." This advice, while proper, was of negative tenor and of no great assistance for it left unanswered what should be done if Kudirka defected without encouragement, which was the possibility the alert had signaled. The section chief then concluded his call with the request to keep him posted, adding that if defection occurred it would have to be handled according to circumstances. "Handled" is an operational term, referring to how a policy should be carried out, but the policy itself was not stated. The section chief never advised, at this time or later, that if the defector appeared to be genuine, he should not be returned (Slip No. 1 in the State Department). This "keep me informed" approach sealed the State Department to a reactive diplomacy.

4:00 — Coast Guard headquarters, preparing to close down for the day (its working hours ending at 4:00), called the section chief to report that no further news had been received. It had not called Boston to make certain, before closing, that it had the latest available information, nor did the section chief request it to do so (Slip No. 2 in the Department). He described that day as having been like all days, hectic, with Kudirka's but one of many problems he had had to deal with.

6:00 or thereabouts — The section chief left for home, without having advised any superior of the alert (Slip No. 3) or having sent (or even considered sending) a Department officer to Boston to preclude any possible foul-up— to keep in touch with the situation, render policy guidance on the spot, ensure prompt communication with the Department and reduce the risk of misadventure in what can always be a tense and tricky situation (Slip No. 4). "There was no one I could send," he said. Furthermore, it would have been "unprecedented" to do so, and he "could not imagine anyone in the office agreeing to it." So he did not raise the issue with any superior. But it would have been an effective way of taking charge and restraining an admiral in Boston from going off on his own tangent.

While the Department's report to the President on this affair states that the section chief informed a colleague (who was to stand duty that night) of the Coast Guard message, the duty officer confided to me that he had not been briefed as to the specific facts or the applicable policy. He had just recently joined the Office of Soviet Affairs, had never before been confronted by a defection case and was specific in his statement to me that there had been no discussion with him of U.S. policy in defection cases, of possible complications or problems to anticipate and what to do if any of these materialized. However, he was a Foreign Service officer, of mid-career rank, with eight years experience, including a year in Embassy Moscow (as a publications procurement officer) and subsequent tours in Paris and Brussels in connection with NATO affairs and in the State Department's Bureau of Intelligence and Research.

This failure to brief a duty officer—especially a newly arrived one—certainly merits identification as Slip No. 5. The section chief did not even ask to be kept informed in the course of the evening or, if he did, the duty officer did not hear him say so (Slip No. 6)

7:45 — The duty officer at Coast Guard headquarters alerted a State watch officer (posted in the Department's Operating Center) that Kudirka had reached the *Vigilant*, requested to stay, and "was being returned at this time at written request of his ship's master." This electrifying report that defection had occurred and the State Department's instructions (to be kept informed of developments) had been disregarded did not electrify the duty officer to whom the message was relayed at his home. Although unfamiliar with the background of the message, the watch officer had the sensitivity to detect the possible need of action and he suggested that the duty officer call the Coast Guard. Instead, the duty officer procrastinated (Slip No. 7). For an hour he did nothing. This was all the more extraordinary since the message was phrased in the continuing present — "was being returned." During this hour he could have saved Kudirka, for the message failed to take account of the struggle which a defector would put up for his freedom and possibly his life.

The duty officer for the Bureau of European Affairs (of which the Soviet Affairs Office is a part) was notified at this time by the watch officer, but never seems to have entered the scenario thereafter, apparently assuming that the responsible office was "on the ball." He did not so much as check with the duty officer for Soviet Affairs to inquire what the report was about (Slip No. 8). Such an inquiry might have activated the latter by generating an exchange of views. The latter simply holed up, paralyzed either by ignorance of all the essential facts, or by a lack of elementary operating training or by an astonishing deficiency in the instinct to act, or all three.

9:00-11:00 — Sometime within this period the duty officer called his Department's watch officer to inquire if further information had come in. None had. Again, the watch officer suggested he call the Coast Guard. This time the duty officer did so, was informed that the Coast Guard duty officer was asleep and, still indecisive, phoned back the watch officer for advice whether he should insist upon speaking to his Coast Guard counterpart. Advised he should, he had the Coast Guard duty officer roused, thereby narrowly averting another slip, but even so Slip No. 9 came precipitately.

The Coast Guard duty officer, reporting that no further message had arrived from Boston, promised to submit a "Situation Report" the next morning. The duty officer could still have spared Kudirka his ordeal and his government ensuing embarrassment of global reach had he requested and insisted upon a call to Boston but, in his irresolute way, was content with the promise of a morning report (Slip No. 9), which, to anticipate the narrative, was never made. Nor did the duty officer call his superior, the section chief, for guidance (Slip No. 10). He did not himself call Boston (Slip No. 11). Nor did the section chief, as a precaution, call the duty officer the entire evening (Slip No. 12). So the duty officer retired for the night as the luckless Kudirka was being brutally beaten and kicked, trussed in blanket and cordage in the presence of the horrified skipper, crew and fisheries negotiators, thrown aboard a cutter lifeboat and delivered to his masters.

What are we to make of this eerie and disastrous sequence of events? Where were all those qualities claimed by the establishment to constitute the hallmark of the career Foreign Service officer and to distinguish him generally from political appointees—unique knowledge and superior know-how, acute and trained sensitivity, a good sense of initiative and timing and professional skill? Except by the watch officer, none of these things were demonstrated. On the contrary, a most excruciating ineptitude, commonly associated with the worst of political appointees, was exhibited—and one of the officers involved was of senior rank.

The diplomatic establishment is forever pleading that the reason it cannot turn in a more air-tight performance than it does is because foreign relations are international in nature, dependent not upon our will alone but on that of other governments as well. But here was one foreign policy situation clearly within the Department's control and it was, just as clearly, bungled. Presidents have long been exhorting the Department to cease being what John F. Kennedy called "a bowl of jelly" and to "take charge." Here was a situation in which, patently, the Department could have done so. It proved to be what President Kennedy had termed it.

All the more disturbing was that this had occurred in the office charged with managing our relations with a government whose dynamic diplomacy exploits every vacuum, every weakness, every mistake presented by its rivals.

The outrage of the President, Congressmen and the public over this incredibly slipshod performance was instant and tidal. With an oath directed at "that god-damned State Department," the President ordered reports from it and the Department of Transportation (in which the Coast Guard is situated). As dismay spread around the world, U.S. reputation for knowing its policies and interests and being able to act effectively in accordance with them took a nose dive. As this came in the midst of our disastrous involvement in southeast Asia, the dive was all the steeper. But when the President received the Departments' reports any follow-through he might have had in mind evaporated. Either he was swamped by other problems or he may have been stumped by the thicket of unfamiliar questions which the situation posed.

The State Department itself, always reluctant to confront basic questions concerning its performance, dismissed the Kudirka affair as an unpleasant episode not symptomatic of systemic weakness. It appointed no board of inquiry, as did the Coast Guard. It issued no reprimands, as did the Coast Guard. And it took no remedial steps save the most obvious, (1) issuing the Coast Guard and other government agencies a statement of U.S. policy on political asylum (which it had failed to do before despite the patent opportunities of defection provided by offshore Soviet fishing vessels), (2) defining for the Coast Guard channels of communication with the Department, and (3) inviting Coast Guard representation on interagency bodies dealing with asylum cases.

These steps took care of locking the Coast Guard stable *ex post facto*, but the basic questions requiring address slipped like quick silver through the Department's fingers. As the furor subsided so did its concern. A brilliant, illuminating flash of lightning had streaked across its sky, revealing a startling sequence of inexcusable slippages, but when the flash was over the tingling disturbance lost all excitement and curiosity vanished. Other problems, other crises, other brush fires closed in. Events conspired with a chronically meager staffing pattern to produce days too hectic and burdened for officers to think beyond their immediate work-load. The latest cable, the latest telephone call, took its customary priority. "Keep me informed, and if you don't call back I'll assume there is no problem" resumed its sway as an operating principle—a reactive stance, not one of positive assumption of responsibility and leadership. Kudirka and his unhappy experience, which should have taught so much, wound up teaching nothing at all.

Were the slippages in this case only personal, as one would like to think, so that any other officers would with certainty, or in all likelihood, have acted more responsibly? Or were they systemic? Even if simply personal, they raised enormous questions of systemic nature:

What weaknesses in the selection system permit incompetent, indecisive officers to be commissioned?

Are officers reasonably adequate when commissioned but inadequately educated and trained when inducted and thereafter?

Does the system fail to instill an adequate conceptualization of diplomacy and diplomatic functions and responsibilities?

Do deficiencies in the promotion system permit unqualified officers to move up the ladder to mid-career and even senior ranks?

Do conditions of service contribute to producing overworked, jaded minds, overly vulnerable to negligence and to incapability of distinguishing the relative importance of situations and taking effective charge of those of highest priority?

Do such systemic factors seal the United States into an excessively cautious and essentially reactive attitude in international politics?

To come to grips with these shadowy questions requires a close familiarity with the diplomatic establishment and, frankly, I have been holding back the publication of this analysis in the hope that someone other than myself would pick up this, or a similar, case and assume the invidious task of analyzing the conduct of colleagues which our general situation requires. But the national interest commands that some such analysis be produced without further delay.

Let us consider first the selection of officers. There is no system for the selection of permanent stationary State Department staff apart from that of the general civil service. Stationary officials other than civil servants acquire temporary sojourn in the Department when some President or influential Congressman wants them to have a government job, or occasionally a political appointee or friend in the Department wants a special assistant. No special orientation or training in the dynamics of diplomacy is provided such appointees or civil servants.

Commissioning in the Foreign Service officers corps has traditionally involved a written and oral examination.* The written tests the range of a candidate's general knowledge and culture and his IQ. It does not test any conceptualization of diplomacy. The oral examination, superceded this year by a so-called "assessment procedure," has permitted a probing of personal qualities, but since the interviewers have been drawn from the diplomatic establishment and that establishment pervasively thinks of itself in pedestrian fashion, as a collection of bureaus, offices, "cones" and "jobs," with no synthesizing conceptualization of diplomacy as a dynamic international political process, they have naturally examined candidates as though

---

*An additional route, called the Mustang program, was added seven years ago. This recognizes officer talent in the ranks of the Civil Service and Foreign Service Staff Corps (secretaries, clerks and administrators) and permits them to enter via oral examination and a probationary period.

they were simply entering a bureaucracy, without reference to political instincts and aptitudes and action mentality. With recruitment itself directed not to the political arena, but to colleges, naturally students of events rather than activists predominantly came before the oral panels, and these put their pedestrian seal upon the recruitment harvest.

Fortunately, the Department's recruitment has been substantially supplemented by self-starters who have come forward as candidates on their own impulses, after trying careers in private business, in the military and in government. Their average hovers around twenty-nine. Still, they constitute a mystifying melange of people prepared and people unprepared for international politics and therefore prophesy an extraordinary range of performance behavior. This has been aggravated by the waiver of the written examination, under the pressures of Equal Opportunity, for candidates from four ethnic groups: American Indians, Blacks, Hispanic-Americans and Asian-Americans.

To give two examples from a recent Foreign Service class of what this is doing to the Foreign Service:

— Officer A graduated from a polytechnic institute with a BS in management and from a university with a masters degree in mathematics education. He taught math and science in public schools for eight years. He thus had no background, educational or employment-wise, in foreign affairs and none in U.S. government and history, including U.S. foreign policy and diplomatic history, nor in international law and international organization. In the whole international area, he was as complete a novice as a high school senior.

— Officer B began his college education at a university but dropped out. After drifting through Central and South America as a tourist and student and through Europe as a tourist, he settled down in the United States as a bricklayer for a year and a half. This was all the preparation he had for representing and explaining this country and its policies abroad, answering questions concerning our history, culture, politics and social problems and engaging in the wide-ranging complexities of international politics.

These two officers came from ethnic groups exempted from the written examination. Such exemption, thus, results in the Department commissioning officers wholly unprepared in foreign affairs. Rather than obtaining learned diplomatic officers, it is inducting the most superficial imaginable. We must recognize, however, that other candidates not so exempt and with better academic backgrounds, still possess serious gaps. Those strong in Americana are weak in foreign affairs and vice versa. Nearly all, exempt or not, are illiterates in diplomacy, untutored in those international strategies and tactics which constitute the essence of international politics. Even if exemptions from the written examination were not being accorded ethnic groups, the Department's claim that the Service gets "the cream of the nation" has become a meaningless shibboleth. "The cream" is no longer good enough for the needs of a World Power.

To assist oral panels in threading their way through a mystifying melange of applicants no psychologist has ever been co-opted either as a panel member or adviser. Since the panels have consisted simply of rotating Foreign Service officers of varying degrees and kinds of experience, with no training in the interviewing art, the weaknesses of candidates have often gone undetected or, at best, superficially explored. In view of the exactions and dangers of modern diplomacy, this is a serious remissness indeed and is surely related to the psychological problems which have overtaken the Service, from aberrant behavior (reported in the media) and alcoholism to disinclination to serve in hardship posts ranging from Moscow to Africa, and indeed to serve abroad at all. This dissipation of zeal for overseas duty, commitment to the nation's needs and discipline have worked to the detriment of our diplomatic performance. Contrasting with the higher degree of commitment and discipline in the diplomatic services of other governments, including the communist, it is inevitable that our effectiveness must have relatively declined. Symptoms of this we witness every week.

For some years, candidates have not been subjected to

any special stress in the course of oral interviews, so that no one could judge how well they might be expected to react to particularly difficult or embarrassing—still less to hazardous—situations, or even to relatively simple ones like Kudirka's. Quite the reverse, for examiners, succumbing to the current easy-going, socializing psychology of our society, have felt that the interview itself is enough of a strain, and so have been making it as pleasant and relaxed as possible. In a hard and dangerous world this has not only exposed the diplomatic establishment and the nation to risks they should not be exposed to but gives candidates a totally false impression of the highly demanding calling they aspire to enter and the unflappable self-control it exacts. One detects, indeed, in the attitudes of three of the officers involved in the Kudirka affair precisely this relaxed, easy-going mentality, devoid of political sensitivity, discipline and teamplay. Thus, the selection system has joined hands with deficiencies, and may have subtly sowed debilitating attitudes where none originally existed.

If nothing in the selection process in recent years has remotely suggested the Ulyssian challenges awaiting successful candidates or tests anything approximating the sensitivity and resourcefulness demanded of them, this particular defect may be somewhat mitigated by an experiment introduced this year of replacing the hour-and-a-half or two-hour oral interview by a day-long "assessment procedure" borrowed from major corporations. This simulates a "day on the job." The candidate is given a stack of material with which he might be expected to be confronted in a typical work-day. He must dispose of this stack, deciding the questions posed. Lacking tutelage in international politics, he will of course come up with some superficial or even cock-eyed decisions, but at least this type of test should help to screen out the indecisive and unimaginative. It is difficult to conceive the two principal officers involved in the Kudirka case taking such a test without raising serious questions concerning their qualifications.

At the same time one must keep in mind the essential

nature of diplomacy, which is not to keep one's in-box contents flowing into one's out-box, but to keep a political process flowing, with an eye to the furtherance of foreign policy objectives. The principal limitation of the innovation is that it is a desk-job test and smacks too much of the widespread anti-humanist, managerial belief that papers, desks and "decisions" are more important than people. It may well reinforce the debilitating conceptualization of the diplomatic process as a mere collection of in-boxes and out-boxes, offices, bureaus, "jobs," "problems" and "cones," rather than a *political* process of international maneuver to obtain certain strategic goals to which all else must be subordinated.

One has to remember, also, that in international as in national and local politics, people of more profound political instinct are most imaginative and resourceful in personal relationships rather than in executive-desk type of in-box, out-box work. The essence of diplomacy is personal persuasion in a cross-cultural, cross-historical context —in which tact and personal agreeableness are important factors—not managing a desk or an office of one's own compatriots and certainly not in a business-oriented type of organization. Some combination of a decisive-minded, management type test with a vastly improved oral examination might provide the ideal combination.

The socializing, make-them-feel-at-ease philosophy which has metastasized American education and had come to characterize our oral examination, pervades the five-and-a-half-week so-called "basic officers course" given to all newly commissioned officers. So much is this the case that officers are commissioned *before* not *after* completing the course, during which *no* examinations are given to test the degree to which material has been absorbed. Indeed, this is not a "course" at all but a fleeting, superficial exposure to a melange of subjects most of which are un-synthesized with either the substance or the objectives of the diplomatic process.

The first priority of the "course" has been to introduce officers not to diplomacy—that is abjured as too "remote" and "high-flown" for new officers (even though their average age is twenty-nine—but to "the work" of the State Department and Foreign Service (a purely bureaucratic concept), to orient officers to the terms and conditions of their employment (including the Department's medical and insurance program, employee-management relations, the career development system and the like) and to make a gingerly thrust at some of the core skills they need in oral and written communication, reporting and analysis of information they gather, negotiating (a one-day simulation) and the supervisory-management skills required of a junior officer.

The second priority is to develop a faint understanding of the relationship between "individual job assignments" and the overall formulation and implementation of U.S. foreign policy, of diplomatic social practice, of some questions of international law which rise to the level of the Department's Legal Adviser (rather than the broad questions which, as diplomatic and consular officers, they can be expected to face), and the roles of the White House, executive departments and Congress in policy formulation and implementation. The general outlines of U.S. foreign policy were once sketched but are not now. Even when sketched important areas have been omitted such as those relating to defection and asylum, basic though these are to what the United States stands for in the world. The interests and activities of the federal foreign affairs community are touched upon, but not synthesized in a total conception of American strategies and tactics. Not even the role and resources of the Central Intelligence Agency have been covered in any meaningful way until recently, when the buffetings to which the Agency has been subjected by Congress and the press have knocked sufficient humility into its head to get it down off its high horse of exaggerated secrecy. This part of the "course" has never included the Coast Guard.

Whether this introduction to the Service provides any grounding in U.S. foreign commitments (including our defense treaties) and the reasons for them or the policies and commitments of other important governments, depends upon the conductor of the course and since there is a constant succession of conductors, both substance and quality in these areas differ astonishingly.

Even when there is some slight genuflection to such vital matters, there is none at all in others equally critical, including the Soviets' political, economic and military strategies and tactics, or in the crucial question of the sources of anti-American feeling around the world, in international law generally (although we profess a consummate dedication to it), in international organizations and the resources and problems they present to us, or— most startling of all—in diplomacy itself, although this is the profession the officers are entering and the principal means by which governments are seeking their objectives. Occasionally, a conductor (such as the present one) explores some diplomatic functions, such as protocol, negotiation, démarches and interviewing skills, but there is never an analysis in depth of diplomacy and the role it plays in our national security and welfare and that of the international community. Hence, apart from negotiation under the present conductor, there are no case studies of a problem-solving nature in the dynamics of the international political process, comparable to those, for instance, which good schools in business management employ to prepare aspirants to business careers. Nor is there the slightest suggestion of the contributions which a complex of sciences is making· to the analysis of our world—cosmography, anthropology, social biology, social psychology, sociology, ecology and the like—especially of the underdeveloped areas. All in all, the basic officers preparation is a resounding hosanna to superficiality and amateurism. Needless to say, the sounds which American diplomatic performance generates include many eerie and discordant ones—as in the Kudirka case—and this accounts in no small part for our slippage in world esteem.

Apart from the one exercise in negotiation, the Department propagates the false conception that diplomacy is hazy, largely individual, instinctive, felt-understood in

encounter experience, incapable of analysis and verbaliza-
tion, to be practiced by people off the seats of their pants,
rather than a sharp, brisk, politico-economic-cultural-
military competition of ideas, moves and counter-moves,
demanding of practitioners the highest degree of learning,
alertness, complex calculation   and systemic teamplay.
This false conception has vast psychological ramifications,
metastasizing the entire diplomatic establishment and
creating a fertile incubation of Kudirka-like slippages and
worse. This is why even in relatively so simple a matter as
dealing with the Soviets on a defection question, or the
siting and construction of embassies in our respective
capitals, and perhaps the more complex SALT negotiations,
we are outsmarted. They know the game and too many
of our officers do not.

Not being conceptualized as professional in nature,
the preparation of officers is cast in the image of its
conductors. These being Foreign Service officers and therefore constantly rotated, orientation content is subject to
equally constant and bewildering mutation as each conductor experiments, adding here, subtracting there, according to his individual experience and perceptions, not to
say victimization by the faddism which periodically in-
vades our conduct of diplomacy. Human rights, for example, is now much emphasized in the basic orientation,
as youth problems were in President Kennedy's time.
If the Department viewed its task clearly and did it well,
such things would be covered all the time and this extraordinary erraticism of content and quality would disappear.

Confronting the same problem, the military establishment has overcome it by reducing courses to writing,
ensuring that basic subjects are covered thoroughly, in
professional manner, while permitting instructors to
contribute their own experience, insights and personality
to instruction. The Department's casual approach to its
instructional responsibilities is symptomatic of a profound
misperception of diplomacy, the modern world and its
own role and cannot but equally profoundly influence
the performance of officers and therefore its own com-

petence relative to our military establishment, our intelligence agency and other governments.

What legal, medical or other professional—not to say artistic—heritage would we possess without written composition?     What diplomatic heritage—and institutional memory—can we possibly create if we do not reduce our diplomatic experience and instruction to writing?

Of equally psychosomatic effect, the course propagates the notion that past experience is of no relevance. No warnings, by case studies or otherwise—apart from anecdotes of course conductors—are given of mistakes committed over the past by either our diplomats or those of other governments to sharpen appreciation of hazards and pitfalls. Of none of the critical analyses of the Department published over the years is study required, to stimulate thinking of some breadth and depth of the kind of an organization officers are stepping into, what inadequacies to anticipate and compensate for and what changes to work for. The excuse is given that all of these studies are "out of date," but all together they constitute a palimpsest of American thinking—and non-thinking—on subjects of foreign policy-making and diplomacy, emitting shafts of light to perennial problems in these two areas. Thus, a wholly passive, irresponsible, even disdainful attitude toward the organization as a whole and its problems is induced.

Not even biographies and memoirs of diplomats are required to be read to stimulate a professional search for clues to the nature of diplomacy, what functions it performs related to the nation's security, and what to do or avoid doing in one's own career to achieve a satisfactory quality of performance in the shortest possible time. Such reading would provide some transfer of conceptualization and experience from officer to officer and from generation to generation, badly needed in a system of constantly rotating officers. Incidentally, also, it would incubate a professional attitude sadly lacking in the diplomatic establishment, as was all too vividly attested by the loose-jointed unprofessional way the Office of Soviet Affairs handled the Kudirka case.

Orientation, thus, is little more than a transient situational disturbance in the lives of the officers and a perfect exegesis of Santayana's admonition that those unaware of the past are condemned to repeat it. It is also an exegesis of the complementary Simpson axiom that those ignorant of the past do not know what good things to perpetuate. It confirms the American insistence of living in a fool's paradise of the present, chopping up history into little daily bits and disregarding the perspectives of the past, which leaves too many officers unable to detect basic trends. Even when we get to know a lot, we understand too little, which explains why World Bank officials say that in their travels they go to American embassies for the most up-to-date information but to others—the British, French and West German—for insights and perspectives into what the information means. This helps also to explain our failure to understand and to attract following in countries respectful and even reverent of the past. The State Department's orientation of Foreign Service officers is thus an orientation away from three-fourths of the human race. (Some modification of this occurs in area studies).

How this slackness penalizes officers anyone of us has observed countless times. I maintain it is one reason— perhaps the principal reason—the China-born officers who became "China Hands" in the 1930-40 period ran afoul of the State Department as well as of the "red-baiting" McCarran - McCarthy - Hurley - Nixon - Chambers - Budenz crowd. For they were simply not adequately trained for their exacting profession and their free-wheeling helped to do them in. I argue it is the duty of the State Department to provide every entering officer with the best possible foundation and discipline, with risks of his committing errors reduced to a minimum. It is not fair either to officers or to the nation to do otherwise by an orientation which is not only superficial but anti-intellectual. It digs for officers what T. E. Lawrence called "a shallow grave of public duty."

One needs only to compare this curious approach to the rigors of twentieth-century foreign affairs with the preparation exacted by the legal and medical professions to see the enormity of its misconception. To be admitted to the practice of law one must have capped a liberal arts education with three years in a law school and further demonstrate, by a rigorous bar examination, a grasp of the substance and procedure of jurisprudence. For the practice of medicine, requirements are even stiffer, since human life is involved—four years in medical school on top of general college work (in which stated pre-med courses are required) and a concluding internship in which further searching examination is made of knowledge, judgment and general capability. Diplomacy, like the law, concerns justice and order and involves maneuvering, bargaining and hard negotiating with these ends in view but on a global scale, encompassing different cultural economic, political and legal systems. Like medicine, diplomacy concerns people's lives, not only those of individuals, as in the Kudirka case, but, again, on a very large scale, with successes and failures affecting the lives, health and fortunes of whole populations. The State Department, instead of measuring up to such formidable responsibilities and requiring, *before commissioning*, a rigorous education and training, coasts along with the most relaxed and minimal standards conceivable.

Even a business like brokerage, which might seem to be relatively simple—merchandising stocks, bonds and units in various types of investment funds—approaches its challenge responsibly. First-class firms put their candidates for account executives through a grueling *twenty-nine* weeks of courses, after which come stringent *examinations* by the New York Stock Exchange, the National Association of Security Dealers and the Chicago Board of Trade. Are foreign policy making and diplomacy really so much less demanding, with so much less of an impact upon the nation and the global community?

Or take something simpler than brokerage: customer service of a public utility. The Philadelphia Electric Company puts applicants through a thirteen-week training to prepare them for work in that department. This provides not only a searching study of all possible customers' problems but psychologically jacks up the applicants' appreciation of the importance of what they will be doing if selected. Just what is the State Department trying to prove by a five-week-plus orientation? That diplomacy is simpler and easier than serving customers of a large electric utility, or its candidates are all that better prepared for their monumental tasks—or that foreign affairs constitute a kind of Willy Loman occupation, "riding on a smile and a shoeshine"?

When, at various times, I have challenged this relaxed, unprofessional preparation of Foreign Service officers, the objection has been made that the recruits would rebel against a thorough and tested preparation. "They are fed up with courses and examinations," I have been invariably admonished. "They have had enough of studying and examinations. They want to get going."

What would candidates for the legal and medical professions be told if they said after finishing college or graduate school they were fed up with studying and examinations and just wanted to "get going," practicing law or medicine? What would first-class brokerage firms or the Philadelphia Electric Company say to applicants who "rebelled" against rigorous preparation? They would all say: "Then you are not for us. Try something else." The State Department says: "Come on in anyway. We'll teach you on the job." The Kudirka case shows dramatically this can be so much malarkey. Few officers acquire on the job everything they need to know to be learned, sagacious, responsible diplomatic officers of a World Power. Few can be intelligent and useful in any profound sense who are simply the product of what John Dewey called his own "undergoings." One needs to recognize that there is a wisdom of centuries not submissive to the fluctuations of time, assignments, daily chores, in-boxes and out-boxes.

The fact that on-the-job training is by fits and starts, by catch-as-catch-can fragments, from supervisors who learned the same way, straps a Kudirka-like time bomb to every

Foreign Service officer. Piece-meal, job-related thinking becomes so fragmentary, limited and pedestrian as to become superficial, a sure way of fusing habit and tradition with anachronism, exaggerated individualism and repeated errors in our conduct of foreign affairs. This is why no government department is so beset by folklore and mythology, by-guess-and-by-God notions and clichés as the State Department. It explains why there is no pervading *espirit de corps*, team play and sustained organizational morale in our diplomatic establishment. To anyone familiar with the casual and disorganized fashion in which that establishment was run before World War II, the Kudirka case is dispiritingly reminiscent, revelatory of how old attitudes, mental processes and operational norms perpetuate themselves in a totally different and far more complex and dangerous age.

On-the-job training also exaggerates the American penchant of viewing foreign affairs not as international politics and therefore in terms of strategies and tactics, which are the dynamics of diplomacy, but as so many "problems." We thereby run the risk of losing sight of the broad political environment in which problems arise and must be resolved. Governments having an overall strategy acquire the momentum we have seen Soviet diplomacy acquiring in Africa and the "arc of crisis" from Afghanistan to the Persian Gulf while we try to separate out from the web SALT, Israeli-Egyptian relations, Rhodesia, Cuba and other "problems" for individual treatment.

Under this system, learning tends to become excessively individualized. This is why the Department, the Service, the basic officers course and diplomacy itself become, each, as I have had occasion to point out before, a kind of Rorschach inkblot, conceptualized not professionally but solely in response to the stimuli of individual experience.

Finally, on-the-job learning is the slowest possible kind. We are a World Power and the state of the planet is such that we can no longer afford the luxury of officers assuming responsibilities of initiative and leadership only after years of service. The Kudirka case dramatically demonstrates that even with eight years experience a mid-career officer can be so unanalytical and irresolute he cannot satisfactorily handle the simplest kind of a situation and a senior officer of *eighteen years* experience does not know how to manage even one subordinate, cannot clearly articulate an important policy for the guidance of others and cannot, therefore, coordinate State Department interests with the operations of another agency.

The fact that the diplomatic establishment has some well-rounded, competent officers is in spite of not because of its commitment to on-the-job training, and these officers are far too few. Only when the average, run-of-the-mill officer possesses a sharp strategic and tactical conceptualization of diplomacy and is trained to act in accordance with it can our democracy hope to contest successfully the kind of diplomacy waged by the authoritarian regimes which have replaced in modern times the Phillips of Macedonia and Alexander the Greats of other times.

This brings us to the metastatic effects which working conditions exert upon the minds and attitudes of officers. These accentuate what the selection procedure and orientation begin: the creation of a bureaucratic instead of a dynamic political mind. For decades the staffing pattern of the establishment has been too lean to permit the development of effective educational and training programs for a sizable proportion of officers, the adequate development of officers by supervisers, or even self-development through individual reading and sabbaticals. The absence of reflective and creative thinking in our diplomacy for which the nation has been pleading for years stems in part from this, for the effect of overly stringent staffing is that officers work with their minds to the grindstone, not infrequently required to perform clerical tasks, as were officers in our consular posts in Iran, and thus so preoccupied with daily chores as to lose sight of the large ends toward which their functions are supposed to be directed.

As one of our officers has written from London: "The tight staffing pattern of the Foreign Service does not only make it practically impossible for an adequate training program at the State Department's training institute to have sufficient in-puts at all appropriate points in officers' careers. It also effectively insulates consular officers from developing political, economic or commercial skills or participating in those functions in connection with their consular assignments. In posts where I have served, I have observed that the sheer pressure of work (brought about in large part by insufficient staffing) leaves officers in such a state of physical and mental weariness at the end of each working day they simply have no energy left to expend on reading or social contacts or other activities ordinarily thought to be part of the responsibilities of a Foreign Service officer."

This could have been written from any of our consular posts in Iran in recent years.

In the Kudirka case, this kind of staffing left the section chief pleading he had no one to send to Boston to take charge on the spot and himself apparently too fagged out to keep on top of a situation brought to his attention during the day. In a wearied condition, he closed the door of his mind as well as of his office at six. He had earlier served a tour of duty at the Treasury Department and noticed that the State Department was keeping that sister department insulated from policies and actions. Yet he could not, even in a specific instance obviously demanding the closest kind of collaboration, breach the insulation of the Coast Guard by issuing it a clear policy instruction and following up on its execution. "Perhaps," he said when it was all over, "we should have a liaison officer over there [at Coast Guard headquarters]." Perhaps we should also have alert, trained, unfatigued, take-charge officers in the State Department. Attitudes, not the lack of organizational devices, are at the root of many of our serious problems.

Year after year, Dean Rusk used to boast before Congressman John J. Rooney's subcommittee on appropriations that he was not requesting any personnel increases for the diplomatic establishment, despite accumulating needs and increasing workloads. "We are just working harder," he used to say. This was demagogy of the worst kind, all the more destructive because two government-wide reductions in personnel (to which President Nixon was to add a third) had already stripped the diplomatic establishment to dangerously reduced staffing levels, and we are traveling that same road in the present Administration. "Working harder" breeds slippages of the Kudirka kind, as constant, day-long, week-in-and-week-out barrages of problems numb the senses, constrict attention span and inevitably induce mismanagement. In a broader sense, "working harder" over the years has also meant working harder at the same old lines of policy, the same old bureaucratic notions of diplomacy, in accordance with the same old shallow ideas of what the United States and the free world community need to do to ensure a preservation of their values and interests. Since some of the policies up to the time of the Kudirka affair had to do with Vietnam, "working harder" had meant digging the nation ever deeper into that disaster. With no time to back off for fresh thinking and fresh perspectives, over-worked minds simply cannot respond alertly and creatively to either immediate or long range, subtle or overt challenges.

The Kudirka affair and Vietnam, each in its own way, are symptomatic of the Department's inability to conceptualize diplomacy in sharp enough terms to relate diplomatic actions to resources. Equally symptomatic—and reinforcing this deficiency—is the absence of a diplomacy planning staff. A Policy Planning Staff has existed since General Marshall introduced it in 1947 in the hope of inducing in the State Department the planning functions and mentality of the military's general staff. But there is still no planning staff for the execution of policy and therefore no coordination of resources—human and other—for the global implementation of the policies decided upon by the President and Secretary of State. Such a staff could, among other things, stimulate adequate educational, training and personnel development programs and conditions and press for a staffing pattern appropriate to the diplomatic needs of a World Power. Every company of any importance has a management action planning system to enable it to operate by plan and anticipation rather than by simply responding to situations. The absence of such a system in the State Department and in each office, such as Soviet Affairs, and proper officer attitudes explain much of the casual, relaxed, reactive way in which all too much of our diplomacy is conducted.

In the promotion of officers the Department has been as inefficient and resourceless as in selection, education, training and staffing, because officers are doing, in too many cases unprofessionally, the evaluations on which promotions are given. Here, again, psychologists have not been enlisted to assist in resolving the problem of supervisors who cannot or fear to write professional, objective evaluations of subordinates. Without such evaluations, the Department can too often fail to make the right promotions or assignments. Nor can it weed out the incompetents, the vacillating, the undecisive, the people unwilling or unable to take charge and prevent them from going through all the ranks even to ambassadorships. The other side of this coin is that officers have not been instilled in the basic course with the professional criteria which would make them willing to accept objective evaluation. In this area, as in others, attitudes are exercising a debilitating influence, making it impossible for the diplomatic establishment to rise above a level of faltering performance. There is not a company of any importance which does not recognize that, to put it in the words of one, "a company's future is only as positive as the capability and attitudes of its key executives," yet the State Department, instead of recognizing this, deliberately sows the very attitudes which degrade its performance potential and make it too little a contributor to national security and too great a contributor to national fumbling.

The Kudirka case, thus, is a lens which brings to a focus what has happened over the years to U.S. diplomacy in Latin America, what happened in Vietnam, what is happening in Africa and the Persian Gulf and what characterizes generally our relations with the Soviet Union and will undoubtedly characterize our relations with the Peoples Republic of China. Other governments are as mystified by our fumbling conduct as was the skipper of the *Vigilant* and they are as traumatized as he by our incompetence in controlling some of our simplest diplomatic challenges. They feel—and many Americans feel—as Wellington said he felt after reviewing inadequately trained troops during the Peninsular campaign: "I don't know what effect these men will have on the enemy, but, by God, they frighten me."

## 19.

# DOES THE UNITED STATES NEED A PARLIAMENTARY FORM OF GOVERNMENT?

*PREFATORY NOTE: The U. S. problem of developing a diplomacy adequate for its global needs is more than one of suitably modernizing and energizing its diplomatic establishment. The problem is also one of developing close working relationships between the executive and legislative branches of our government. Joint and responsible leadership of these two branches is essential if the national security is to be adequately served and the requirements of the world community as well. As this essay argues, we need a diplomacy which will help to knit together the world on the basis of civilized values.*

It is becoming clearer every day that a better way must be found to evoke a strong, effective yet responsible leadership in our Government.

We are experiencing a political paralysis on so wide a range of critical problems, with a President unable to elicit sufficient Congressional support either for positive programs or needed restraints, as to invite disaster.

Energy conservation, one of the more critical problems that face the nation—and the world—is a case in point. It continues to be the victim of inadequate treatment.

The imposition of effective budgetary restraint is another problem whose evasion invites disaster.

A citizens' storm is building against the size of government, its spending and its appalling waste, yet both the

Reprinted with permission from *The New York Times*, December 31, 1978.

executive and legislative branches, organized in a system of checks and balances rather than one of joint and responsive leadership, are powerless to effect the needed change in direction. The separation of powers provides an open plain on which Congress can wage its outrageous battle for more and more expenditures while the executive is obliged to back off and sue for compromise.

A myriad of previously legislated expenditures, a veritable wildwood of mandated outlays, complicates this problem, frustrating every Administration's effort to make good on its promise to balance the budget. Divided power and responsibility imposed by the checks-and-balances system renders it impractical for any Administration even to suggest the revision of this situation, yet without such reform the budget cannot be balanced.

Hence, in comparatively good times, as in the last years, national budgetary deficits, instead of diminishing or disappearing altogether so as to permit the scaling down of a national debt whose servicing annually costs in excess of a billion dollars, actually soar higher and higher. There is no visible end to this condition under our present system.

Similar irresponsibility besieges our conduct of foreign affairs. The executive branch cannot conduct these affairs —including the intelligence function—without Congressional pulling and hauling this way and that, all with vociferous hullabaloo and unaccountable leakages of secrets, rendering all but impossible a thoughtful, consistent integral pursuit of the national interest.

This chaotic rivalry with the executive is accompanied by defamatory bluster that humiliates other governments which themselves would not tolerate such unseemly behavior were it not for a common threat from the Soviet Union.

In other words, we are not knitting together a world on the basis of civilized values but are forced to manipulate working relationships on the shifting foundation of our own political convenience.

With our present system so invading the conduct of diplomacy with raucous disputation over rival prerogatives, our national interest is not adequately served nor our national security, bolstered. The quiet, methodical, sustained strategy demanded by the challenge of a resolute, systematic enemy becomes impossible.

The crowning failure of our system has been made painfully patent in the election of our prime national leader from outside all national and international experience. This is pure, unadulterated folly and we have been witnessing its effects each passing month.

A parliamentary system would preclude such nonsense, for the prime national leader would rise from the ranks of the legislature, would know how it works, would have acquired some familiarity with national and international affairs, would be regarded by his party not as an arch rival but as its leader and therefore possess adequate authority for the purpose.

A real danger exists that the continuation of our present political system will perpetuate paralysis, leading to such ineffectiveness and frustration as to jeopardize more than the system.

The possibility should not be pooh-poohed that it could lead to such a drift to disaster as to invite dictatorship.

The world is not exactly a seminary of democracy and the seed plot is being narrowed and defertilized progressively by the increasing magnitude and complexity of problems demanding decision. Our best hope of avoiding a drastic remedy is to effect in good time a rational one.

Since, as a practical people, we do not want a Constitution that is but a "gilded halo hovering round decay," I suggest the assembling of a national convention to draft a constitution based upon the parliamentary system, which I believe would come closer than our present checks-and-balances arrangement to meeting our requirement of a united, decisive, responsible national leadership capable of moving expenditiously to meet the challenges that confront us.

# 20.

# WHAT NEEDS TO BE DONE

What I am pointing out, basically, are three things. We must:

1. Conceptualize diplomacy as serious, highly competitive, international politics, which other leading powers and the more sophisticated smaller ones have professionalized because it demands the utmost learning, training, perceptivity and finesse;

2. Elevate our own performance, accordingly, to professional standards so as to perfect our utilization of diplomacy as a factor in the equation of our national defense and the preservation of civilization; and

3. Revise our system of government in such a way as to steady our diplomatic performance and keep it constantly focused on our long-term national interests.

Any improvements in any of these respects over our present superficial and erratic ways of conducting our foreign affairs will have some corrective effects upon the quality of our diplomacy. However, if we are to compete successfully in the major league of world affairs, drastic reforms are needed.

These reforms may be summarized as follows:

First, we must educate ourselves from high school through university levels in diplomacy. We do this with respect to local and national politics. We must do it for international politics. This will broaden our citizens' conception of the real world in which we live and the peaceful resources we possess to work out our destiny. Since international politics involves governments representing not only different states but different cultures, psychologies, periods of human history and stages of civilization, instruction in diplomacy provides a good vehicle for instilling a realistic, even profound view of the world and the ways it works. It would also promote a recognition of diplomacy as our first and a constructive line of national defense.

Accordingly, expenditures upon the diplomatic establishment must be viewed as contributions to our national security and therefore substantially increased over the niggardly levels to date. I say that as one who is committed to a general reduction of government spending, a balanced federal budget and a scaling down of the national debt. If equipping the diplomatic establishment to do its work effectively must be at the expense of social welfare programs at home and aid to foreign countries, so be it. It is no good helping the needy to survive in a world which will crash in ruins upon them. The security of the nation and the world come first.

Since national defense and that of the world community require that we have the best possible people in diplomacy, recruitment of personnel must be directed to that requirement. We must stop handing out commissions in the Foreign Service as a compensation for intellectual poverty. Equality in employment opportunity must be visualized in terms of equality of competence. A candidate for the diplomatic service who is a college drop-out and bricklayer cannot be favored over better prepared, more competent people simply because he belongs to an ethnic minority. He must compete with all other candidates just as, if admitted to the service, he will have to compete with the diplomats of every other nation for influence, initiative and leadership in the advancement of national interests.

It follows from this conceptualization of diplomacy that a major reform step must be to professionalize it—to state the professional qualifications of diplomatic practitioners and to apply these to the admission, the education and training, the assignment and the promotion of officers. These qualifications must include an acceptable level of learning in the history, philosophy and social characteristics and problems of our own country, sufficiently in depth to enable our diplomats to accurately represent us, conveying convincingly to other peoples our principles, philosophy, objectives and experience. With this must go an equally in-depth knowledge of world history, international relations in all its aspects, including legal, organizational, economic and geographic, along with diplomacy itself. Our dallying with these important ingredients of an effective diplomacy must end. Since the degree of erudition demanded is rarely achievable in our educational system, a foreign affairs academy of graduate status must be established to bring candidates to the required professional level of learning and competence.

Those who have passed qualifying written and oral examinations for admission to the academy —passed in fact, not as a result of re-grading on the curve —should be provided this education at public expense, just as is done in the military academies. Before commissioning, they must be required, as in all professions, to demonstrate in examinations their intellectual and other readiness to take on the nation's diplomatic responsibilities.

Such an academy must train officers to discharge their responsibilities in the milieux in which they are required to perform, from the politico-bureaucratic at home to the terroristic abroad. Only in this way can the art of diplomacy be married to present-day demands so as to serve adequately the needs of both the national and international communities. Officers must be thoroughly instructed in the activities and resources of the federal government as a whole, including covert and military, so as to be prepared to contribute effectively to an integration of our strategies and tactics in the world community. This would help to restore the diplomatic establishment to its proper role in the conduct of our foreign affairs and serve the

need of retaining an effective civilian control over the utilization of military force in international situations.

Included in the academy enrollment should be the appointees of the Central Intelligence Agency. It is unacceptable that the CIA should operate abroad virtually as an
independent agency. Inclusion of their candidates in
academy enrollment should induce them to feel they
are a part of the government, subject to our political
philosophy, not an agency operating independently, with
its own philosophy and rules. This would assist chiefs of
missions and consular posts to bring the CIA into a more
effective partnership with the rest of the government and
at the same time give the rest of the government a more
understanding insight into the objectives, needs and procedures of the CIA.

The academy must educate and train not only diplomatic and CIA officers, but all of those who deal with
foreign affairs in the federal government. This would provide not only a community of knowledge, perception of
the national interest and understanding of the resources
available for pursuing that interest, but an *esprit de corps*
needed to effect that degree of policy integration and coordination of maneuver which communist and other totalitarian states achieve by their party ideology, organization
and discipline and which provides them an appreciable
edge over democratic countries in the rough and tumble of
international politics. Democracies must move in their
own ways to redress this in-balance and enhance their
effectiveness.

Such an academy should contribute significantly to a
change in the American attitude toward diplomacy—an
attitude manifested within the diplomatic establishment
itself, including presidents, their advisers on national
security affairs, secretaries of state and even career practitioners—that this is something that can be dabbled in
successfully by anyone, whatever his education and experience. The art and science of international politics
would come to enjoy the respect which professionalization

has brought to the art and science of war. We are still much influenced by frontier mentality in regard to diplomacy and force and this is far from relevant to the world in which we live.

In facing the fact that it is absurd to base our strategy vis-a-vis the Soviet Union on the credibility of mutual destruction, we must recognize what this means, namely, that our survival and that of Western values depends basically upon diplomacy and its resources , and do all that is necessary—rapidly—to master them. By multiplying nuclear and other technological resources, we and the Soviets have reached the point at which neither seemingly dares to use them, but the Soviets have been quicker than we to realize and act upon the implications of this technological stalemate. They are using, in coordinated fashion, all the dimensions of diplomacy, including covert operations, to press their ambition for dominance, while we continue to play the game of diplomacy like uneducated and confused adolescents not sophisticated enough to comprehend what is going on. So we are playing not only amateurishly but defensively, simply trying to catch up with the Soviets' maneuvers, while they press the competition here, there and everywhere in vigorous and resourceful pursuit of their own objectives.

Indicative of this discrepancy in perception is the Soviet decision to make their ambassador in Washington a member of the Kremlin's Central Committee and to keep him in the United States for over seventeen years, while ours in Moscow is not a member of the President's cabinet and has difficulty in keeping informed of what his own government is thinking and doing, in seeing the Kremlin leaders and in serving more than three or four years. This is not using our heads and can only end in defeat.

Moreover, our career diplomatic officers are given to understand that generally they can count on serving but once as ambassador and then must retire to "give others a chance." This, too, is nonsense of the worst sort. If an athletic coach applied such a concept to his team, he would never produce a winner. We cannot do it in diplomacy. Winning in all kinds of competition requires ability and team play developed by training and experience. We must get it through our heads that winning should be our objective, not confusing the means—adjustment and accommodation—with the end. We need not Andrew Youngs and short-time career ambassadors but Anatoly Dobrynins in order to do this. An academy would help to propagate and reinforce this conception.

A diplomatic academy would also assist in the clarification of diplomacy as not simply a process of international accommodation, of adjustment, but also of leadership and must necessarily be so as an ingredient of national defense. The best defense lies not in reacting to others, but in initiative—in leadership. Since the United States has not so viewed diplomacy, it must exert every effort and command every available resource to do so and put it to work. For this, an academy for the training of diplomats in leadership techniques is essential.

In the selection, education, training, assignment and promotion of foreign affairs officers the full resources of the behavioral sciences should be enlisted. With psychological factors and personal qualities being important in international politics, it is inexcusable that in the latter half of the twentieth century, a ministry of foreign affairs should have disdained the use of psychologists in these various stages of the diplomatic process.

Greater care in all these stages of officer selection and development would solve many problems which now plague our diplomatic establishment and appear as "inevitable" or "insoluble" because they seem to be stemming from general social causes. Proper education and training would off-set such causes by the development of values, motivations and attitudes appropriate to the demands of international politics. This in turn would obviate much of the recourse to a grievance system which now so distracts and delays needed substantive decisions and actions as to erode the will and ability of senior officers to lead decisively.

The educational and training process must be viewed as a continuing one. To enable officers to participate in it—not only through classes but self-educational effort as well—the size of the diplomatic service must be expanded to make possible the release of officers for educational and training assignments and the leisure required for self-development through study and reflection. Reading programs must be instituted in every mission and post. Sabbaticals must be provided every officer on a regular basis. No one, except in crises, should be worked, as American diplomatic and consular officers are today, as some kind of a draft horse, driven long hours, too exhausted by the end of his day to think of anything but flopping into his stall and bed of hay.

We cannot afford the shallowness which such working conditions and the lack of adequate educational training programs have induced in the great preponderance of our diplomatic officers. The age-old parsimony of appropriated funds which has prevented release and leisure for educational purposes, and which no Secretary of State since Henry L. Stimson has dared to contest, must be ended.

I repeat, this is not some desirable social program but a defense requirement.

The responsibilities imposed upon diplomats by our complex and hazardous world raise the issue of the musical-chairs rotation of officers which the State Department perpetuates as the basic means of broadening officers' horizons and experience. This practice once had validity. It was a way of assisting diplomats to become sort of Renaissance men—well-rounded, versatile jacks-of-all-trades —and to preclude the formation of undesirable connections. What it does now, however, is to reduce diplomats to superficiality and ineffectiveness in the influencing of foreign leaders. Merry-go-round diplomats simply cannot command the respect of such leaders or indeed anyone else. Other ways are available to broaden horizons and perspectives and to discourage undesirable personal attachments, and at the same time effect the profound specialization in subjects and countries on which influence and

leadership rest. Professionalization and continuing education are among them.

Our overseas representatives must be viewed—and with
these reforms will be viewed—by presidents and secretaries
of state as members of a total diplomatic team, kept
fully informed not only of discussions and debates in
Washington on matters relating to the countries in which
they are posted but the regional and global play of international politics as well, and their advice solicited and given
proper consideration. Overseas missions must be viewed
as an integral part of the infrastructure of our national
defense, essential to the pursuit of our national destiny.
This is the kind of integration which produces success in
international politics. Nothing short of it will.

These reforms can only come about and be consistently
developed over the years through a permanent general
manager of the State Department. There must be such
an official to oversee operations, initiate improvements
and see them through to fruition over the long pull, fill
in gaps, tailor resources to policies, effect really fundamental adjustments to changing world conditions and assure
that these will have the needed follow-through and reinforcement. Presidents and secretaries of state changing
every four or eight years cannot do this. Rotating diplomatic officers cannot do this. We must abandon the
tomfoolery of blow-torch efforts to improve our diplomatic
performance which dissipate as soon as the blow-torch
operators are rotated. We must keep in mind that a seven-
teen-year ambassador in Washington is more seasoned in
international politics than any top U.S. official who floats
in and out of Washington according to the swells and tides
of national politics—more seasoned than our presidents,
who serve eight years at most, more seasoned than our
secretaries and deputy secretaries of state, more seasoned
than other cabinet members, more seasoned than presidential advisers on national security affairs. When one
adds to this fact that the Soviet Minister of Foreign Affairs
has held his position as long as Ambassador Dobrynin has

held his and had previously served through the diplomatic ranks, it is clear that the Soviets possess a combination of continuity of experience, strategic conceptualization and drive which we do not so much as approximate.

This brings us to the point of our constitutional system. While a general tightening up of our diplomatic performance will result from such changes as those recommended in our diplomatic establishment, serious handicaps are endemic in a system of checks and balances presided over by presidents unable to impose party discipline and to give our diplomacy the thrust of dynamic, consistent and flexible leadership. Nor are we consistently bringing to our presidency and cabinet positions people experienced in national and international politics. Global problems and the strategies and tactics employed by the various governments of the world in approaching those problems are too often beyond the reach of their experience and comprehension. As Dean Rusk used to say, the members of congressional committees dealing with foreign affairs knew more than he. They spend years investigating, studying, debating and voting upon foreign policy issues and do a good deal of overseas traveling for these purposes. We should, accordingly, base our national leadership upon that extensiveness and continuity of experience. We should adopt a system which brings to our prime political office and to cabinet positions men and women who have such a background and may even have served previously in these positions and in shadow cabinets when their party has been out of power. Our present grab-bag method of choosing our prime political leader is not conducive to a wise and seasoned exercise of power.

Furthermore, we cannot afford the misadventures which come from irresponsible congressmen meddling in diplomacy. Some discipline, some national purpose, must be imposed upon our legislature. We cannot lead in world affairs by a disjointed, chaotic relationship between two separated branches of our government.

What we must keep in mind in all of this is the dual

exigency of ensuring our national security and a planetary environment as promotive of that security and the values and processes of freedom as we can make it. We Americans have a lot of catching up to do in this whole matter of diplomacy. We had better begin doing it now. The place to begin is with our conceptualization of diplomacy. When that is clear, all the rest follows. And we had better start the process before the rapid erosion of recent years places our one-time position of leadership in the world beyond retrieval.

# INDEX

204 (*see also below*, Preparation, lack of adequate educational) African assignments resisted, 269

anti-intellectual attitude pervasive in, 137, 199, 254

basic officers course (orientation), q.v.

candidates: unprepared for, 117ff; illiteracy in diplomacy, 254, and in background knowledge of State Department, 288

CIA and covert operations, relationship to 48, 148-149, 195, 304

China Hands, q.v.

Civil Service differentiated, 12, 13, 32, 37

clannishness, 208, 227

conceptions of, 77-78, 149, 205, 207, 292

cone system: proposed, 188; problems of, 77, 84, 136, 200, 203, 208ff

consular and diplomatic services merged (Rogers Act), 209

consular contribution to policy making and implementation overlooked in orientation, 146-147, 247

consular officers: education/ training of, 145, 146-147; effect of working conditions on, 294

consular responsibilities: importance of, 48; nature of, 29, 94, 146-147, 209; need of synthesis with diplomatic, 139, 151, 209-210

development of officers: (*see also* education and training, below); Basic officers course; computers; consular functions, need of synthesizing with diplomatic; Junior officers; On-the-job training; Transfer-of-experience problem); leisure, crucial factor of, 125, 169, 190, 196-197; lack of, 125, 157, 169-170,

179, 195-196, 254, 279, 293-294; relationship to reform, 208, and to size and funds of Foreign Service, 125, 136, 157, 169-170, 179-180; through: adequate analysis of errors, 50-52, 177, 207; assignment to other government and nongovernment organizations, 190, 194, 197; conceptualization of diplomacy, 16, 19, 73ff, 139, 293, and of their role, 139-140; correspondence courses, 166, 211; education and training, q.v.; rotation versus other means (*see* Rotation); self-efforts, 154, 157-158, 199-200, 293-294, 307; supervision, 57, 64, 168-169; 293

diagnostic approach to filling gaps in officers' knowledge, 153, 199

dilettantism of, 248, 249, 165, (*see also* 168-169 and Rotation)

diplomacy, conceptualization of, not used in recruitment for, 53; in testing candidates, 280, 284; in orientation, 284

drop-out of junior officers, 145, 146-147

economics, intensive training in, 170

education and training: areas needed to be covered, bureaucratic politics, 15; intelligence work, 48, 177-178; inter-agency coordination, 147; management, 63; parliamentary diplomacy, 49; politico-military relations, 42, 84-85; public clarification, 19-20; career-long nature, 130-131, 157, 307; commitments and policies, importance of meshing with, 25, 50, 51, 61, 173, 194-195, 295 (*see also* Basic officers course and Counter-insurgency); covert operations to a minimum, relationship with reducing, 48,